Fly-Fishing Pressured Water

Fly-Fishing Pressured Water

Tying Tactics for Today's Trout

LLOYD GONZALES

PHOTOGRAPHS BY NORM SHIRES

STACKPOLE
BOOKS

Copyright © 2005 by Stackpole Books

Published by
STACKPOLE BOOKS
5067 Ritter Road
Mechanicsburg, PA 17055
www.stackpolebooks.com

Printed in China

First edition

10 9 8 7 6 5 4 3 2 1

Photographs by Norm Shires
Paintings and drawings by the author

Library of Congress Cataloging-in-Publication Data
Gonzales, Lloyd.
     Fly-fishing pressured water : tying tactics for today's trout /
  Lloyd Gonzales ; photographs by Norm Shires.-- 1st ed.
        p.   cm.
     Includes bibliographical references and index.
     ISBN 0-8117-3220-7 (hardcover : alk. paper)
     1. Trout fishing.   2. Fly fishing.   3. Fly tying.   4. Flies, Artificial.
  I. Title.

SH687.G63   2005
688.7'9124--dc222004028004

ISBN 978-0-8117-3220-8

To my dear wife, Barbara, who once quipped to Ed Koch
that my love for her was second to my love of trout.
I swear that the reverse is true but have little to offer as proof.

And to my parents, for their gifts of sport and art, and for
the tolerance that allowed me to explore both in my own way.

CONTENTS

FOREWORD

by Ed Koch

There are books, and then there are *books*—no matter what the category. This is one of the *books,* in a very special category—a fly-fishing book by a fly-fishing and fly-tying expert. Lloyd has done some thirty years of research on aquatic insects. His patterns are exact—and I mean exact—duplicates of the scores of naturals described in the book. If you can duplicate his patterns, you will catch (and release, I hope) more trout than you ever thought possible.

Ed Koch
York Springs, Pennsylvania

FOREWORD

by Norm Shires

How I wish our paths had crossed those thirty some years ago that Lloyd Gonzales refers to in his introduction to this book. It was then that he, as a youngster, was fishing the Yellow Breeches and beginning to study its abundant population of aquatic critters. It was about the same time that I began to study and photograph those same critters. The coincidence goes beyond that; he moved to the Pocono area of Pennsylvania, where he honed his fly-fishing and fly-tying talents on many of the streams of my youth.

My dad was a fly fisherman; thus I was introduced to the sport at a very early age (much to his consternation, I suspect, when I pestered him to allow me to cast his trey of wet flies). Back then, the art of fly tying was a closely held secret; dad would drive about thirty miles to buy his flies from the only person he knew that tied commercially. All we knew about back then were wet flies (fished three at a time), dry flies, and streamers. Nymphs, emergers, duns, spinners—never heard of them. Times have surely changed, and Lloyd's contribution to the sport we love promises to change them even more.

Lloyd is often asked if he fishes with flies like the ones in this book. The answer is, without a doubt, yes. The flies in his fly boxes are exactly like the ones shown here. They may not be tied with the same care for obvious reasons, but they are the same patterns. Lloyd is a perfectionist like no one that I have ever known; witness the numerous rejected photos that were discarded because of some minor flaw in the tying that showed up in the photograph. In such cases the fly was retied and rephotographed. If there is one question that surfaces frequently, it is this: Will typical fly tiers take the time and go the extra mile to tie extended bodies, add distinct legs, hinge the abdominal portion of the fly, and do the other little things that result in a very realistic imitation of the natural insect? If they fish waters where catch-and-release is routinely practiced, where the fish are fussy or have seen and been fooled by the same typical patterns over and over, I think they will.

Norm Shires
Carlisle, Pennsylvania

ACKNOWLEDGMENTS

Rare and unexpected gifts, like the invitation to write this book, deserve very special thanks. The personal debt of gratitude that I owe to the many friends, authors, and anglers that have helped me over the years is hard to express in a few public words. But, I will try.

Above all, my undying thanks go to two limestone legends, Ed Koch and Norm Shires, who have been the patron saints of this fly fisher. The idea to write a book was Ed's alone, and the generosity he displayed toward a nearly forgotten face from the past is almost incomprehensible. His random act of kindness will never be forgotten. And Norm Shires, my colleague and collaborator, endured endless hours of tying and photographing flies around his kitchen counter with unwavering good fellowship and hospitality. It is hard to find words that adequately express my appreciation for his support and encouragement. These fine gentlemen carry the mantle of Vince Marinaro and Charlie Fox, and do so proudly.

Many thanks are also due to my editor at Stackpole Books, Judith Schnell, who gambled on an unknown and untested author, and who shepherded me through an unfamiliar process with uncommon patience and skill.

I also wish to acknowledge an unpayable debt to angling heroes who fish with us now only in books and memory. The exploits of angling immortals A. J. McClane, Lee Wulff, and Joe Brooks inspired my early angling fantasies in the same mythic way that Roy Rogers fired my childhood cowboy dreams. And, closer to home, Pennsylvania angler and masterful fly tier Chauncy Lively attracted my attention to fly tying at a time when I should have been doing my homework.

I would also like to recognize the literary gift of inspiration from one of the greatest living fly fishers, Ernest Schwiebert, whose books revealed the wonders of matching the hatch. Likewise, I am grateful for the contributions of those who followed in his wake—the hatch-matching teams of Doug Swisher and Carl Richards, and Al Caucci and the late Bob Nastasi. Without such creations as the Wiggle Nymph and the Compara-dun, my tying and fishing would both be poorer. And on the caddisfly scene, the singular contributions of Gary LaFontaine are valued as much as he is missed.

While acknowledging literary debts, I must say that whatever meager writing skills I can muster should be credited to my high school English teacher, Gloria Stewart, who encouraged me to think clearly, read critically, and write frequently (even if not always well).

And, on the professional side, I would like to take this opportunity to thank my comrades, brothers and sisters, of the two ski schools that have been a much-loved extended family for my wife and me over the past quarter of a century. Thanks, too, to my fellow examiners with the Professional Ski Instructors of America, who accepted an unworthy flatlander into their elite company, and among whose ranks I am growing old without having to completely grow up.

Finally, I would thank all of my fishing partners, past and present. In particular, much-belated thanks must go to the brilliant Steve McBeth, schoolmate and best friend, who shared my early fly-fishing experiences on the streams of our Cumberland Valley home. And, of course, thanks to Jim Coyne, my long-time Pocono compatriot, whose efforts to master the sport lead to many discoveries and fine adventures. And a note of encouragement goes to Don Sensenig, one of the finest skiers I have known and also a budding fly fisher of great promise.

INTRODUCTION

The opportunity to write this book was happenstance. There was no plan, no anxious expectation, no tattered manuscript shopped around to publishing houses. There was only a strange confluence of random and seemingly insignificant events. The incident that set all of this in motion was an erstwhile encounter with a pair of spectacular mayflies on a central Pennsylvania stream.

Thirty-some years ago I was in high school, and aside from suffering the usual throes of virulent adolescence, I was further afflicted with fly fishing (age has largely cured the former, but the latter still fluctuates between fervor and fever). At that time, Swisher and Richards' *Selective Trout* had just been released and was causing something of a stir among the then-small fly-fishing community. Much of the fuss centered on the authors' no-hackle dry flies. For me, the most immediately useful revelations were the photographs of mayflies. These gave me a visual reference for some of the common mayflies found on the streams of the Cumberland Valley in Pennsylvania, where I lived and fished. The only downside to this new information was that for every answer provided by these photographs a new question arose. Old puzzles resolved into new ones.

My usual spot for observing or collecting mayflies was on the campus of Messiah College, which surrounded a pastoral stretch of the Yellow Breeches Creek. Evenings I would inspect the streamside lights, recording what I found there on a copy of Charles Wetzel's "Trout Stream Insect Emergence Tables." There were no real surprises until the last days of June, when an enormous mayfly—the largest I had ever seen—appeared in the lights. Its numbers increased throughout July and into August, when another similar mayfly, slightly smaller and much darker in color, gradually replaced it. I turned to *Selective Trout* for answers, but these were not forthcoming.

Yellow Hex: The hatching of this Hexagenia *dun (tentatively identified as* Hexagenia rigida*) from the Yellow Breeches coincides with the yellow drake* (Ephemera varia).

Dark Hex: The hatching of the slightly smaller and darker Hexagenia *dun* (Hexagenia atrocaudata) *from the Breeches coincides with the famous white fly* (Ephoron leukon).

The only clue that offered any promise was the photograph of *Hexagenia limbata*—the giant Michigan mayfly. It was close, but I couldn't reconcile the photograph with the twin giants of the Yellow Breeches. The earlier of the two was much lighter in color than the pictured insect and lacked the dark staining around the rear margin of the hind wing. The later-emerging mayfly was a better match but still so different that I wasn't convinced I had found any answers. Even more baffling was that the authors indicated that *limbata* was primarily a Midwestern insect, with heavy hatches occurring in the streams and rivers that drained into the Great Lakes, such as the legendary Au Sable in Michigan. No one I knew had any knowledge of *Hexagenia* in the Yellow Breeches, yet I was reasonably sure, based on the keys found in *Selective Trout,* that both insects were members of this giant mayfly genus.

In those days, one of my fly-fishing haunts was the Little Run that flowed out of Boiling Springs Lake and into the Breeches at Allenberry. Ed Koch owned and operated a little fly shop that was situated at the head of the lake. His was the only local shop devoted to fly fishing, and he was the only famous fisherman I knew. After fishing the Little Run, I would often stop by the shop to pester Ed with questions about fly fishing or fly tying. He was always extremely patient with my inquisitive intrusions, whether or not I had a few dollars to spend on assorted bits of feathers and fluff. He was, and is, my idea of a fly-fishing gentleman.

One day late in the summer of 1973, I was in the shop talking with Ed about bugs and fish, and I mentioned the Hex hatch. He wasn't acquainted with it and asked if I would collect some specimens for him. A few days later, dusk found me at my station beside the Breeches, plucking the large duns from the lights and placing them in a plastic vial. After I had gathered a half-dozen or so, I got in my car and drove to Boiling Springs. When I arrived at the shop, the windows were dark. I tried the door, but it was locked. Finding some paper and duct tape among the clutter inside my car, I wrote a note to Ed and taped it, along with the vial of mayflies, to the doorknob. In the fall I departed for college. I didn't see Ed again for thirty years and didn't know what had become of my little package of *Hexagenia* duns.

Recently, my wife and I came to reside in Boiling Springs. I had spent the quarter of a century that followed my premature departure from college living and, of course, fishing in the Pocono Mountains. Upon my return, I naturally resumed fishing in the familiar streams of my youth. Although much has changed, the fly shop still stands watch over the little lake. Now greatly expanded and owned by Emily Zeiders, the Yellow Breeches Fly Shop continues to be a hub of fly-fishing activity in this area.

On one of my visits, I was in the shop to purchase some tying materials and to order some hooks that were curiously absent from their extensive stock of curved and pointed metal. While there, I overheard Mark Altland, one of the knowledgeable staffers, discussing the Hex hatch with a customer. When I returned to pick up my hook order, I was armed with a few of my Hex ties, the annotated Wetzel tables, and a condensed version of this story. I shared all with Mark, almost expecting to get a dismissive look that said, "Yeah, sure you did, buddy!" Instead, Mark told me that Ed Koch still frequented the shop and that he would ask Ed if he remembered me. I was happy to be provisionally believed but expected nothing to come of the incident.

Later that week, my phone rang. It was Ed Koch. He asked if I would meet him at the shop and bring some of my flies. I was elated about the opportunity to meet and talk with Ed again. We got together and chatted for a long time, sitting in the shop's comfortable little library. He was very enthusiastic about my fly patterns, and it pleased me to get the master's approval. But I was surprised when he suggested—to someone he hadn't seen in thirty years and only half-remembered—"You should consider writing a book." This I took as a kindly, but casual, compliment until the more surprising follow up added weight to his suggestion. "My publisher might be interested." These were serious words.

I was enormously flattered by Ed's recommendation, but I also voiced immediate reservations. I was concerned that much of what I did in my fly fishing and fly tying might be too involved or specific for many anglers. My fly patterns were developed to solve problems and fill needs in my personal and, until now, very private fly-fishing style. At times I made adjustments to the tying or adapted the materials to suit the requirements of a fishing partner but never made an attempt to make these flies commercial or universal. Because of this, I worried that the flies and the type of (mostly Eastern) fishing they reflect ran contrary to the trends that seemed to be driving the popular patterns appearing in magazines and catalogs.

Ed's steadfast encouragement caused me to reconsider these assumptions. It made me look at my private pursuits in a different way and from a new perspective. I came to realize that the lack of certain commercial or universal qualities was precisely the thing that made many of these patterns and techniques valuable in my own fishing. My next realization was that there was little likelihood that my approach would ever become the norm in either tying or fishing. This also meant that sharing these flies and techniques with others through a book should not diminish their effectiveness. In a rush of new awareness, I knew at once what this book had to be about. There it was, underlying and unifying my experiences and my creations—the thread that ran through all of it was *pressure*. My approach to fly fishing and the style that grew out of it was built upon a lifetime of fishing in pressured water. I knew what I wanted to do.

It may seem that I am saying that this book will only benefit those who fish in crowded conditions or that my Eastern orientation will regionalize or limit the application. I don't believe that this is the case, although I certainly hope that those who share this common ground with me will find it useful. The unfortunate truth is that pressure is no longer just a local or even regional influence. If the waters you fish are not crowded, you are blessed. Even so, that blessing may only be a temporary reprieve. Today, few places are so distant or inaccessible as to be immune from the effects of pressure.

Pressure is a relative term and requires a relative or progressive strategy in order to cope with its challenges. When the salmon and trout are running in New York state's Salmon River (or Alaska's Kenai, for that matter), anglers are often forced to time their casts in order to avoid fouling with others around them. On intensely pressured special regulation streams, like Pennsylvania's Little Run, casting more than a rod's-length of line can be a luxury. In contrast, an angler accustomed to fishing a tiny tributary in complete solitude may feel an unacceptable degree of pressure upon encountering another angler. At some level, pressure is a concern even when you have the water to yourself. I have long understood the importance of considering the pressure that I created on the places I fished. As I point out elsewhere in this book, we create our own fishing pressure and carry it with us wherever we go. This is where the relativity of pressure comes to a point that is irreducible and inescapable. It is at this point that we stare into the waters we fish and meet our own reflection.

What I will attempt to share within these pages is an approach to fly tying as an important part of a strategy for dealing with the demands of pressured waters. I hope to help you unravel some of the tangled mysteries surrounding the thorny questions about fly selection and to provide a rationale for understanding when simple, standard patterns can succeed and when more complex or unusual flies have an edge. Through this process, I also hope to inspire you to investigate, to create, and to learn the lessons that the challenging trout of difficult waters can teach. And I will admit that I am humbled by this unexpected task, just as I have often been humbled by the teachings of my own trout tutors.

And so, dear reader, I hope you will enjoy this book and these flies. Most of all, I hope you will forever enjoy the blessings of brooks and rivers, tiddlers and trophies, solitude and communion. Fly fishing offers all of this and more. It is essentially and always a hopeful endeavor. You never know what will come from a modest meeting with a mayfly. They can guide you to encounters with trout, or they can capture past and future in a moment. Serendipity flies on ephemeral wings!

Lloyd Gonzales
Boiling Springs, Pennsylvania

PART ONE

Grace Under Pressure

CHAPTER ONE

A Perspective On Pressure

. . . anything that makes the fish harder to catch improves the sport.
—Ernest Schwiebert (paraphrasing G. M. L. LaBranche), 1955

Nobody goes there anymore. It's too crowded.
—Yogi Berra, commenting on Ruggeri's restaurant, 1959

Fish hooks boy . . . funny how that works. A youngster sets the hook on his first good fish and finds himself impaled for life, with no desire to be released—happily hoisted by his own petard. So it was with me, some forty years ago.

At that time, fly fishers were rare sights in the places I fished. The ease of spinning and spin-casting had "cornered the market," and the tools of the fly fisher had become unpopular and obscure. The practitioners of the sport seemed to be members of some exotic secret society, their knowledge and rituals passed by some unknown process and spoken about in whispers. I can remember times spent sitting on the bank of a trout stream amid the early season throng of bank-bound anglers, all of us hoping that our lifeless lines would be suddenly jerked into animation by an unseen fish. In a moment of distraction, my gaze would drift along with the stream, and in the distance an apparition would catch my eye. There would appear an angler quite unlike the hapless fellows sharing the shore with me. He would be wading in the water, moving quietly along a stretch of stream inaccessible to the rest of us. His line would curl back and forth in a way that seemed to defy the laws that governed the fling and plop of our casting. And sometimes, in the most compelling of these instances, the angler's rod would ease into a deep, dancing bend. The rhythm of my heart would start to quicken, and then, as if to heighten the mysterious nature of what I beheld, he would bring the object of all of our desires to hand and silently let it swim away. I

longed to learn the secrets of this strange art. I wanted to know the things fly fishers knew.

Fast-forward to the present day. No one who had come to the sport in a similar way and at a similar time could deny that things have changed. The sport has become an industry, replete with all the baggage that change implies. Today's initiate into the still strange world of fly fishing is often overwhelmed by a flood of information, advice, and expectations pouring out of magazines, books, videos, and cyberspace. What's worse, perhaps, is that the crowds in and along the streams are no longer the temporary influx of Opening Day enthusiasts. Fish any stream with a reputation for fine fly fishing and your first challenge may be finding a patch of open water upon which to place your fly. The secret is out, the society is no longer exclusive, and some streams, once rich in fish and insect life and known to but a few, are in danger of being trampled to death.

It is hard not to feel at least a little ambivalent about the present popularity of fly fishing. After all, I doubt that anyone packs his gear and heads to the water hoping to find a crowd. It is not surprising that some long-time fly fishers complain bitterly about the spate of newcomers that cramp the space along their favorite streams. Some even rail against a particular book and movie, both innocent in their intent, as the source of all evil and the font of congestion. I, too, have cursed the crowds at times, and, while I enjoyed both the book and the movie, I cannot entirely dismiss their impact. I even confess that I have been tempted to discourage the newly afflicted by warning that fly fishing could ruin their lives; that they will expend inordinate amounts of time and money in pursuit of a quarry that will do its level best to frustrate them at every turn; that should they ever ascend to the pinnacle of fly-fishing skill and travel to some remote Shangri-la rumored to contain the huge, wild trout of dreams, their floatplane will no doubt be met at the mooring dock with that most useless of all fishing advice—"You should have been here last week!"

I have always restrained myself at such moments, knowing that I have no right to shatter the illusions of the innocent. Beyond this, I understand (however cliché it may sound) that there can be strength in numbers. And if ever we needed strength to protect our streams and rivers, it is now. Certainly, the prospect of fishing in solitude on dead waters is no fishing at all. Can we all agree on that much? And really, how can we fault others for being attracted by the same qualities that drew us to the sport, however long ago. At our best we can ask, "What took you so long?" and move over and make room. Or we can admit that the only sure way to lessen the pressure on our favorite streams is to stay home. If you are at all like me, that is one remedy too extreme to contemplate.

So here we are, left to deal with the changes that have occurred and facing an immediate future that, like it or not, is usually something other than the idyllic image of the contemplative angler plying the water in solitude. Pressured water is the medium in which most of us will play this game in the near term. Much of our continued success and enjoyment will depend upon our ability to work within this context. Our respect for these beleaguered resources and our respect for one another will both be tested if we are to continue to reap the gentle harvest of this ancient art.

Whether you are a fly fisher who seeks an escape from pressured water or one who revels in the added challenge it provides, it is important to recognize that either approach involves a strategy. Both acknowledge that this is the world in which we fish now. Today, an escape from pressure is largely either bought or earned. If you, like me, are an angler who suffers from a perpetual state of financial embarrassment, then solitude is earned with boot leather. That, and by holding what secret spots remain close to the vest and sharing them only with a trusted few. If, on the other hand, you are the sort who can afford to buy your solitude, don't bother to ask me about such spots—unless you are willing to pony up an extra seat on your next wilderness excursion. We all must do what we can.

It is with the second strategy, confronting pressured water and accepting its challenges, that I offer my help. Of true wilderness I have tasted too little and would be out of my depth. Besides, in such places most of the help you would need comes in the form of a guide with a big, noisy gun and a keen eye for bear sign. The majority of my experience draws from places where the paths are deep and battle scars are more likely to come from the hooks of encroaching anglers rather than the claws of marauding grizzlies. But trout are no less worthy for being found in the shadow of civilization. This is particularly true of wild fish. They are treasures wherever they are found, and I value their opinion above all others. Wild trout will not tolerate the careless approach that is common among anglers whose senses have been dulled by fishing for hatchery substitutes. A wild trout that is educated by constant exposure to modern angling techniques, being "well-tried," as the Brits say, is the most wary and demanding of all fish. On heavily fished public water where the average fish is neither large nor wild, the act of releasing a large wild trout brings a kind of satisfaction that only pressured water can provide.

I do not mention this to convince you of my point of view, nor in any way to disparage the value of experiencing wilderness. I only suggest that civilized waters have their own virtues and offer their own rewards. An angler who fishes the Beaverkill, the Brodheads, or the Letort may not find solitude, but unseen among the crowds wander the persistent ghosts of legendary anglers—Gordon and Hewitt, LaBranche and Leisenring, Marinaro and Fox. To fish in their presence, even if that is an act of imagination, is an honor. To fish well enough to fool the trout of these haunted waters is a test of skill and a rite of passage. A sense of history and respect for tradition are values too often lost in the crush of competition. That these streams are still worth fishing is a living testament to the legacy of the anglers that brought them fame.

The roots of our fly-fishing heritage run deep in my home waters in the Poconos and the Cumberland Valley. In those waters, history endures, and wildness is not exclusive to wilderness. Wilderness is an endangered species, driven into corners of our country and surrounded by the scars of development and exploitation. But wildness survives in surprisingly tenacious ways. It clings to scraps of undeveloped land. It conceals itself in suburban backyards and beside shopping malls and behind factories. Like a child playing hide-and-seek, it hides best where few would think to look. Amid the overwhelming angling pressure and the overflow of information, surprising secrets remain to be uncovered for those willing to dig a little deeper, and fascinating fish remain to be revealed to those who look behind the shroud of civilization.

I know a rough stretch of Pocono water where wild brook trout run to a size that would be hard to match in the woods of Maine. Wild, big-water brook trout are a faded memory in most of Pennsylvania, and these fish hark back to a time long ago when our state fish could be a fish of rivers as well as the brooks of its name. The water in which these fish reside is hardly unknown or unfished, but, because other sections of it are heavily stocked, the easy fish draw all of the attention. I know of no one (who has not fished it with me) aware of the brook trout, though I suppose that others could be reluctant to reveal the truth. In an unguarded moment, I have even discussed this situation with a member of the Pennsylvania Fish and Boat Commission, who expressed complete surprise (and perhaps disbelief) that such a place existed.

But the place does exist, and the fish survive as relics of the past because they are isolated in unusual ways from pressure and exploitation. Some of this has to do with the dangers and difficulties involved in fishing this stretch, but it is also related to circumstances that favor—sometimes in rather perverse ways—the particular needs of these exceptional fish. This water is also host to brown trout, mostly wild, and stocked rainbows that stray into this stretch from upstream areas. Yet unlike the usual outcome of the interaction of wild brook trout with these two alien species, the invaders have not been able to usurp the dominance of the native species. Peculiarities of brook trout biology (regarding their response to limits imposed on spawning habitat and by predation) and their tolerance to a condition that is less than optimal for the other species allows this situation to persist. Of course, the benign neglect of this area by

irresponsible developers and insensitive anglers is also a major factor.

There's another Pocono paradise where the big water produces sly, wild brown trout that average about two pounds and four-pound fish are always a possibility. These big browns are as fine and strong and fussy as any I have encountered, and they seldom surrender to the casual angler. Here again, I am not describing water that is unknown or unpublicized, and stocking disguises the presence of these fish—a situation that fills me with conflicting emotions. Even though the numbers of wild fish decline in the stocked areas, few anglers other than dedicated locals seem aware that they exist at all. Probably tactics that are geared toward the dull pursuit of stub-finned, trough-reared pseudotrout do not fool many of the wild fish, or perhaps those that are caught are not recognized for what they are. This last possibility is a sad prospect in so many ways. It is one thing to catch an extraordinary fish; it is quite another to do so without any appreciation of the event. We only see what we know, to paraphrase Goethe.

A further reason that these wonderful wild fish are not better known is due to the quirks of the Pocono fly-fishing culture. Large numbers of visiting fly fishers frequent the Pocono streams, and they tend to belong to two distinct camps. One camp is comprised of public-water anglers who crowd into areas where stocking by the state is the heaviest. These anglers generally have neither the time nor the inclination to explore the areas that offer the best wild trout fishing. The other camp consists of the members of the many private clubs that

River Brookie: This wild, eighteen-inch male brook trout came from an isolated section of a well-known Pocono river. An unusual set of circumstances allows brook trout to maintain their dominance in this section at a time when large river-dwelling brookies have long since disappeared from other Pennsylvania waters. Because the majority of the angling pressure is focused on other areas stocked by the state, this population is largely unknown.

Pocono Brown: A wild, twenty-two-inch male captured during an evening hatch on a favorite Pocono stream. This watershed hosts abundant wild trout of all sizes, but due to heavy stocking in the popular sections, few anglers are aware that a wild population exists. Angling methods geared toward stocked fish are unlikely to fool many of the sly and sizable wild browns in the lower water.

appear (to the visitors) to have locked up most of the best water and even much that was never very good. These clubs are expensive and exclusive and reward their membership by stocking massive numbers of large, easily-caught trout—sometimes into waters that are incapable of supporting them. One club, for example, stocks five hundred large trout biweekly into a short stretch of a small, acidic tributary. Obviously, with such an artificial abundance close at hand, few of the club members have much incentive to look elsewhere.

I don't mean to be overly critical of either group. If casual and convenient angling is what appeals to a person, who am I to condemn it? However, it does explain how the wild trout get overlooked, and I will freely admit that I have been the beneficiary. And to be fair, I will also gratefully concede that some of the Pocono clubs have served the valuable function of protecting critical areas from development and other forms of abuse. In such cases, the fishing in the waters above or below would certainly be much poorer without this significant intervention. Where such protection exists, for whatever reason and by whatever mechanism, the benefits can accrue to the entire watershed, and the stream under discussion is an example of this. If size is not the primary consideration in the pursuit of wild fish, then the other end of this stream offers a different, but equally intriguing, experience. And sometimes the rewards can be even more unusual.

Far up in one of the headwaters of this stream, a waterfall forms a natural barrier between the dominant wild browns below and the brook trout above. Here the little browns are brilliant fish, closely rivaling the neighboring brookies in color. They are so liberally splashed

with red that, in addition to spotting their golden flanks and staining their tails and adipose fins, many display crisp red spots on their dorsal fins. This dorsal peculiarity ranges from a single, central spot of red to twin rows of spots, and I have rarely noticed this on other browns. In fact, the only account I have found that describes these red dorsal spots comes from an eighteenth-century description of the brown or common trout, written by a French nobleman. Perhaps this trait is more common among native European strains. Certainly, the coloration of these browns betrays their German heritage, and they appear just as I imagine their forebears did in the streams of the Schwarzwald.

The even more colorful brook trout above the falls are not only wild but, in all likelihood, native. They are the original denizens of these hemlock-sheltered and laurel-shrouded streams. Their ancestral birthright entitles them to the protection that the falls provides from the attractive, but alien, browns below. The abrupt shift in population that the falls represents serves to accentuate in a dramatic way that the real contest isn't about which species wears the most splendid coat-of-many-colors. An earnest struggle for territory exists, and the browns have conquered all but this last refuge. While the browns are clearly the victors, among that rival horde beneath the falls, in a miracle of role reversal, a solitary and stubborn brook trout can have its all-too-rare revenge.

For a short distance below the falls, a few stray brook trout mingle with the browns. There, late in the spring of 1993, my fishing partner caught the rarest fish I ever hope to see—a wild tiger trout. This cross between a female brown trout and a male brook trout (a true trout and a char) is sometimes produced by hatcheries, but

Headwater Gems: Brilliant little brook trout crowd the sanctuary above a barrier falls on a tiny Pocono headwater. Below the falls, strikingly colored wild browns hold sway over the rest of the stream.

even under hatchery conditions their hatching and survival rates are low, making them an expensive product to produce. Without hatchery manipulation, the odds against such a fish surviving are overwhelming, and records of its occurrence in the wild are hard to find.

Yet here, in this tumbling rill, was the hybrid progeny of that valiant male brookie who found himself trapped among the hostiles—our champion had sired a tiger. This little freak of nature was a coppery, dark-headed fish, the vermiculations from its father's back descending along its sides to form the tiger's stripes. While not as ostentatiously colored as either of its parents, it was, nonetheless, a strangely striking fish that imparted a lasting impression. We had no camera and no desire to kill the fish, so we released it after careful admiration. Later, I painted a portrait to commemorate the event for my friend. Actually, I painted the fish four times—until I was satisfied that the rendering matched my recollec-

tion. We carry a camera when we are on this stream now, though we have no expectation of ever catching another wild tiger to photograph. So it almost always goes. Memory is a poor camera, but a precious one.

Development and angling pressure have had an even older and more obvious impact upon my other home waters in the Cumberland Valley (though the Pocono region, which contains some of the fastest growing counties in the state, is currently running hard to catch up). But even among the suburban sprawl of this once mostly rural valley, interesting and unheralded fishing for wild trout still exists if you know where to look.

One example that comes easily to mind is a painfully brief, but classic, little spring creek. It is a portrait in miniature of all that makes these valley limestone springs so special. It is cold, clear, and cress-lined and produces trout in sizes and numbers that are all out of proportion to its diminutive scale. One of its more

Wild Tiger: The tiger trout is a cross between a male brook trout and a female brown trout and is sometimes produced by hatcheries. In the wild, the odds of one hatching and surviving are extremely low. This rare fish was found on an isolated Pocono headwater in 1993.

novel attributes is that the dominant population consists of gorgeous wild rainbows. Wild rainbow trout are rare in Pennsylvania. Falling Spring, a better-known limestoner that lies to the south, is famous for its rainbows, though it probably supports a nearly equal number of browns. Some wild rainbows are occasionally encountered in other limestone creeks such as Big Spring, the Yellow Breeches, or the Little Lehigh. And, of course the upper Delaware River has the most extensive population. But other than a very few isolated tributaries, that's about it.

Rainbows are not the only trout to be found in this tiny creek, though they are the most numerous. It also has a fair number of sizable wild browns. And on one memorable occasion I caught a remarkable thirteen-inch male brook trout, securing my only species slam on this creek. As is characteristic of limestone-enriched waters, all of the trout in this stream are well-fed and robust, but the brook trout was so rotund that its shape was reminiscent of a humpback salmon. To further embellish an already satisfying experience, the brookie was caught on the last day of the season and was adorned by spawning colors already in full bloom.

The short course of this little spring creek terminates where it enters a warm-water creek. This confluence of dissimilar waters yielded another revelation that had eluded me during all of my earlier adventures on this stream. While the condition of these trout indicates the abundance of food available to them, the variety of foods is extremely limited. In fact, I usually imitate only one prey item in order to catch these fish. It turns out, however, that the fish have an interesting way of adding variety to their diet.

When water temperatures allow, the trout move into the sluggish, warm-water stream to feed among the bass, carp, and suckers. I discovered this during an unusually cool season when the little creek seemed nearly devoid of its usual inhabitants. On one of my visits, the only reward had been one tiny, parr-marked trout. Attributing my lack of success to clumsy fishing, I was about to leave when I noticed troutlike rises on the surface of the normally warm, larger flow. There I found the spring creek's resident rainbows feeding on white millers. I had no imitation, but some extreme improvisation eventually allowed me to catch a few of the rising fish. I was struck by the sturdy resourcefulness of these fish and impressed by their ability to make the most of their situation. I was also embarrassed by my failure to recognize the potential of this situation, but the fish eventually imparted a bit of their character to the angler.

In my youth, I favored another tiny suburban limestoner, thoroughly abused by its location and neglected by anglers. In it, I found the remnants of America's two original immigrant brown trout, the Von Behr and the Loch Leven, coexisting as apparently separate strains. These two were long ago blended in hatcheries to produce the muddy brown trout stocked in most places today. One could assume that the same would happen in the wild, but in that place and at that time, they were starkly different.

The Von Behrs, which crowded the riffle water, were golden-brown fish with characteristically brilliant red spots, blood-tinged adipose fins, and blue eyespots on their cheeks. The Loch Levens, which preferred the slack areas, were sleek, silvery fish, black-spotted with no trace of red, and looked very much like miniature Atlantic

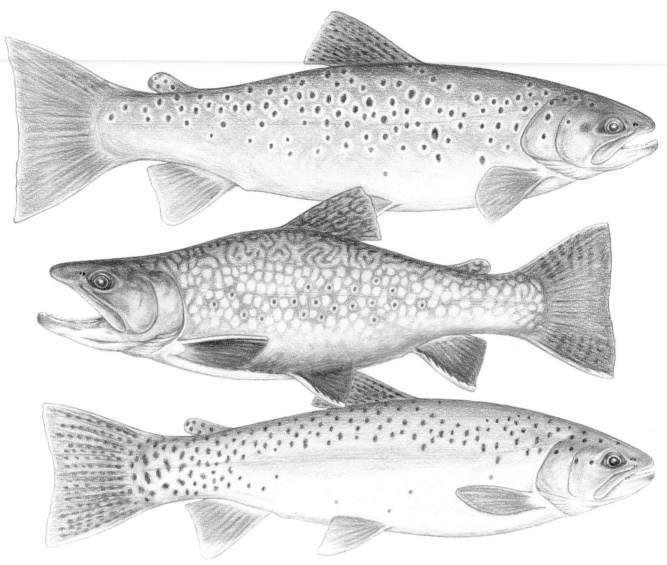

Spring Creek Slam: A fifteen-inch brown, a thirteen-inch brookie, and a fourteen-inch rainbow constitute an unusual species slam on a tiny Cumberland Valley spring creek. Rainbows are the dominant species and a fair number of browns share the water, but the brook trout is an oddity.

salmon. Many even sported the Atlantic's X-shaped marks on their sides. Except for their spotted dorsal fins and the length of their jaws, they bore more of a resemblance to the salmon than to any brown trout that I had caught before.

Both strains were remarkable, wild fish, made more so by their unusual circumstance. In odd and coincidental ways, these immigrant Germans and Scots mirror the human history of this rich valley. Despite their non-native status, I have always had enormous affection for wild brown trout, and I pursue them at every opportunity. Few, however, have made as lasting an impression on me as the residents of this unfortunate little stream. They have inspired lifelong questions about trout genetics and about the limitations of taxonomy in expressing differences between distinct populations.

Such questions have even assumed current political significance in a time when we have been told that hatchery fish are the legal equivalent of wild fish when they are the same species.

The story of how the Loch Levens came to adopt this little creek is a curious chapter from the glorious past, circa 1930. But that story has already been told, and to recount it here would give too much away. To the best of my knowledge, the descendants of these fish are still there, perhaps still retaining their original appearance. I have recently tried to confirm this, but the section I fished as a youngster is no longer recognizable, let alone fishable. I will keep trying.

Forgive me for not referring to these streams by name—the few who know them well will probably recognize them immediately. Should you somehow stumble upon these places, I hope you will treat them with the respect due their history and their fish. In truth, the identity of these streams is only thinly disguised, and anyone who wants to do the homework should be able to discover their names. They are all public waters (at least in the portions I have described), and they receive no special protection, other than the unlikely nature of their existence or the difficulty of their fish and fishing. In fairness, I should also caution that a casual visit to any of them is likely to yield disappointment—they are not the sort of streams that surrender their secrets easily. I only mention them because I want to tease you with some of the possibilities that still exist for the fly fisher willing to invest the time and effort required to learn the secrets of home waters. I worry that I have already said too much about some of mine, but I also worry that secrecy is not always the best protection for frail resources. This paradox troubles anyone who cherishes a special place in this time of unparalleled pressure.

Despite the competition that we face today, there are still fine fish to be caught and wonderful waters to be explored. These are the rewards for the skill, effort, dedication, and special, intimate knowledge that grows from a personal relationship with the waters we love. The rewards do not come easily. I won't even pretend that I can make it easy for you—I cannot. Yes, there is easy fishing to be found. You can chase hatchery trucks or fish pay-to-play parks or hire experienced guides to do the hard work for you. If you are severely overcapitalized, you can even fly off at a whim to places where the trout have rarely seen a fly. None of this is bad—guides and wilderness lodges, especially, have a respected and time-honored place in the traditions of the sport. But some of this is just plain lazy. Patience is a virtue of fishing; laziness is not. While I cannot make things easy, what I can do, perhaps, is clarify the process so that it is less confusing and so that less of your effort will be random or wasted. If there is one simple rule I have learned in my time on

Immigrant Browns: The German Von Behr (top) *and the Scottish Loch Leven* (bottom) *shared a suburban spring creek without any apparent mixing of the two strains. The stream in which these fish resided was abused and ignored, but between its overgrown and littered banks an unusual story unfolded. The unique characteristics of these two original strains have been blended in the brown trout stocked in most places today, and relatively pure specimens exist only in isolation.*

pressured waters, it is that *success comes from a willingness to do things that others consider too much trouble.* Simple, but not easy.

At times, this can leave us with a sad and wistful longing for the good old days, when men were men and trout were trout, and the only thing between them was a tight line stretched over virgin waters. With all the negative pressures bearing upon our sport today, I suppose it is forgivable if we succumb to such whining. But before you become too greatly discouraged, let me offer some older words which are not my own:

> A million boots have plowed the sand and pebbles of this stream bed, a million flies have whipped its surface. It is old, old fishing landscape, scarred with its human contacts, familiar and friendly and kind to the childlike frailties of anglers. It will accept you and take you to its heart. But it will challenge your fishing skill today, as it never challenged anyone's a century back. Its fish are inured to the grosser solicitations of mankind; only the most deftly placed lure, the subtlest and most inobvious persuasion will win them.

The words belong to Howard T. Walden II, author of *Upstream and Down* and *Big Stony.* They are from an article he wrote for *The Sportsman,* dated April 1937. There is a kind of strange solace in these words, for they add the perspective of the ages to the problem of pressure. The difficulties facing trout and trout anglers may increase with time, but they are not new. Each generation of fly fishers must confront the pressures of their time and devise new ways to master their situation while retaining the delights that have always attended our sport. When we face these pressures squarely and defeat them on our own terms, the rewards are as sweet now as they were then. And the communion we feel with our fellow anglers at such times is as ancient and timeless as the lovely fish we seek.

CHAPTER TWO

Principles of Fly Selection

I seldom write about angling in primitive areas where good trout fishing is easy to come by, because object lessons are on difficult streams.
—A. J. McCLANE, *The Practical Fly Fisherman*, 1953

A great trout rises, and a fly is presented in its line of drift. The fly passes untouched. The trout rises again. Perhaps the timing was off. The trout rises, and a steady countdown begins—"one alligator, two alligator, three alligator . . ." until the enumeration coincides with the rise. Now the countdown begins anew, and at the appointed moment the fly is delivered. The trout rises on cue—to a natural fly, inches from the artificial. The process is repeated. So is the outcome. Is it the fly? Maybe it's too large (or small or dark or bright). A change is made, and the new candidate is delivered on the count. The trout no longer rises. Two . . . three . . . four more casts cover the spot. Nothing. Dejected, the unhappy warrior moves silently upstream, scanning for a new prospect, a fresh hope. What went wrong? Should he try the first fly over another fish? Was the presentation flawed? Should he study the naturals for clues? Questions without answers. Doubt rises, and in the abandoned water below, the trout rises . . . again . . . and again. Damn!

These are the things that vex our days and the fish that force us to question our assumptions and compel us to try harder. And, for the truly obsessed among us, these are the fish whose coy rejection keeps us coming back for more.

It would be sad if trout had no defense against the onslaught of our age. To their infinite credit, this is not the case. Somewhere in their miniscule brains lies the uncanny ability to learn from and adapt to our increasingly sophisticated attempts to fool them. Of course, these defenses depend, more and more, upon being given the opportunity to learn. The advent of the catch-and-release ethic in our sport plays an important role in facilitating that education. In many heavily fished waters, trout are subjected to an almost constant barrage of artificial flies of every description. In the face of this parade of phonies, some fish seem to have developed an immunity to the allure. These fish can appear to taunt us with their acquired resistance. Even when they choose to rise to the fly, they can turn away at the last instant, leaving nothing but an insulting disturbance on the surface.

Pennsylvania's Cumberland Valley is home to many such supremely schooled fish. The names of many of the streams that drain this limestone-laden region are famous. The Letort, Yellow Breeches, Big Spring, Green Spring, Falling Spring—names that recall waters winding among elodea and watercress beds, beneath willows and sycamores, and alive with beautiful, fat-bellied trout and their handsome avian associates: kingfishers, great egrets, and great blue herons. As kids, we called this place Cow Valley, although that appellation is less appropriate now that the farm fields of our youth are rapidly being replaced by housing developments and strip malls. Then, as now, many of these fabled waters contained specially-regulated sections where catch-and-release produced fish that were particularly jaded and generally uncooperative.

I could often be found on one of these sections, flailing away at some hypereducated trout that was thumbing its spotted nose at every fly in my arsenal. On one

Letort Spring Creek: This classic limestone spring creek is world-renowned for its large and finicky brown trout. It epitomizes the challenge of spring creek fishing and has inspired many thoughtful anglers over the years.

such occasion, a grizzled old veteran of the fishing wars sidled up to me, apparently amused by my vain attempts to slap the fish into submission.

"Giving you fits, isn't he?" he asked with a sly grin. I grunted something in reluctant acknowledgment of his unwanted attention and continued casting. But the voice of experience came again. "That old boy is too smart to be fooled by your flies anymore." I said nothing and set about whipping the water with renewed fierceness. "Toss him a big fat nightcrawler, and I bet he'll take it." Now I was irritated. The very mention of worms was insulting.

"*That* isn't legal," I replied curtly.

"Yep," the old man agreed, "that's why he'll take it." I redoubled my efforts and eventually the old guy wandered off, shaking his head in a knowing way.

I can be motivated by a form of spite—there is no surer way to spur me on than to tell me that I can't do something. My greatest successes and my greatest failures spring from this stubborn resistance. "We grow too soon old, and too late smart" goes an old Pennsylvania German expression I remember from my youth. With

the belated grace that comes with age and experience, I now recognize that the old fisherman was offering me a secret that I was too impatient to accept. He wasn't suggesting that I break the law or that I should resort to worm fishing. Rather, he was quietly trying to get me to take a moment to reflect upon the reasons for my failure and to understand the nature of my opponent's defenses. Here a stubborn fish and a stubborn fisherman were locked in an obvious stalemate; the fish wouldn't take, and I wouldn't quit. The wise old guy wanted me to see that the fish's familiarity with flies had bred contempt and that only the unfamiliar offering stood a chance of breaking the deadlock.

In the intervening years, I have learned, time and again, the lesson that my unwanted mentor had tried to teach. Long before I left Cow Valley, I was using this strategy to fool the cagey trout that swam its springs. The idea was not to break the laws that govern those specially regulated waters, but to break the rules by which the trout of those waters discerned the fakes that drifted above and around them on a daily basis. The essence of the strategy I've come to use so frequently on difficult fish was contained in an old fisherman's unwelcome advice.

WHY THE FLY MATTERS

Pattern versus presentation is the basis of a fairly old debate among fly fishers. Despite the durability of this debate, I have a hard time believing that any experienced fly fisher would come down strictly on one side or the other. Dismissing either seems limiting and narrow-minded and ignores the important relationship between the two. Some presentations are greatly enhanced by the choice of fly, and vice versa. There *are* situations where an inverse relationship exists between the two; conditions requiring difficult presentations may be less demanding of the fly, and conditions allowing simple presentations may demand more of the qualities of imitation. But this doesn't negate the importance of either; it just weighs them in the light of circumstance.

On the other hand, we are all shaped by the waters we fish, and our attitudes may merely reflect the character of those waters. This is an understandable provincialism, and we need to overcome these place-specific prejudices in order to be successful on waters of another character. I feel fortunate to have been schooled by home waters with very different dispositions. Pennsylvania is a diverse state, and the limestone springs of the Great Valley are a sharp contrast to the rough-and-tumble streams that fall from the Pocono Plateau. From a fishing standpoint, about the only thing these places have in common—other than trout and a few hatches—is a certain level of fishing pressure. From a fly-tying standpoint, however, the common ground between these two different geographic regions is that both have inspired many developments in the design of flies and continue to do so. The connection between fishing pressure and the evolution of fly patterns is no mere coincidence. In fact, it is a valid generalization to say that the evolution of the fly is a pressure-driven phenomenon. Put another way, the fly becomes more important in direct proportion to the amount of fly-fishing pressure an area receives. This in no way serves to diminish the importance of presentation, but it does establish that, while presentation may be the most important aspect of fishing effectively on lightly pressured waters, presentation coupled with astute fly selection is the formula for success on heavily-pressured waters. We should embrace all the skills of fly fishing if we want to be adaptable anglers. So, if we can agree—at least for the moment—that pattern choice can be important, let's investigate a few fundamentals that regulate the selection of an appropriate fly.

Trout see what they need to see. Trout are simple creatures and respond to simple stimuli, no matter how layered their responses may become through experience. It is normal and even entertaining to anthropomorphize trout, but it is a mistake to let this contaminate our appreciation of their nature. Stimulus and response determine a trout's feeding pattern, and risk and reward

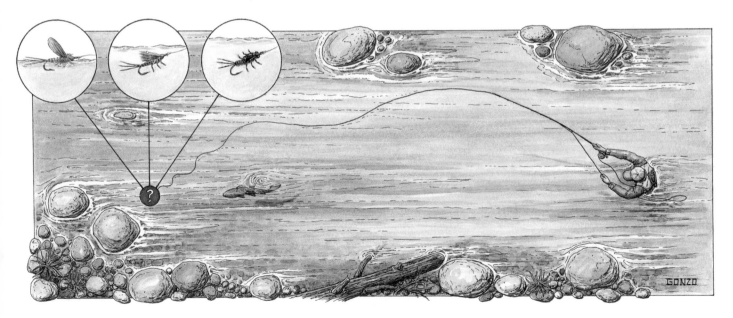

Pattern and Presentation: Presentation is an essential fly-fishing skill, and on some waters it is most important. But when trout are fixated on specific prey or are subjected to heavy fly-fishing pressure, fly selection cannot be ignored. Under these conditions, knowledge of the trout's prey and the imitative or beguiling elements that convince the fish to take the fly is a critical part of a successful strategy.

motivate the trout to continue or alter that pattern. If a single distinguishing trait is used to identify and capture prey, and the trout is consistently rewarded, then it has no need to further complicate things.

Let me provide a rather notorious example. Visitors to Boiling Springs are fond of feeding bread to the ever-present population of ducks, geese, and swans on Boiling Springs Lake. Many of these visitors find their way to the Little Run, which is the outlet channel of the lake. There they feed the trout, which are clearly visible in the shallow water of the run. If you are fishing when this occurs, the fish that had been treating your favorite flies with disdain suddenly behave like pigs at a trough, jostling each other to get at the free meal. The fish that reside below the little footbridge that crosses the run are so accustomed to this handout that they will often rush to take up positions at the mere appearance of someone standing on the little span. At such times, something white wrapped on a hook may be the only subterfuge required to fool the fish—the sight of something white falling to the water is sufficient incentive to send several fish charging to intercept it.

Of course, this lowly tactic is well-known to anyone who has spent much time fishing the run (I was first introduced to the ploy more than thirty years ago), and sooner or later, most of the fish get exposed to bread flies. With exposure, the response of the fish changes. Several fish may still rush the fly, but now they will usually turn away at the last moment. Under these circumstances, subtle refinements of the fly are required to make it more convincing. I will refrain from describing these refinements for fear of being accused of promoting the use of junk flies. The point is that the fish have learned from experience that the simple white-equals-food equation is no longer reliable. Their needs dictate that they find a way of distinguishing between white food and white nonfood. And even though trout have no ability to conceptualize the difference, they are remarkably adept at finding a distinction when they need to.

The primary job of the fly is to make a positive appeal to the trout's scan. To succeed at this task, the fly needs only to show what the fish needs to see. As long as this requirement is met, it doesn't matter what else the fly does or does not represent. In this way, a very simple fly and a very elaborate fly could be equally effective provided that both possess the traits that satisfy the trout's identification process. It would seem, then, that all one needs to do in order to create an effective fly is to determine the key characteristics and incorporate them into the pattern. Sounds simple, doesn't it?

It can be. When the quarry of the moment is an uneducated trout that is conducting a nonspecific food search, most flies will succeed if they can be presented without alarming the fish. Here, the job of the fly is simply to offer a general suggestion of food. If that naive trout is a wild fish, approach and presentation will far outweigh the importance of fly design. If the trout in question has been recently stocked, has missed a few feedings, and has had time to overcome its initial trauma and disorientation, then even approach and presentation are not critical. A familiar plop on the surface of the water may be all that is necessary to ring the dinner bell. For the unfortunate stocker, as the pangs of hunger and the pressures of competition grow, most any fly (lure, bait) stands a good chance of being tested for palatability. This vulnerability leads to what Vince Marinaro called the "slaughter of the innocents."

In contrast, when the targeted trout has been educated by fishing pressure and is fixated on a particular food form, most flies will fail no matter how careful the approach or presentation. Now the job of the fly is to present specific characteristics without calling attention to any elements that may have negative associations. Educated trout are sophisticated scanners. Usually no single key can unlock their jaws. They are protected by a combination-lock sequence. Penetrating these multilayered defenses requires the skills of a master locksmith. This is when fly selection becomes an artful blend of knowledge and intuition. Determining which qualities of a fly have positive or negative functions is no longer simple, although we can assume we are onto something when a trout takes the fly. When numbers of trout take the fly, either they were all keying on the same traits, or the fly possessed elements that satisfied the various criteria of different fish.

Through the years, many fly-fishing texts have presented attempts to prioritize the characteristics that are important in successful flies. Size, shape, color, light pattern, and other traits have been arranged and rearranged by various authors. Even when limited to the dry fly, which was often the case, all of these systems had inevitable flaws. The notion that the same aspects have the same significance to all trout in all situations is an untenable generalization. The significance of any of these elements is specific to the fish and its situation. The variables involved are too numerous to be represented by rigid priorities. Nevertheless, I do believe that it is possible to organize one's thinking and to approach the questions of fly selection in a logical way.

The easier something is to see, the more likely it is to be noticed. This may seem like a redundant and obvious statement, but it goes to the heart of practical imitation. Fly patterns, mine included, are frequently guilty of representing things that the trout cannot see or will not see in a particular situation. For example, I will often imitate the colors or markings found on the backs of mayfly duns. In dry-fly patterns, the trout cannot possibly see these things. I do this for my own entertainment; the patterns will work without these embellishments. These superfluous elements typically do no harm, but they don't contribute to a trout's decision to accept or reject a fly. Wings obscured by hackle, details hidden by the posture of the fly, colors masked by light and shadow—these are some common, and occasionally unavoidable, instances of imitating the inconsequential.

It may seem, as you consider the flies presented in this book (especially the more elaborate ones), that I am obsessed with realism. I plead guilty . . . and not guilty. I do enjoy making flies that look, to me, like the real thing, but that is never my first priority. That they appear realistic and convincing to the trout is the only important consideration, and such *practical realism* is best evaluated in the stream, not in the vise or a display case.

Realistic imitation is often maligned in fly-fishing literature, with the detractors leveling the incomprehensible accusation that such flies are poor fish-catchers because they are too realistic. That is not possible, and what they really mean is that the materials used to achieve a realistic appearance are often stiff and lifeless, producing a fly that does not move or drift in a convincing fashion—in practical terms, such flies are not realistic enough. The only valid knock against realistic imitation is when we attend to the things that make the fly look real to us, while ignoring the aspects that appeal to the trout. I am never satisfied with a fly until I can make it behave like the real thing. My true fly-designing obsession is with copying the characteristic drift, posture, and movement of the natural prey. If I can address these things, then I feel free to enhance the fly's superficial appearance, knowing that I have done all that I can (short of flavoring the fly) to appeal to the trout's sensibilities.

The issue of how realistic a fly needs to be for effectiveness in a given situation is another question entirely. Extremely realistic flies are usually more troublesome to tie, and questioning why one should bother is completely legitimate. Knowing when the added bother is warranted is the key, and these are questions I will attempt to answer or at least illuminate.

There is one factor that influences imitation directly and is somewhat independent of the other considerations that will be discussed in this chapter. Some trout foods are easier to imitate than others. Consider fish eggs and midge larvae, for example. Both are abundant and important on certain streams at certain times, and both are the models for some of the simplest flies an angler could hope to tie. Curiously, both are also subject to all sorts of embellishment that do not contribute anything to the imitative quality of the fly. Beadheads, fuzzy thoraxes, and other extraneous additions are often added to imitations of midge larvae, yet the real thing has none of these traits. Egg imitations undergo even more bizarre modifications, although in some cases, these are added to make the fly legal under certain regulations.

Large prey with complex characteristics, on the other hand, can be very difficult to represent accurately. Large mayfly and stonefly nymphs have many easily discernible traits that are absent from most of the simple representations of these insects. Postures, movements, appendages, and other elements can be distinctive and, when absent, can be a reason for rejection by a discerning trout. The larger the object to be imitated, the easier it is to notice what is missing.

One of the things you will notice about the series of flies presented in this book is that all of the more complex flies are designed to imitate larger prey. I have long adhered to a dictum borrowed from one of my angling heroes, A. J. McClane. Roughly paraphrased, it states that *when fish are fussy, give them less to find fault with.* This is a good rule for pressured water. Anglers often find that tiny imitations succeed with difficult trout more readily than large flies. Some attribute this to the abundance of midges and other tiny prey found in the waters they fish. This can be true, but the fish also have a much easier time detecting the fraudulence of larger flies. *Flies need to get better as they get bigger.* If you want to catch difficult trout on simple flies, imitate small, simple organisms—like midge larvae and fish eggs.

Whatever is distinctive and consistent can be a trigger for acceptance or rejection. For a trait to be useful to the discriminating trout, it must be a reliable way of distinguishing between food to be eaten and flies to be avoided. These traits can be either positive or negative, promoting confidence or triggering suspicion. If focusing on a distinctive trait is rewarded by a satisfying meal, the trout is emboldened by positive associations. If not, the trout is educated by negative associations and constrained by suspicion.

As the feeding trout scans its environment, it uses distinctive and consistent characteristics to recognize familiar food. A distinguishing trait could be a distinctive color, such as the vulnerable white of a newly molted stonefly or the vivid green of a free-living caddis larva. It could be a sparkle or flash, such as the reflective bubbles surrounding an emerging caddisfly or the silver sides of a feeding dace. It might be a peculiar shape, such as the defensive curl of a salmonfly nymph caught in the current, or a special movement, such as the up-

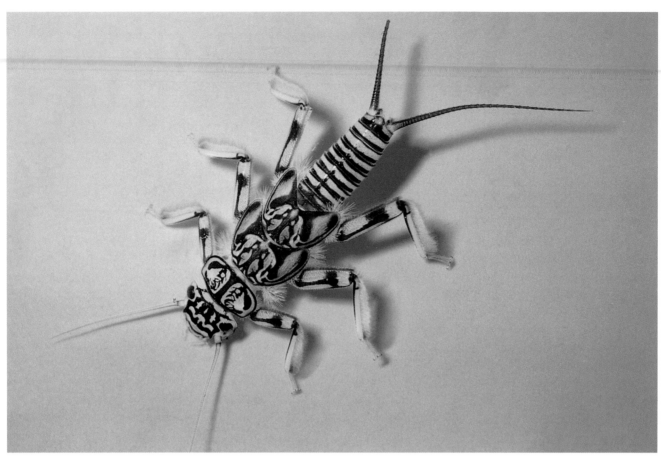

Bigger and Better: Large prey, such as this beautiful stone nymph (above), *possess many obvious and distinctive traits that present problems for fly tiers who attempt to imitate them accurately. The design of this nymph imitation* (below) *follows the premise that flies need to get better as they get bigger.*

and-down wiggle of a slate drake nymph darting in a rif-fle. Often, it can be a combination of traits that identify a particular prey, or various traits may be more or less useful under different conditions. For example, the gas bubbles that form inside the pupal skin of a caddisfly normally stand out, but near turbulent water that suffuses the surrounding area with air bubbles, it is camouflaged. Under these conditions, the color of the caddisfly's body or the pulsing movement of its legs may be the only ways that a trout can tell which bubbles contain food. Similarly, the flashing dace may signal a potential meal to a trout on the prowl, but when combined with the simultaneous flashes of a school of its kind, the flashing becomes a bewildering distraction. The trout cannot effectively target the dace unless it becomes separated from the school. Because of such variable circumstances, selecting only one trait as the basis of an imitation is not always successful, even though that trait may often predominate. This is a flaw, albeit an occasional one, of *impressionism*—the fly-design theory that suggests dominant traits while leaving the rest to the trout's imagination (which is limited, at best).

On the negative side of the equation, distinguishing traits also allow the educated trout to recognize pseudo-prey that it needs to avoid. An unnatural drift or uncharacteristic movement may alert the trout, or the fly may simply lack sufficient elements to satisfy the trout's criteria for identifying a familiar prey. Whatever sets the fly apart from the prey (whether generalized or specific) may become a reason for rejection. The more distinctive the difference, the greater the chance of discrimination.

Hooks and leaders are often suggested as obvious reasons for the rejection of our fraudulent offerings. In fact, these things have been used by fly fishers who reject the notion of imitation as justification for their beliefs. After all, they say, what natural prey has a piece of curved steel protruding from its abdomen or a string attached to its nose? That this argument appeals to human logic is the flaw—it views hooks and leaders from a human rather than a piscine perspective. We understand the concept of hooks and leaders; trout do not.

When a trout recognizes key characteristics of its current prey, the presence of hook or leader is usually no deterrent. It is when those things interfere with the impression that they become significant. When a leader impedes the drift or movement of a fly, or when an unbalanced or improperly weighted hook ruins the imitative effect, then the trout may be alerted to a problem. This is more often the case than the appearance of either hooks or leaders being the source of rejection. However, in constantly fished water, trout may see more artificial flies than naturals drifting past their noses. Under these conditions, hooks and leaders that are obvious and consistent in their appearance can become traits that foster suspicion. The trout never know what they are, but they can learn to avoid them. I believe this is especially a concern with dry flies, because the leader and the hook are more consistently displayed. This true hook or leader shyness is one of the most advanced stages of education, and anglers who pursue scholarly trout are justified in looking for ways to disguise or minimize the appearance of both the hook and the leader.

The ideas presented up to this point provide a raw, unfinished overview of the reasoning behind my approach to fly tying and fly selection. These ideas have grown and changed with my experience astream and will no doubt continue to do so. Please don't take anything I have said as immutable law, because I do not. Instead, I offer this as a starting point from which to develop some more situation-specific considerations that form a set of open-ended guidelines for fly selection. I hope these will help to make some sense of the factors that influence this mysterious process, especially for less experienced fly fishers who may be struggling to sort out conflicting theories or incomprehensible events. For experienced fly fishers, who undoubtedly have theories of their own, I hope these guidelines will provide food for thought and perhaps a worthy challenge to some popular dogma.

MATCHING THE CATCH

What is a trout? I know that sounds like a stupid question, but I'm not sure I can answer it—at least, not with any degree of scientific certainty. I have known since the early days of my trout-obsessed life that the brook trout is really a char, but more recent taxonomic revisions have further clouded my confidence about what constitutes membership in troutdom. The rainbow trout and its trout-titled relatives—cutthroats, goldens, Apache, Gila—are now assigned to the same genus designator as the Pacific salmon, *Oncorhynchus.* Doesn't this make them salmon in the same way that the brook trout, lake trout, bull trout, and Dolly Varden trout are char? And doesn't this leave the introduced brown trout as the only true trout in America? But wait a minute. The brown does have a close relative that is native to America, the Atlantic salmon. Does that make the Atlantic a trout or the brown a salmon? Maybe there's no such thing as a trout! In that case, most of my life has been spent chasing a hopeless delusion. Despite the truth that may be lurking in that depressing observation, I do know that, whatever they really are, trout can be different things in different circumstances.

It is accepted in most circles (scientific, as well as angling) that some trout species are easier to catch than others. The usual order places the brown in the top rank of elusiveness, the rainbow following, and either the brook or the cutthroat bringing up the rear. I can't dispute this as a generality, but I do think there are factors other than sheer brainpower that contribute to this division. The brown's tendency to favor calmer water, to hold tight to cover, and to be photophobic (especially large browns) may add to the difficulty of its capture. The rainbow's penchant for faster water and willingness to feed in open water in the middle of the day (if temperatures allow) may make it easier to fool. The brook trout's habit of overpopulating small waters contributes to competitiveness, which motivates it to throw caution to the wind. And the cutthroat . . . well, the cutt is just dumb—but lovely and loveable in spite of its gullible nature, and perhaps the fact that it is more likely to be encountered in wilderness situations contributes to its indiscriminate reputation.

Experience shows, however, that there are exceptions to the rule. I haven't found fast-water browns to be noticeably more difficult than fast-water rainbows. And the wild rainbows that inhabit the slick, weedy segments of Falling Spring are notoriously tough. Likewise, the wild brook trout that formerly resided in Big Spring could be as shrewd as any brown. They succeeded in frustrating me more times than not and their disappearance has robbed this stream of one of the main reasons for its renown. Even the cutthroat, when it inhabits slow, food-rich water, can be surprisingly finicky—though it may still inhale a Chernobyl Ant with disturbing frequency, sometimes in the midst of a hatch of pale morning duns!

Of course, when any of these species is the recently deposited product of a hatchery, the distinctions, even though they still exist, are pretty much moot. They are all dumb as posts. To its credit, however, the adaptable brown will likely outlast the others. Wild trout of any species are far more wary than the pellet-fed intruders, and this difference remains even after the newcomers have had a chance to acclimate to their unfamiliar surroundings. Should a stocker be fortunate enough to survive the initial period of dull indiscretion, it still retains the taint of hatchery socialization. It takes a long time for stocked fish to learn to flee from humans rather than looking to them for a handout. Wild fish have no ambivalence about us and are always more difficult from an approach and presentation standpoint. I do have to concede, despite the aspersions I cast toward stocked fish, that the lowly stocker, when allowed to hold over and become educated in the ways of fish and fishers, resumes some of its latent appearance and redeems a measure of worth. As long as this occurs without damage to wild or native fish, such holdovers can be challenging and worthwhile adversaries.

Resident trout are usually more demanding of our flies than nonresident trout. This obviously applies to stocked fish, but it is also true of wild fish when they are not full-time residents of a stream. Consider the gaudy or fanciful concoctions used to entice a steelhead fresh from the sea or a big lake-run brown. Such flies are several layers removed from the flies required to fool a resident rainbow or brown in the same water (though all will take simple egg imitations when the time is right).

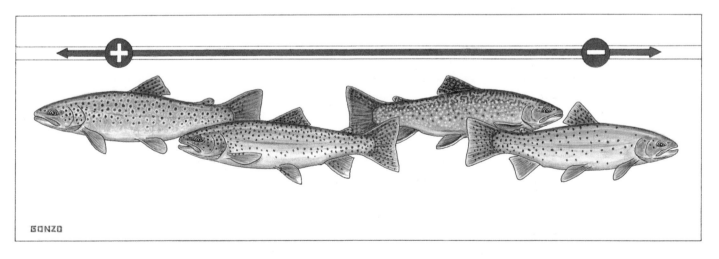

Scale of Difficulty: Brown trout, rainbow trout, brook trout, and cutthroat trout are arranged here with the more difficult-to-catch brown on the left. Few anglers would argue the arrangement of the illustrated scale, but the reasons for the differences are open to speculation. Actual intelligence probably plays an insignificant role, and exceptions are easy to find. This suggests that situational factors probably play a large role in the perceived shrewdness or gullibility of these species.

Big Spring Brookie: The brook trout that inhabited Big Spring were the exception to the rule. They were free-rising fish that could be as fussy as any brown. The late Vince Marinaro, the author of A Modern Dry Fly Code, *caught this lovely specimen many years ago.* V. MARINARO PHOTO.

The sea- or lake-run fish may be hard to catch at times, but that usually has more to do with a diminishing feeding urge than any initial fussiness about flies. The trouble with these great fish, however, is that they draw fishing pressure like a magnet. Before long, they are so harassed that flies are treated as an annoyance rather than a temptation. Sooner or later, fly fishers who pursue the pressured runs from the Great Lakes learn that the most telling secret for fooling these fish is to locate a few that haven't been hammered into a state of lockjaw. The other secret is to select flies that are smaller, less garish, and more like the patterns used for the resident fish as the inevitable pressure mounts.

The most significant factor for determining the resistance of a fish to the fly is its level of education. No matter the species or the origin, when a fish survives long-term exposure to fishing pressure, it becomes a much more astute critic of fly patterns. These noble fish have earned their degrees the hard way, and our own education as fly fishers suffers without such worthy oppo-

nents. May their tribe increase. With the levels of pressure today, they likely will—if we treat them with the respect that is their due.

EATING HABITS

Are trout really as inscrutable as they are sometimes portrayed? Probably not, but no fish has been the subject of so much investigation and speculation by anglers, and no part of our sport has been blessed (and sometimes burdened) by so many words as fly fishing for trout. The vast body of literature devoted to the attempt to understand these fish suggests that there is something about our angling relationship with them that defies precise and definitive explanation. In part this is because that relationship changes and evolves with each generation of trout anglers, requiring us to refine and redefine our understanding. And in part, the popular acceptance of explanations that are inadequate or simplistic can contribute to confusion rather than promote understanding. I believe that the standard, short-

South Sandy Creek, New York: When large lake-run fish enter tributary streams, their initial naivete about flies diminishes rapidly as angling pressure mounts. Smaller and lesser-known waters may hold fish that are less harassed. This stream, where I had my first encounters with steelhead many years ago, receives a small fraction of the pressure found on the nearby Salmon River.

hand description of the feeding behavior of trout is an example of this misleading oversimplification.

This behavior is routinely described as being either opportunistic or selective. It is a convenient division that seems to represent the times we have all experienced when trout were susceptible to a wide variety of flies and others when they wanted something specific. This creates a picture of a fickle creature, alternately indiscriminate and discriminating, manic and moody. With these as the accepted alternatives, it is no wonder that we are sometimes left scratching our heads over the vagaries of fly selection. It is my contention that one term is too narrowly applied and the other is used too broadly. Trout are supreme opportunists and seldom very selective.

In trout, true selectivity is rare. This statement may be a surprise coming from one who obviously believes in imitation and matching the hatch. But, despite the immense debt I owe to the authors of the book, I believe the title of *Selective Trout* is a misnomer. This is a pet peeve

of mine, so I hope you'll pardon me for being peevish about what is partially a semantic point. Selective feeding implies that a choice is being made and that trout are feeding on a prey item disproportionately to that item's availability. We abuse that notion when we use the term to describe all situations in which trout are feeding on a specific prey or when they refuse all but a particular fly.

I don't mean to say that selective feeding does not occur. It does. But such instances are the exception rather than the rule. There are reliable studies that support the idea that trout, especially large ones, will positively select larger prey. And it is possible that trout living in places blessed with a superabundance of food, as in some limestone or tailwater streams, may have the luxury of indulging their tastes. But that is what it is—a luxury, which most trout can't afford.

Yet this is not what most anglers or angling authors refer to when they speak of selectivity. Usually they are describing a situation where a hatch or temporary abundance of specific prey captures the trout's attention. At some point, this preoccupation is so complete that other prey items and most flies are no longer investigated. But is this selectivity? Or is it efficient opportunism? When trout lock onto a predominant food form, I don't believe that the typical mechanism is one of choice. Whether it involves instinct or conditioning or both, I can't say, but it doesn't seem to be driven by the intent to reject other food. Instead, it appears to be something quite different. Rather than making choices about whether to accept or reject potential food, a trout can feed more efficiently on abundant prey by scanning for certain key characteristics and putting its feeding response on autopilot. This explains why the minority prey items (or dissimilar flies) are ignored. Ignored, not rejected. It also explains why fish seem less fussy early and late in the hatch; only abundance engages the automatic response.

I am suggesting that a trout feeding on a heavy hatch is not like a child who eats everything on the plate except the vegetables. That's a choice. Instead, this type of feeding induces a kind of tunnel vision. As in the case of a horse fitted with blinders, things that would interfere with the efficient performance of the task at hand are eliminated from consideration. This may be one reason that trout feeding on a heavy hatch can often be approached more closely than when they are not hatch-feeding. To me, the more accurate term to describe this phenomenon is *fixation,* not selectivity.

I know that there are well-known examples of the selectivity of trout. These may be accounts of a trout feeding on a particular phase of a hatch (say, emergers rather than duns) or only one sex of an insect (such as female Hendriksons) or one hatch to the exclusion of another concurrent hatch (dark blue sedges instead of green drakes). These must be proof of trout exercising selective choice, right? Perhaps, but ease of capture and immediate availability are more likely to be the cause of the perceived preference. I believe that closer inspection will usually reveal that these are simply instances of trout feeding opportunistically on whatever is most available around their particular station. For a trout to do otherwise would be counterproductive. On those occasions when they do ignore abundant food, it is usually due to our interference rather than their preference.

I believe that trout display five feeding behaviors or modes—two common modes, two relatively uncommon modes, and a fifth mode that can overlay and alter any of the other four. Trout adjust their feeding behavior according to the relative abundance or scarcity of food and according to the pressures they receive from either population density or angling. Let's begin with the common modes.

General feeding. This mode corresponds to what is usually described as opportunistic feeding. Trout operate in this mode when food is being encountered intermittently and in a variety of forms. Those that live in impoverished streams where food is scarce will operate in this mode nearly all the time. The trout will usually accept whatever food is present, and the same will be true of their response to flies provided that the fly can be delivered without frightening the fish. This last proviso is usually the key to success in a general feeding situation, and it places a premium on approach and presentation. In this mode, trout remain fully alert to their surroundings, and their level of spookiness is high. The relationship between food and safety is always a balancing act for the trout. When there is no immediate bonanza to distract them and they are not starving, the balance will often swing in favor of safety.

Most flies stand a reasonable chance of succeeding when trout are feeding in this mode, and the selection of the fly is more a matter of deciding what can be most easily and effectively presented to the trout in a given situation. I will usually select an imitation of a familiar food—a medium nymph (such as a slate drake or a sulphur nymph) for runs, a large nymph (usually a stonefly) for pocket water, a medium dry (such as an Elk Hair Caddis or a yellow sally imitation) for shallow riffles or tiny tribs, a small crustacean (scud, sowbug, or little crayfish) for quiet limestoners, and a baitfish imitation (usually a sculpin or a dace) for stretches that might harbor something of size. I will rarely turn to attractor flies unless off-color water or the need to get the trout's attention from a distance suggests that they might have an edge. I can't argue that attractor flies won't perform well for general feeding at other times—it's just a personal prejudice.

Fixated feeding. This is the mode that trout enter, perhaps involuntarily, when an abundance of a particular food appears. As I have stated, my belief is that this response is a kind of efficient opportunism, and very little selection, if any, is involved. When trout become preoccupied with a particular food, two things usually change—they abandon some of their customary caution, and they ignore any potential food (real or imitation) that doesn't possess the distinctive characteristics of their prey (as they perceive it) until the abundance subsides. The fixation phenomenon can be observed in wilderness trout and civilized trout alike, and it exists regardless of fishing pressure.

When confronted with an abundance of a particular prey, whether from a hatch or other seasonal spike in availability (such as behavioral drift, annual migrations, or wind-induced terrestrial falls), most trout will become fixated to some degree, but they will not always fixate on the same phase of the hatch or on the same characteristics. These variations will usually reflect the conditions around the trout's lie. During a pale evening dun (*E. dorothea*) hatch on New York's Esopus Creek, the majority of the fish that came to my nymph imitation were rainbows, and most that responded to my dun imitation were browns. This situation might seem to suggest selectivity, but I believe it had more to do with the type of water favored by each species. Most of the duns emerged in the slower water and were easy targets for the browns. The rainbows probably saw more migrating nymphs and paid little attention to the few scattered duns in the faster water. Each species fixed upon whatever was most available and easiest to capture around their feeding stations. Fixation is often confused for selectivity, but the former is far more common than the latter.

General feeding and fixated feeding are the two most important feeding modes that anglers will encounter day in and day out. General feeding will dominate the day on food-poor streams, and fixated feeding will often predominate on food-rich streams. Two other minor feeding modes will occasionally be encountered, but they are far less important and occur only in atypical environments or under unusual conditions.

Competitive feeding. If you have ever tossed a handful of food into a hatchery raceway, you have witnessed competitive feeding at its frenzied extreme. The response of the Little Run trout to bread that I described earlier is another example. Hatchery trout are reared in a competitive feeding environment, and when they are stocked in concentrations they retain this behavior until angling, predation, or attrition thins their ranks. Population pressure motivates this behavior, and it is usually the least demanding situation for fly selection. The fish only have time to respond to a crude initial impression before charging the fly—any further investigation would mean that they will lose the potential meal to a hastier competitor. I once had a conversation about terrestrial fishing with a fellow angler who mentioned that he tied a size 12 beetle imitation that was deadly in the early spring when few beetles were in evidence and fewer were on the water. I think he was trying to support my point that terrestrial feeding is often nonspecific. I didn't have the heart to tell him that when his beetle plopped on the surface the hatchery fish were rushing to the memory of Purina Trout Chow and not to the appeal of a land-dwelling insect.

I don't want to leave you with the impression that competitive feeding is exclusively a trait of hatchery fish. When population pressures are high, whether as a nor-

mal or temporary condition, wild trout will feed competitively as well. I mentioned previously that when brook trout overpopulate small waters, they are compelled to feed competitively and that this may contribute to their reputation for gullibility. There are also times when water temperatures become so warm during hot, dry spells that trout crowd into any refuge that offers relief. Such spots become the natural equivalent of hatchery raceways, and as long as the temperatures and oxygen levels remain comfortable, any fly that is dropped to the surface is likely to be swarmed by competitive trout. This is hardly uplifting fly fishing, though, and I hope that if you encounter such a situation, you will simply enjoy the company rather than exploit the situation.

Selective feeding. Yes, selective feeding does exist, but it is my guess that it will play an insignificant role in your fly-fishing success or lack thereof. Specific selective preferences are individualized, and they only matter when your focus is to capture quirky individuals that occupy extremely rich streams. This is an entirely honorable obsession, but it is a rare possibility, and I can only recommend that you read or reread Vince Marinaro's delightful story "A Game of Nods." For most fly fishers and for most trout, the only role selectivity plays is in the more generalized tendency of most trout, when given a choice, to select larger prey. Or, to be more precise, to select the most meat for the least effort. This often means that trout will show a preference for larger prey, but sometimes superabundance and ease of capture will tip the scale in favor of a smaller item. Here is the only aspect of selectivity that really has any widespread significance, and I hope you can see that there is a strong element of opportunism even in this.

OK, I can hear you asking the question, "If all of this is true, and trout are such opportunists, then why do they sometimes ignore abundant and vulnerable prey or spurn a fly that they accepted the day before?" The answer to this question is simple, and we are it. Remember I said there is a fifth feeding mode that can overlay and alter any of the other four. We are the cause of that mode, and you will not witness it among trout that have not been exposed to fishing pressure. Trout that have no experience with anglers and their deceptions can exhibit general, fixated, competitive, and even selective feeding behavior. The fifth behavior, however, is exclusively pressure-driven. It can be mistaken for either selective or fixated behavior, but these are both responses to positive associations.

Suspicious feeding. Trout enter this mode whenever a particular food, fly, or associated activity has had negative consequences in the recent past. They can enter this mode out of any of the previous behaviors, or it can co-exist with any of them. In other words, a trout can feed in a general and suspicious way, or a fixated and suspicious way, or a selective and suspicious way. And, yes, they can even feed in a competitive and suspicious way—refer again to my earlier example of the trout feeding on bread in the Little Run and their increasing fussiness about bread flies.

Some fish can become so wary of the deceptions adrift in their realm that even the genuine article is subject to suspicion and scrutiny. Witnessing this behavior was one of the early lessons I learned from the embattled trout of the Little Run. I can remember watching one well-trained trout feeding boldly near the bank in the clear, thin water. It had developed an unwavering strategy for discriminating between floating food and dry flies. It would follow either, drifting back an inch below the surface, until it reached the critical point where a fly cast above its lie would normally begin to drag. If drag set in, the fish would calmly return to its lie and await the next candidate. If the object continued to drift with no drag, it would confidently tip up and inhale the bug. I caught that fish by dapping—touching the fly, but not the leader, to the water and slowly walking back with the fish until it took. It was a dirty trick, and my success was tinged with guilt. But I continue to use the tactic, so the regret was not insurmountable.

A trout's response to the fly when feeding in the suspicious mode appears to present itself in two slightly different ways. As best I can determine, these seem to be related to the nature of a trout's short-term memory. I am not at all confident of my conclusions, but I will provide you with the evidence from which those tentative conclusions are drawn. The clearest examples I can offer for this also point out the importance of considering the pressure one's own fishing creates. I have become acutely aware of the influence that my own fishing activity can have on the waters that I fish frequently.

In the East, the sulphur mayfly hatches are among the most reliable and popular hatches of the season. Emerger patterns are often recommended during sulphur hatches because, it is said, warm weather allows the duns to fly soon after emergence, and the fish will focus on easier targets. I'm sure that there is some truth to this, but it is not the only explanation. A few years ago on the Brodheads, I had occasion to fish the sulphur hatch on the same pool on consecutive evenings. This was not by design, but the preferred alternatives were occupied on the second evening.

On the first evening, I attended the rising fish with a tandem arrangement—a dun imitation with a wet emerger suspended behind it. This is not my usual practice, but I was testing my options. The fish responded very well to the dun, so I removed the trailing fly to unencumber my fishing. When rising developed on the second night, I started with the same fly that had worked so well previously. The response was poor, and again I added the trailing emerger. Now, this was the fly that they wanted, and I took all but one fish on the emerger that evening. Had the trout shifted to feeding on emerg-

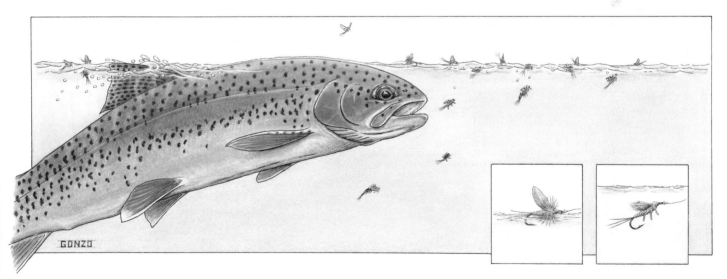

Eating Emergers: There are many rationales used to explain why fish may ignore duns and feed on emergers. On pressured waters, sustained exposure to dry flies is as likely to be the cause as any natural phenomenon or preference. Notice that the depiction of a sulphur emergence shows some of the insects emerging at the surface and others below. This is common for many Ephemerella *species. Emergence is seldom as clear-cut as it is often described, and sometimes we need to look to ourselves for the reasons that fish turn to emergers.*

Olive Eater: This twenty-inch wild brown from the Brodheads took my nymph imitation during an olive morning dun (D. cornuta) *hatch. In order to fool such fish during your favorite hatches, you should be careful not to overexpose the fish to the fly. Success is often followed by failure if we try to repeat the same experience in the same spot during the course of a hatch.*

ers? I don't really know, but they had clearly learned their lesson about my dun imitation.

Trout remember, but in my experience, their memory is relatively short-lived. Salmon "remember" the scent of their natal stream for several years, but I believe that is a different mechanism—more of an instinctual sense rather than a memory of recent experience. Just how short a trout's memory for events is, I can't say for sure, but a related incident may give some clues.

Ten years ago, I was fishing the Brodheads during the olive morning dun hatch *(D. cornuta)* on the last day of May. This is a favorite hatch and has produced many fine fish for me, so I always meet it with great anticipation. As with any favored hatch on favored waters, however, it is easy to overfish a particular stretch in our zeal to make the most of these precious opportunities. On this occasion, I had selected a rough stretch of pocket water for the morning's fishing because these duns are fast-water flies and because many anglers dislike wading on this section. The trout came so willingly to my olive nymph that I never bothered to switch to a dry during the course of the hatch. By the time the hatch ended, I was at the top of the stretch and had landed about twenty trout. As is often the norm with nymphing in this kind of water, I had also missed a fair number of the trout that had intercepted my nymph. It was a morning of fast action.

Six days later, I found myself on the same water, fishing the same hatch. The hatch came later on that cool, overcast morning, and here is the essential statement from my notes—"tremendous response to nymph, but possibly thirty missed hits." I only landed six fish on the nymph that morning, and while I did manage to add four on dries, the lesson was obvious. The fish couldn't stay away from my nymph—a positive comment on the quality of the imitation—but when they realized they had grabbed a fake again, they were remarkably quick to get rid of it.

The tentative conclusions that I draw from these and many similar experiences may or may not be valid, but I live by them for now. If you find that the trout are snubbing an imitation that is usually reliable for a given situation, it's possible that another angler did well with a very similar fly on the previous day. The negative memory of a particular fly seems to last for a day or two, unless exposure to similar flies continues. I know that there are instances of trout being caught on the same fly twice in one day, but I believe these are abnormally desperate fish. The one that comes to mind for me was blind in one eye and could only afford to be half as picky.

On the other hand, if trout are taking your fly but you are missing most of the takes, they are showing their more lasting caution from having been previously caught. This general suspiciousness endures somewhat longer than the specific memory of a fly and is probably cumulative. Trout that are well-fooled take the fly deeply and confidently and are consequently easier to hook. Suspicious trout nibble and nip at the fly and expel it at the first sign of fraud. These fish will take, but few will be hooked. So, if you must fish the same water in which you experienced success a day or a week before, you'll be well-advised to fish different flies or a different hatch. Better still, give the fish a break and find another spot!

Of course, if you are a catch-and-cook angler, these precautions are meaningless—education stops at the frying pan. You should also be aware that a steady diet of wild trout has been shown to severely impair your sex life. I'm kidding about that—the same could probably be said of fishing in general—but it is a reality that catch-and-cook pressure does change the equation. Unlike predominantly catch-and-release water where education is a primary concern in fly selection, general regulation waters present different conditions. If there are any fish left, their education to the fly is much less of a concern.

WORKING THE WATER
In our quest for trout, water is an intermediary—a fickle go-between that can serve as either friend or foe. As an ally, it can conceal our approach and disguise our deceit, hiding our intentions from the trout until the trap can be sprung. As an enemy, it can betray our presence by magnifying every movement and broadcasting every misstep. It can reveal the flaws in our carefully laid plans and present our devices as obvious and ineffectual frauds. Water is a fascinating and contrary medium, and it is no less capricious toward citizen trout. They, however, are far better adapted than we to cope with water's inconstant ways. The essential fluid of a trout's world is alternately a window and a mirror, a transmitter or scatterer of light, a transparent veil or a dirty shroud, and, ultimately, the bearer of rich gifts or the source of stern poverty.

For the fly fisher, understanding the advantages and disadvantages presented by each watery situation is a critical aspect of both pattern and presentation. I have already mentioned that the reputations of trout species for coyness or gullibility may be influenced by the water they prefer, and this is true of individual trout or trout populations as well. The relationship between a trout and the water it inhabits demonstrates many important considerations that influence fly selection. So much about this relationship is intertwined with other influences that they must be considered cumulatively.

Trout that hold in or near fast water strike a compromise. In exchange for food being delivered by an accelerated conveyor-belt, they sacrifice time and clarity in drawing distinctions about their prey. Even though the water in which the fish rests is never as fast or turbulent as it appears to us, the broken surface and surrounding confusion of bubbles and debris make clear vision impossible except at extremely close range. When food is caught in the current instead of being flushed into the slower water of the trout's lie, the fish is compelled to dart into the fray without ever gaining an accurate picture of the intended target. Sometimes, they must rely on taste or feel in order to make the final determination to accept or reject questionable objects.

This provides an advantage for the fly fisher, and the demands on the fly are greatly reduced. The fly must present a simple suggestion and mimic only those things that are blatant and quickly perceived. Fast water is a great leveler for the dub, as the trout may fall for approaches and flies that no self-respecting slack-water fish would entertain. But the angler's reaction to the take must often be swift—a fast-water trout seldom has complete confidence in its decision and is quick to expel distasteful flies.

In contrast, the trout of smooth, slow waters have a much clearer view of the objects they would eat and have plenty of time to make up their minds. They take full advantage of this leisurely opportunity, and when pressured into suspicion, can develop extensive and excruciating inspection regimes. These fish hold most of the cards in our little game, and no refinement of the fly or its presentation should be overlooked in order to improve our odds.

Further complicating this already challenging situation is that pools concentrate fishing pressure. Many fly fishers are drawn to the placid water. They come because the fishing seems easy, even if the catching is not. Obvious rising, easy wading, and simplified casting are the attractions, but none of these are truly as they appear. The obvious risers see countless flies and treat most with casual disregard. The wading is easy, as long as you don't mind alerting every fish in the pool to your presence. And the casting is simple, but the best fish in the pool always seem to be just beyond reach. Inexperienced anglers are particularly beguiled by these places, yet most would find more success where the water is faster. When I was young, we called these places sucker holes, and not just for the fish that occupied their bottoms.

An incident from one of my fishing logs serves to illustrate this point. Ten years ago, in early June, I decided to fish the Big Bushkill. The six-mile stretch of special regulation water within the Resica Falls Scout Reservation is the most popular fly-fishing destination in the Poconos—especially for visiting anglers. It is a ruggedly beautiful stream, with spectacular waterfalls and a number of fine hatches. The Big Bushkill was once a formidable trout stream with wild fish to match its wild water, but those days are long past. It has never been a favorite of mine, for the sole reason that its trout are almost exclusively hatchery fish. Despite this, they become educated by heavy pressure, and that pressure is focused on the popular pools.

A well-worn path leads downstream from Resica Falls to one of the largest and most popular pools. On that occasion, I arrived at this pool to find it already crowded. There were fish rising throughout, as is often the scene. Anglers had taken up all of the casting positions and were working furiously to cover the risers. One fellow stood idly near the edge of the pool. I wasn't sure whether he was just watching or waiting a turn at the risers, but I offered the traditional greeting as I passed. "Any luck?"

"Not yet!" he hollered back. There was something impatient about his tone, which I interpreted to mean that he was, indeed, waiting for an opening to fish. Not wishing to form a queue, I decided to try the unoccupied pocket water that reached around the corner below the pool. I tied on a simple Elk Hair Caddis and began to pick pockets. In short order, six trout came to the fly, and I landed four. Encouraged, I decided to make the short walk to the bottom of the pocket water stretch and work my way back upstream to the pool.

On the way, I noticed a smattering of light cahill duns emerging from the pockets. A smattering is about all you usually get from an emergence of these duns (the spinners are a different story), so I wasn't prepared with a matching imitation. As a compromise, I picked a large sulphur imitation to replace the Elk Hair. The wading was treacherous in the fast water—it almost always is on the Bushkill—but the fishing was as fast as the water. By the time I reached the pool again, about an hour had passed. In that time, sixteen nice browns had come to hand, with several more either missed or lost. I was satisfied. As I made my way past the pool, I saw the same fellow as before standing near the edge. "Anything yet?" I asked.

"No, not yet," he replied. His earlier impatience was now muted to a tone of quiet desperation. I was tempted to suggest that he might have better luck if he found another place to fish, but I decided to leave well enough alone. I made my way back along the trenchlike path, stopping for a while to watch the fish rising in the deep sanctuary pool (closed to fishing) at the base of the falls. When I arrived back at my car, I met another angler who was packing up his gear. He claimed to have spent most of his time on the popular pool and swore that he hadn't seen more than two fish landed all afternoon. When he inquired as to how I'd done, I related my experience on the fast water below the pool.

"No kidding?" was his response, but the arch of his eyebrows indicated that it wasn't a question so much as an indictment. My habit is to be tight-lipped about my fishing success, especially when guarding a secret spot, but when I am honest I get viewed with suspicion. Reticence is the answer.

I'm not sure that my decision to change flies played much of a role in events, but I seldom miss a chance to match a hatch if I can. Anyway, it wasn't much of a hatch, and it wasn't much of a match. I strongly suspect that my decision to fish the faster, less-pressured water was the only important one. I also suspect that had the pool been uncrowded, this might have been a tale about frustration—it is, of course, but not mine.

As we survey the water for clues to fly selection, another consideration is the clarity of the water. Any obvious staining or clouding of the water will affect the acuity of a trout's vision. An off-color condition can have either a positive or a negative impact on the fishing—a slight stain can make the trout more forgiving, but mud never fishes well. This seems like a simple matter, and it is when we are dealing with things like tannin stains in acidic watersheds or silt roiling the water from the runoff of a thunderstorm. For those who fish tailwater streams, however, it can have a more serious impact.

When the Cannonsville Reservoir becomes low in late summer, releases into the West Branch of the Delaware increasingly contain weeds and silt. At first, these releases produce a slight stain that generally improves the fishing. The fish are easier to approach and less critical of imitations. But, as the reservoir draws down, the fishing conditions worsen. Streamers become a fly-of-last-resort as visibility declines. In very dry summers, it can eventually reach the point where the fish can barely spot a fly through all the interference—not to mention the annoyance of having to remove the clingy junk from the hook on every other cast. Fortunately for the West Branch, this is usually a temporary, at worst seasonal, condition.

On the Catskill's Esopus Creek, a much more severe and sobering condition exists. In recent years, the legendary creek has developed a silt problem that makes fly fishing frustrating at best. Long a favorite of mine for midsummer fishing, the unfortunate Esopus is declining by way of the same underground tunnel that made it famous. The Esopus below Allaben was always somewhat discolored whenever the Shandaken Portal was running, but recent events have exacerbated the condition by turning a forgiving tint into a cloud of doom.

There were many things to love about the Esopus. It ran cold and bankfull at times when my Pocono home waters were warm and shrunken. It was filled with wild, silvery rainbows that, though small, were always feisty yet forgiving. At one time it held more wild trout per mile than any stream in New York. So many, in fact, that I had to discipline myself not to move on after catching a fish or two from a particular structure or cover. Often, a half-dozen or more could be gleaned from each stop along

Esopus Rainbow: The wild rainbows of the Esopus have many fine traits that are attributable to the character of the water in which they live. Their color, shape, strength, and willingness to take the fly are all a reflection of their environment. Unfortunately, that environment has declined drastically in recent years, and the mechanism of that decline is the same as the source of its former glory—the Shandaken Portal.

the way. Even the silt-laden water of the Portal contributed to making this a memorable stream. It influenced the character of the fish and the fishing. Not only did it contribute to the trout's forgiving reception of my flies, but it also affected the shape and color of those fish. Esopus rainbows are pale, slab-sided, muscular fish, with a pink blush and irregular parr marks. There are large, colorful rainbows in the Esopus during spring and fall when they run up from the Ashokan Reservoir, but these are not the fish that populate my memory when I think of this stream. Sadly, the Esopus has become a memory for me now, though I hope it can recover.

The last time I fished the Esopus, the water was so thick with silt carried in from the collapsing clay banks of the Schoharie Reservoir that I wondered how the fish could breathe, let alone find a fly. It was painful just to look at the stream in this condition, and the experience contaminates my recollection of a cold, summer stream rich with brilliant wild rainbows.

Certainly the stifling silt of the Esopus is an extreme that extends the discussion well beyond any question of fly selection, but it does show how powerful the simple consideration of clarity can be. Not only is a stream being robbed of fishing opportunities by too much silt, but its fame, the fortunes of the surrounding community, and the very productivity that supported it all are threatened. Fly fishing, which depends so heavily on visual appeal, seldom benefits from dirty water. A slight stain can be a helpful way to take the edge off of a hypercritical fish's eyesight, and most fly fishers would agree

that there's no harm in being a little off-color occasionally. As a constant thing, however, it's just plain filth.

This brings us to the ultimate issue of productivity, and the way the character of the water shapes all things that depend upon it. Trout streams cover a range from impoverished acidity at one end to rich alkalinity at the other. Failed streams fall off the scale at either end. Naturally acidic streams are pushed over the brink by acid rain or mine-acid deposition. Rich limestone streams can be overfertilized by agricultural runoff or, as was the case with Big Spring before the belated hatchery closure, smothered by the discharge of hatchery effluent. Short of these extremes, the more acidic streams normally feature hungry fish that are eager to snap at any fly, while the alkaline waters hold fat, well-fed fish that have a reputation for being fastidious diners.

Limestone streams, or chalkstreams as they are called in England, are the richest and most productive waters on earth. Infused with cold spring water, embedded with water weeds and the insects and crustaceans they shelter, and endowed with trout that enjoy the best of all possible worlds, these streams are also rich in fly-fishing legend and lore. Many of our most sophisticated practices and most elegant flies were developed to match the demands of these waters and their trout. For many they are the ne plus ultra of fly fishing for trout.

But there is another, equally powerful paradigm in trout fishing. It is found in the youthful ebullience of a splendid mountain stream. Dramatic and enthralling, these rugged waters have different charms and present different challenges. In the English fly-fishing traditions that inspired our own, this is the classic contrast between the gentle chalkstreams of Hampshire and the swift North Country streams. In Pennsylvania fly-fishing traditions, that contrast is mirrored by the limestone spring creeks of the Cumberland Valley and the quick, boulder-strewn streams of the Pocono Plateau—both my beloved home waters.

In my mind (and my heart), the best mountain streams and the best limestoners attain a rough parity of virtues. The rich spring creeks have more of the most difficult kind of water—slow, smooth, weedy, and with hatches of long duration and incredible density. While this is generally acknowledged as the ultimate test of fly-fishing and fly-tying skills, spring creeks often lack vari-

ety. The best mountain streams offer a greater diversity of hatches and water types. These require different flies and techniques and are a valuable complement to the skills developed on their spring creek counterparts. Both types of streams hold important lessons. They are the bookends of fly-fishing lore. Learning to fish these contrasting waters well is like earning a degree in the classics.

LOCATION, LOCATION . . .

Today, the unmistakable influence of fly-fishing pressure is so widespread that it reaches deep into remote wilderness destinations. Have you noticed how many of the glossy, grip-and-grin photographs show otherwise-beautiful Alaskan rainbows sporting Joker-face smiles? This grotesque disfiguration results when the maxillary

Pennsylvania Trio: Pennsylvania is blessed with a wide diversity of trout waters. The Letort (above) *is the quintessential spring creek, and its smooth, rich, weedy currents define the experience. Penn's Creek* (top right) *has limestone spring origins and is fed by other limestoners, but it has many different types of water. This variety of habitat is reflected in the greater variety of its hatches, and its fast-water stretches present very different fishing conditions that the Letort. Cherry Run* (bottom) *is a tributary to Penn's Creek outside of the limestone belt, and it displays all the traits of a tumbling mountain brook. Such streams may have a diversity of insect life, but hatches are typically so sparse that imitating them is not necessary. The fishing on such streams is nearly the opposite of the spring creek experience. Each stream has unique and valuable lessons to teach, and the adaptable angler will try to learn them all.*

flap is torn away. It is a sure sign that the fish has been hooked before and is aggravated by the practice of pegging an egg imitation on the leader well above the hook. The argument for this arrangement is that it prevents a fish that has swallowed the egg from being deeply hooked, but it results in most fish being hooked on the outside of the jaw and tearing the maxillary during the fight or a rough release. It is true that wilderness fish sometimes gulp their food with little of the defensive testing and tasting that their more educated counterparts display, and they deserve some protection from their own gluttonous tendencies. But one also wonders if another reason behind the wide adoption of this practice is that guides are compelled to cater to a great number of neophytes who cannot recognize when a fish has taken the lure.

Anglers are drawn to the wilderness for many reasons. Unbroken beauty, a sense of adventure, an escape from the tedium of civilized life—these are all attractions, and any one is sufficient to plan a wilderness trek. But the angling attraction is unspoiled fishing. Wilderness fish are big and easy to fool. Fly selection is a simple, sometimes whimsical, task. Sure, a heavy hatch or other abundance of prey can produce fixation even in wilderness fish, but standard imitations will usually suffice. When they will not, pressure is often the culprit,

Rough and Tumble: The rugged streams that descend the Pocono escarpment present a very different character from the gentle limestone creeks that traverse the Cumberland Valley. Precipitous terrain also creates protected stretches or pockets where difficult access shelters trout from extreme angling pressure. The trout that feed in these protected areas are generally less critical of our imitations than trout in surrounding areas where exposure to the fly is far more frequent.

even in these unspoiled places. Uncontrolled pressure has spoiled countless wilderness destinations in the past, and lodge owners, guides, and guests must all exercise restraint in order to preserve pristine fishing.

The type and quantity of fishing pressure that a location receives leaves a distinctive mark in many ways. The scars of mishandled fish are among the most obvious. It is important to realize, however, that whether we fish in relative wilderness or in severely civilized environs, fishing pressure is never distributed evenly. Just as the sure sign of pressure can be found even in wilderness waters, the lingering vestiges of wilderness can be found even in the most pressured streams.

Easy fish are found in difficult places, and difficult fish are found in easy places. If we apply the principles of large-scale wilderness to the conditions of pressured waters, we can develop a valuable parallel in miniature. There are sections or spots on every stream where the fish see little pressure and are less demanding of our flies. These could be places where access is limited by the lack of roads, the presence of rugged terrain, or both. Any section of a stream that is described as a gorge, narrows, or canyon always piques my interest. On more accessible sections, microwilderness may exist as an

isolated feature that protects trout from all but the most determined and creative anglers. Deadfalls, overhanging brush, steep banks, and tricky currents can all form areas where the trout are relatively unmolested.

Three of my favorite Pocono streams have long stretches that are known locally by the same descriptive title—the Gorge. Without exception, riding shanks' mare into these places earns opportunities at trout that see a small fraction of the pressure that educates their more accessible kin. Two of the three can be floated by adventurous or foolhardy anglers (the appropriate adjective depends upon water levels), but the length of the float between access points severely limits fishing time. Hiking into these gorges is also time-consuming, but fishing on foot permits a more thorough exploration of a small section of stream. This is usually more productive than covering many spots in a cursory fashion, which is the norm when floating these waters.

Not all streams are blessed with such gorges. On many, the search for microwilderness must be scaled-down. Deadfalls and blowdowns create isolated pockets of protection that intimidate most anglers. The trout that seek sanctuary in these places may pass seasons without ever seeing a fly or lure. Some of these spots are truly unfishable, but others await anglers who are patient enough to wait for an opening and daring enough to seize the opportunity when it comes.

There is a piece of the lower Brodheads that I call the Woodslot for the large woody debris that collects there. The exact location and configuration of these tangles of trees changes from year to year, but they are always a feature of this stretch. For a while, there was one large blowdown that would catch my eye every time I fished this stretch. My basic appraisal of fishing this knotty prospect was that one of two things would happen. The most likely was that my fly would sweep against the debris, being immediately and irretrievably snagged. The other, should the fly manage to encounter a trout before a tree, was that the fish would instantly bolt into the branches—different mechanism, same result. On one visit, however, the prevailing water level seemed to present the possibility of a third outcome. In order to avoid the other two, everything would have to work perfectly. On this rare occasion, it did.

With the first drift of the fly, I managed to feed the offering through the narrow opening between the trunks of two downed trees that framed the top of the protected slot. Upon entering, the nymph was quickly seized by a fish, and I responded by applying every ounce of pressure that I thought my tackle would stand to the task of getting the fish's head up and guiding it back through the tunnel. To my delight, the tackle held and the tactic worked. The trout proceeded to tear up the surrounding water, but in the end, I managed to land a stunning seventeen-inch wild brown. I'm not sure which was more satisfying, the fish or the method of its capture. In such situations, one crowns the other and they are hardly separable.

Sometimes, the sanctuaries that shelter trout from fishing pressure can be as subtle as a quirk of the current. Preston Jennings, in *A Book of Trout Flies*, recounts just such a situation that occurred more than seventy years ago but only a couple of miles upstream from my Woodslot conquest. Jennings tells of a "free riser," a "constant feeder," that occupied the far side of the Brodheads,

Deadfall Denizen: No matter how much angling pressure a stream receives, it is never distributed evenly. There are always places where the fish see few flies due to the difficulties presented by their lies. Fishing for these fish is hard, but fooling them with the fly is usually easy. Deadfalls are obvious examples of sanctuaries from pressure, but sometimes a tricky current is all that is needed to protect the fish from the unimaginative angler.

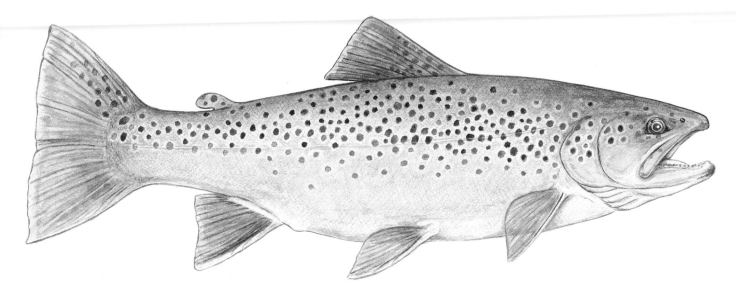

Breeches Brown: This twenty-three-inch female took a simple streamer fished from an unusual angle. She appeared to be the stream-born product of hatchery parents and was protected by a tricky eddy in the middle of a famously pressured spot—the Allenberry dam. Fooling exceptional fish in pressured water often demands a degree of novelty in either the presentation or the fly or both.

across the tracks from a small hotel in Analomink. He tried this fish and allowed others to try it, but after two hours of trying, the fish could not be caught nor put down. When he finally conceded defeat, he retired to the hotel bar where he reluctantly confessed his failure to his host. The proprietor, a Frenchman that Jennings only identifies as Charley, responded by describing a fish that had held the same lie in the previous year and was reputed to be untouchable. In answer to a wager to that effect, the Frenchman had taken the fish by wading into position on the far side of the stream. "He had said enough!" exclaims Jennings in his book, and following the insight offered by his host, he proceeded to take his fish the next day—on his first cast and with the same fly it had so thoroughly spurned the night before. The crucial difference was the trouble of crossing the stream and sneaking along under the alders.

Even on extremely pressured waters, sometimes all that is needed is a fresh perspective from which to view a situation. The dam at Allenberry on the Yellow Breeches is a familiar landmark to any angler who has fished the popular catch-and-release section of this stream. Several years back, I was fishing above the dam on a hot July evening when the fishing was off. A handful of yellow drakes had emerged, but there were too few to generate any interest. My count for the evening was one stocked rainbow and three rock bass, and as dusk approached, my attention was drawn to the other side of the dam.

Under medium or low water levels, current peels off either corner of the dam and a slow, eddying pocket forms near the middle against the dam face. When I fished below the dam, I usually had success fishing along the current on either side but had seldom been able to solve the riddle of the eddy. From my point of view above the dam, I saw a fresh angle on an old tactic. I would often fish a large streamer at dusk as a last-ditch effort when the anticipated hatch failed to develop or was otherwise disappointing. Here was a chance to show that streamer to the fish in a way that they seldom see it.

I cut back my tippet and tied on a large black streamer. I was fishing a wimpy six-and-a-half foot, three-weight rod (I had intended to fish the Little Run for old time's sake, but it was too crowded), and I lobbed the streamer over the dam breast and started to swim it into the eddy. There was an enormous swirl, and a few seconds later the little rod bowed all the way into the grip. "Now that you've got it, what are you going to do with it?" was the old expression that came to mind.

I held the fish on a loose rein as I made my way to the near corner of the dam. I carefully lowered myself over the face of the dam and eventually managed to find a position where I thought I could land the fish, which had been cavorting freely through the lower water. When I finally brought the fish to hand, I saw that I had a fat, twenty-three-inch female brown. From her markings I could tell that she probably had hatchery parents, but she appeared to be a wild fish. Her fins were perfect. Holdovers, even when they survive long enough to regenerate their stubby fins, usually retain a bent dorsal—her dorsal was crisp and square. It goes without saying that this fish made a perfect ending to an otherwise forgettable evening, but what was even more elevating was that my fortunes had turned on a simple change of perspective.

Situations like this point to the inverse relationship that sometimes exists between pattern and presentation on pressured waters. Where the casting is easy and the presentation requirements are simple, the fish see flies from every passerby and become very critical of pattern. However, in tricky microwilderness spots, the closer the casting and presentation come to the impossible, the more likely that fly pattern will be a minor concern. Easy fish are in difficult situations and vice versa. The difference in levels of education and resistance to the fly that exists between fish in a given stream can simply be a matter of location.

READING THE MENU

The next time you encounter a heavy hatch on heavily pressured water, take some time to observe the anglers around you. OK, that may be asking too much, so let me describe a typical scene. If you could exercise such improbable restraint, you'd likely see extremes of emotion reflecting the fortunes of anglers rising and falling with the vagaries of the hatch. An angler who has found an answer to the puzzle of the moment will be happily engrossed by the business of catching and releasing fish, a fish-on grin plastered across his face. Nearby, another

angler will be frantically searching for a solution, staring into a fly box, mumbling and fumbling, and stealing envious glances at the commotion caused by the grinning angler's fish. Sooner or later, we all wear that grin, and we all are reduced to manic frustration. The best we can hope, as our skill and knowledge grow, is that we grin more often than we grumble.

If you follow the cycles of abundance in a trout stream, you will inevitably experience times when catching fish during a hatch is relatively easy and times when it is excruciatingly difficult. Sometimes the same hatch on a different moment, day, or stream will be the cause of these opposite experiences. As incomprehensible as these variations can appear, there are ways of making sense of these situations. The density, duration, and popularity of a hatch will influence the trout's response to it—and ours, if we are to be successful.

A sparse hatch may or may not be noticed by a trout, but it will rarely place many demands upon the imitation unless the insect has been a reliable resource for the trout over an extended period of time. Sparse hatches of long duration can provide very productive fishing to a reasonable facsimile. Dense hatches command the trout's attention, and usually produce the fixation phenomenon that I described earlier in this chapter. When this occurs, the fish feed as though in a trance, seemingly oblivious to anything except the immediate

Two Tactics: During an extremely dense hatch, the imitation faces overwhelming competition from all of the natural flies on the water. Spoon-feeding the fly to the fish so that it arrives at the exact moment when the fish is ready to rise is a very demanding, but effective, approach. A less demanding, but sometimes successful, tactic is to mismatch the hatch by offering a very different fly, such as an ant, a beetle, or a baitfish imitation. This ploy is more likely to appeal to fish that are on the fringes of a hatching concentration or, in the case of the streamer, to a large, non-rising fish that was waiting for a more substantial meal.

bounty. These hatches typically require accurate imitation of the prey's characteristics, and the longer the hatch lasts, the more critical the trout become.

Extremely dense hatches present the additional problem of competing for the trout's attention amid the scores of naturals available to it. This embarrassment of riches promotes two very different tactics, and each has its day. The first, known as *spoon-feeding,* requires extreme accuracy and near-perfect timing in order to feed the imitative fly to the trout. Trout develop a predictable rhythm when feeding on a heavy hatch, and the fly must arrive in front of the fish at the exact moment when it prepares to open its mouth. The idea is to make it as easy as possible for the trout to eat your fly rather than one of the multitude. *Unmatching the hatch* is a less demanding but occasionally effective approach. This tactic presents the fish with a tempting alternative to the hatch, such as an ant, a beetle, or a streamer. The hope is that the discordant image will break the mesmerizing spell the hatch has cast. My preference is to go with the first tactic and to keep the second as a back-up plan should the first prove too frustrating. Success is not guaranteed with either approach, but having options improves the odds. I have even seen anglers play both cards at once with a tandem arrangement, but I consider this to be a desperate ploy that makes it hard to be accurate with either fly.

Most dedicated hatch followers have had the unfortunate experience of a heavy hatch that the trout seemed to ignore. The hypothesis that the trout have become sated from prior gluttony is often put forward. I suppose this does happen during dense hatches of very large insects (*Hexagenia* mayflies or Western salmonflies, for example), but I have caught too many trout with distended bellies and overflowing gullets to believe that this is the only explanation. Popularity adds a further dimension to fishing the hatch and should not be discounted. I have already mentioned how early success with a particular pattern or type of fly can lead to resistance later in the hatch. Days of heavy dry-fly pressure can make the fish reluctant to feed on the surface, and it may appear that the fish are not feeding at all. Switching to a hatch-matching nymph or subsurface emerger pattern should soon reveal the truth of the situation.

Weather and water conditions can dramatically affect hatching and alter the timing of a hatch, but I believe they can also contribute to lackluster feeding during a hatch. I have no firm theories to offer on how this works—I have had too many contradictory experiences to reconcile at the moment. What I will offer, however, is an example of how another form of outside interference can mess up a perfectly good hatch.

Five years ago, near the end of April, my fishing partner and I witnessed one of the finest Hendrickson hatches we had seen on Pocono waters. The little gray sails of the duns covered the water from bank to bank, but not a rise could be seen. The stream was unusually crowded, but no one, not even the bait and hardware

Surface Rejection: Trout have difficulty making up their minds about surface offerings because they seldom have a clear, unobstructed view of these flies. Educated fish often subject surface flies to prolonged inspections in order to detect some clue that will eventually trigger either acceptance or rejection. While this reaction appears to convey extreme fussiness, it actually suggests the advantages surface flies have over subsurface offerings. Trout can only discriminate based on the elements of fly design they can perceive in a given situation, and these elements are limited in dry flies by the two-dimensional nature of fishing at the interface of air and water.

Deep Rejection: Subsurface flies are seldom subjected to extended inspections, even by educated fish. These flies can usually be seen clearly, and the fish have little trouble deciding whether to accept or reject the fly. Even in fast-water situations, trout often feed on subsurface food in places where they are protected from the turbulence and can view their food clearly at close range. This is less likely to be the case with surface food under the same conditions. For these reasons, subsurface imitations should be tied to a higher standard of accuracy in order to be more consistently successful.

component of the crowd, was having any luck. We had been fishing Hendrickson nymphs prior to the appearance of the duns without a touch. Now, with the duns blanketing the surface, we were completely baffled. We wandered the stream looking for any sign of feeding fish. Eventually, I spotted two steady risers, tight to a rock wall and well below the crowded access point. Both fish took an imitation Hendrickson dun, and I landed one fish. It was a heavy fifteen-inch wild brown that fought brilliantly, leaping head-high three times during the contest. My honor was satisfied, and we departed the scene still mystified by the day's events.

On the way out, we stopped to commiserate with some members of the crowd. My partner commented that he'd never seen the stream so apparently devoid of fish. Then the other shoe dropped. In fact, we were informed, the stretch was full of fish due to an in-season stocking. The state, in all its beneficence, had just deposited a generous load of fish shortly before our arrival. The pieces of the puzzle fell into place. Dump a huge mess of disoriented and well-fed hatchery trout into cold water (forty-eight degrees F at our arrival), and most of the wild fish will be occupied by defending their territories or else hiding in a crevice until the commotion dies down. Apparently, the two risers we had located were in a section too far downstream for the stocking crews to reach. Because of my love of wild fish, I ignore stocking schedules—sometimes to my regret.

Generally, popular hatches that are heavy and of long duration will be the most demanding in terms of imitation. Obscure, sparse, short-term hatches require

less effort. Of course, there are sources of prey abundance other than hatches—concentrations of baitfish or terrestrial insects or the regular downstream migration of some aquatic insects and crustaceans (known as behavioral drift)—but these usually abide by the same considerations.

THE FLY FACTOR

Clear waters reveal much, and the opportunity to watch trout feeding under these conditions is always enlightening. I have already commented on educated trout feeding in slow, smooth pools and the extensive inspection process that often ensues. If you take the time to observe these rituals in clear water, you will probably notice that the most patient routines are reserved for surface food. Some have taken this observation to mean that educated trout are fussier about dry flies than they are about subsurface offerings. I take just the opposite meaning.

Because surface food, or a dry fly, can only be seen in its entirety when it enters the trout's window, trout have difficulty deciding about these objects. This is an advantage of dry flies, not a disadvantage. Underwater, fish usually get a clear and undistorted view of potential prey. For this reason, they do not need to extend their inspections to such extremes. This is a disadvantage for underwater flies, and the reason that I believe nymphs need to be tied to a stricter standard. This runs contrary to much popular practice, but I have complete faith in this interpretation.

Often the interaction of light and water creates opposite conditions for surface and underwater flies. Over-

Streamer Stimulus: Most traditional streamers rely upon movement to fool the fish. When not actively fished, they are far less convincing imitations of the trout's prey. If fish are constantly exposed to traditional streamers and typical presentations, they will follow, but seldom strike, ordinary offerings. This resistance can often be overcome by baitfish imitations that resemble the targeted baitfish even when they are not actively fished. Such imitations offer presentation options that can suggest vulnerability in a way that rapidly-retrieved streamers do not.

head sunlight can reduce a dry fly to a mere silhouette, changing or negating color and obscuring depth and distinction. Only the outline of its shape and the drift or movement of the fly remain as means of identification, and imitation becomes a simplified task. Underwater, the same angle and intensity of light can reveal the color and detail of a nymph imitation in stark display. Sharp-eyed trout will have no trouble distinguishing a shabby fraud beneath the surface, but the dry fly will prove more problematic.

The misconception that trout are tougher to fool on dries is rooted in the practice of fishing dries to rising fish, while using the nymph as a generic tool for fishing the water. Apples and oranges. This notion is further perpetuated by the fact that most casual nymph fishers have no idea how many times the fish ignore or reject their fly. When a dry fly is presented to a rising fish, on the other hand, rejection is assumed every time the fish doesn't take. If you are not convinced by this argument, turn the situations around. Imagine that, contrary to typical practice, we reserve nymphs for fishing to rising fish and dry flies for fishing the water. Wouldn't we be inclined to conclude that fish are fussier about nymphs than they are about dries? What we are really reacting to is the simple fact that fish that are feeding on specific prey are more demanding than fish that are looking for food in general.

Clear-water observation of educated trout can offer insights into other aspects of fly design. The reaction of these fish to traditional streamers is especially interesting. On waters where most of the pressure is of the nymph or dry-fly ilk, streamers retain a degree of novelty and may be attacked aggressively. On other waters, where the fish are regularly exposed to traditional streamers, they are either ignored or become the subject of a curious response. Educated trout will often follow a moving streamer, only to stop or turn away when the streamer stops moving. Sometimes a fish that has stopped or begun to turn away will resume the pursuit as soon as the streamer starts moving again. This pursuit hardly ever results in a take. At best, the fly receives a tentative nip, and that contact concludes any further expression of interest by the trout.

Most traditional streamers are rather poor imitations when not in motion. They rely on motion to create the illusion of life, and that is the secret of their effectiveness. When not in motion, the illusion is shattered and they are perceived differently. Flies that are intended to be fished in motion don't need to be accurate representations in ways beyond the establishment of this illusion. Motion disguises the details and makes all but the most obvious elements unnecessary. Such flies can be made more versatile, however, through the addition of elements that are more convincing when the fly stops or is moving very slowly. For example, I tie imitations of swimming mayfly nymphs (true swimmers and burrowers that swim to the surface to emerge) that contain elements that are probably extraneous when they are actively fished. These elements come into play when the fly is drifted or fished with a slow, stop-and-go retrieve, making the fly more effective for a number of different presentations.

Selection Guidelines

Less Demanding	Influential Factors	More Demanding
cutthroat, brook newly stocked, non-resident wild naive	TROUT	rainbow, brown holdover, resident wild educated
general competitive	BEHAVIOR	fixated, selective suspicious
fast, broken stained poor, acidic	WATER	slow, smooth clear rich, alkaline
remote section protected lie difficult presentation, far cast	LOCATION	accessible section exposed lie simple presentation, near cast
short duration sparse distribution unpopular, obscure	FOOD	long duration heavy concentration popular, well-known
small dry, damp swimming, twitching	FLY	large wet, nymph drifting, still
Ordinary Flies	**Fly Design**	**Extraordinary Flies**
generic suggestive simple	TYING	specific accurate complex

For today's pressured trout fishing, useful flies cover a spectrum from simple, suggestive standards—flies with ordinary virtues—to flies that are uniquely and elaborately suited to very specific situations—flies with extraordinary virtues. Where within that spectrum your fly choice should fall is determined by the cumulation of the influences I have described in this chapter. I know I have given you a great deal to consider in order to guide your selection, and such decisions may seem overwhelmingly complex. Sometimes they can be, but in order to further clarify and simplify this process, I am including a cheat sheet. This condensed outline provides an overview of all of the influential factors, displayed in a quick-reference format. If you are so inclined, or if you simply want to try an interesting exercise, it can be used to chart the requirements of a particular piece of water or to compare that water to others.

I am not a huge fan of the systematization of trout fishing, but we all do it to some extent, less consciously and more intuitively as we gain experience with the waters we fish. Nor do I have any wish to remove the appealing mystery from trout fishing. That is unlikely to happen because the paradoxical nature of this obsession is that the closer we draw to the heart of the mystery, the deeper it becomes. My hope is that, through the application of these guidelines to specific situations, you will be better able to find the fly to try. When you do, you will fish with greater confidence and a greater appreciation of all that makes this sport so fascinating.

CHAPTER THREE

Simple Tools and Modern Materials

The tools of fly-tying are few and simple: a vise, a couple of pairs of hackle pliers,
two pair of scissors and a bodkin are about all that are necessary to turn out excellent flies.
—PRESTON JENNINGS, *A BOOK OF TROUT FLIES*, 1935

. . . nor are plastics excluded from grace . . .
—ANNIE DILLARD, *TICKETS FOR A PRAYER WHEEL*, 1974

Among the many attractive aspects of fly fishing are the opportunities for handcrafting it presents. Today, especially, handcrafting is a satisfying antidote to the overwhelming influence of technology. We can build our own rods, tie our own flies, and customize our tackle in endless and interesting ways. All of these help to make the experience more personal and sometimes more effective. The extent to which we exercise these options varies. Some are quite content to fish with factory-built rods; the quality and variety of these has never been greater, and the best still display elements of handiwork. For others, who place a premium on both craft and tradition, the process of acquiring a new rod is a lengthy one that begins with the painstaking selection and splitting of a long, blond culm of Tonkin cane.

The flies we fish provide an even more pervasive example of the craft of fly fishing. With the exception of certain quasiflies (such as the infamous Alaskan Pegged Egg—a plastic bead and a toothpick), all flies are still tied by hand. Even mass-produced flies had a human hand guiding the thread. Admittedly, the fact that the hand may have done its work in Sri Lanka, where trout are remarkably scarce, somewhat detracts from my point. But the offshore industry typically produces high quality flies at extremely low prices—supply and demand. Fly fishers who tie their own flies, however, put their own indelible stamp on the experience. The act of fooling a fine fish is heightened by having personally crafted the fly that did the deed. That the chances of fooling a fine fish may also be heightened is another reason for learning to tie.

Beyond the artsy-crafty aspect of tying, the fact is that fly tiers have an advantage over nontiers in some of the more practical considerations of fly fishing. The tier is not at the mercy of the commercial menu, however vast it has become. This is particularly valuable when fishing extremely pressured waters, where the trout can become indifferent to the latest hot flies, almost before we have a chance to try them. Tying offers the opportunity to fish with flies that are decidedly noncommercial—flies that will never become popular except with the fish. And tying allows us to imitate prey items that are not imitated, or not well imitated, by mass-produced patterns. I have always felt that, at some level, matching the hatch becomes a fly tier's game. Only the most widespread and popular hatches are specifically imitated by mass-produced flies. Local fly shops may stock some specific patterns to address important local hatches, but even this practice is becoming less common as more of their stock is provided by large commercial suppliers. The diversity of trout stream insects and other trout foods is too great to be represented accurately by mass-produced flies.

TRADITIONAL TOOLS

For most of my fly-tying life, I have produced my flies with the assistance of an old Thompson Model B vise (if you are not old enough to have seen or used one, it's recognizable by the big red knob that opens and closes the jaws). It's not that I have anything against the current generation of intricate rotary vises; many of them are beautiful just to look at. It's just that the B has never let me down, and it does everything I ask of a vise—to quickly and securely hold any hook I care to use (OK, I'll admit that stubbornness and poverty also factor into the equation). I did not, however, use the Thompson for the tying demonstrations that are shown in this book. That vise was an inexpensive Cabela's import that allowed the flies to be positioned at different angles for photographic purposes. The smallest set of jaws (it comes with three) was re-shaped and re-blued, and the vise stem was shortened to accommodate a pedestal base. These changes were made to facilitate the photography, and I found it to be a convenient tool, but I haven't abandoned my trusty Thompson. I wholeheartedly agree with Jennings that the tools of tying don't have to be extensive or elaborate in order to produce high-quality flies. The tools that are found in a moderately priced fly-tying kit are probably superior to many that I use.

I would certainly add a bobbin to Jennings' list of basic tools, as the old practice of securing a length of thread with a pair of hackle pliers (the reason that he mentions needing two pair) is unnecessarily cumbersome. Like most tiers, I find a bobbin indispensable, though I have only one. Many tiers prefer to have several bobbins, either for different applications or to minimize the need to reload each time the thread is changed. Reloading the bobbin isn't much of an inconvenience for me, but I suppose I'm just not very fussy in this regard.

Where I am fairly picky is with the scissors I use in tying. These are not expensive (some came from disposable suture kits that I was given by a friend who is a nurse), but I have learned to sharpen them properly and I perform this ritual frequently. If you don't want to bother with this, there are many superb fly-tying scissors on the market that don't require the constant attention. I would particularly recommend those with fine serration on one or both blades, as they are terrific for cutting slick, synthetic materials without slipping. Eventually I will get around to buying a pair for myself.

The other additions that I would make to the fundamental tools of the trade are less traditional and more specific to my fly-tying style. These include some homemade devices (described in the next section) and three

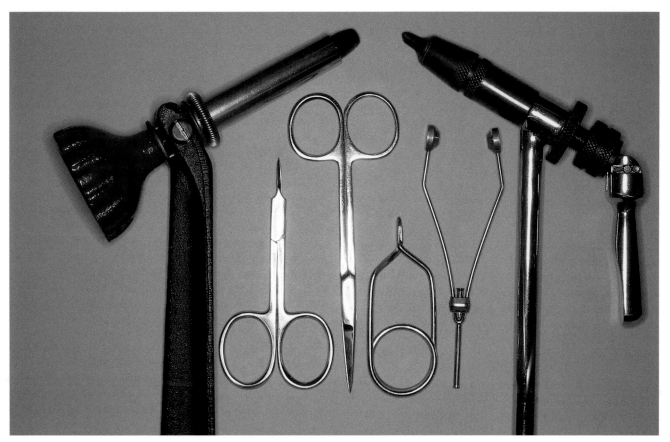

The basic tools of fly tying need not be elaborate or expensive.

A selection of pliers that are useful for crimping, bending, and cutting hooks, and also the more specialized application of embossing monofilament.

or four pair of pliers. The pliers are for uses that Jennings did not envision.

First, because I crimp the barbs on all of my flies, I find that fine-jawed pliers with smooth faces perform this job nicely. I also do a fair amount of bending and re-shaping of hooks. I used to do all of this with my thumb and index finger performing the work of pliers, and though this method can minimize breakage, it also be-comes fairly painful after a while. I now use a round-tipped pair of wire-bending pliers for this purpose (if you have trouble finding these, check your local hobby or craft shop). Another thing I do in my tying—and this really does qualify as abuse—is cut the hook bend from perfectly good fly-tying hooks in order to produce two-part, hinged flies. The only tool for this task is a decent pair of diagonal wire-cutters.

Finally, there's a very specialized and rather perverse pliers application; I have found that the fine ridges on the jaws of my Leatherman pliers produce an attractive, em-bossed segmentation on monofilament used for tails or antennae. To achieve this effect, just place the mono lengthwise in the jaws and squeeze. I don't recommend trying this with an ordinary pair of needle-nosed pliers be-cause they are typically too coarse and rough, and can cut or otherwise weaken the monofilament; the Leatherman jaws are especially fine and well finished. They are also the only expensive pliers in this collection, and can very well be omitted, as this technique is strictly for gilding the lily.

I'm not really an advocate of minimalism with regard to the tools of tying; I'm just an experienced practitioner of it. Learning to do without is a practical way of reduc-ing needs. But I wouldn't want to deny any tool to a tier if it makes the task more enjoyable, as long as that tool doesn't actually interfere with learning some of the im-portant skills of the craft. I do hope that fly making will always be manufacture in the root sense of the word—to make by hand.

HOMEMADE TOOLS

In the event that you haven't already guessed, I should probably confide that there is some Scotch blood in my thoroughly mixed ancestry (Scots-Irish, to be exact and correct, as well as Basque, Cajun, Pennsylvania Ger-man, and Chippewa). Perhaps because of this, I am loath to buy a tool if I can make one. Fly-tying bodkins are a case in point.

The lowly bodkin is among the most useful and least expensive tools in a fly tier's kit. Bodkins are used to pick out fur bodies, to separate fibers, to apply cements, and because I whip-finish by hand, to catch the loop of tying thread as I draw it tight. I like to have several in different diameters. I make these by gluing the eye ends of different sizes of sewing needles into small pieces of cork. The needle is then clamped into the chuck of an electric drill, and the cork handle shaped with sandpaper. I stain the cork and finish it with epoxy, but this is optional.

Along the same lines as the construction of these bodkins is a more specialized tool that I call an *eye holder*. This device enables you to hold small objects, like burnt-monofilament eyes or commercially molded eyes. The pesky mono eyes are prone to slipping from my grasp and getting lost in the carpet; the molded eyes are hard to attach by hand without smearing adhesives across the face of the eye, ruining their appearance. The eye holder solves these problems, as well as being handy for holding other tiny items while attaching them to the fly. It is made by gluing a round toothpick into a piece of cork, shaping as with the homemade bodkin, and then molding a small lump of beeswax to the tip with your fingers. The sticky beeswax picks up and holds the ob-

ject, but is easily removed after affixing the piece to the fly. Personally, anything that allows me to spend less time on my knees doing a carpet scan is welcome.

Another homemade tool that I find useful is a *Velcro dubbing teaser.* This is made by attaching the hook side of adhesive-backed hook-and-loop material to a Popsicle stick (craft stick, if you don't indulge). Smaller versions can be made by splitting and shortening the stick and then rounding the ends with sandpaper or a grinding wheel. Again, I like to finish these, but that's up to you. One advantage of Velcro over commercial dubbing teasers (which often resemble the little wire brush used to clean the bore of a .22 caliber rifle), is that they can be used over relatively fragile ribbing materials—like Krystal Flash—without catching or tearing them. This is not an original idea, but I can't remember where I first heard of it.

I like to incorporate burnt wings and wing cases into many of my fly patterns. A *wing burner* is a requirement for this work. Usually, these tools are intended for shaping breast or other body feathers. I mostly use them for burning synthetic yarn and plasticized paper (Tyvek). Commercial wing burners are fine for this purpose, but they are available in a limited range of sizes and shapes. Fortunately, wing burners are not hard to make. Most

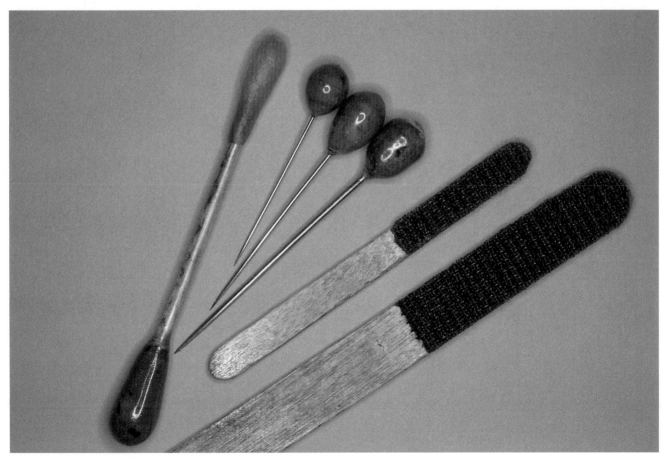

Homemade tools (left to right): *eye holder, bodkins, and Velcro dubbing brushes.*

An assortment of commercial (Renzetti) and homemade brass burners for shaping wings and wing cases.

hobby shops stock flat strips of brass in various widths and thicknesses. Almost any of these can be used to construct a burner, as long as the strip is wide enough to accommodate the shape that you want to reproduce. I make wing burners that range from large, four-inch models to tiny, inch-and-a-half versions.

To begin, cut the brass strip (with a fine hacksaw for the thicker stock, tin snips or heavy shears for the thinner material) to twice the length desired for the finished tool. Fold (bend) the strip in half across its length. Trace the shape to be used on the tip (the open or cut end), and grind or file around the outline. The rough shape is then refined with a small triangular file or fine grinding tool (such as those available for a Dremel or similar hand-held rotary tool) and smoothed with fine sandpaper or steel wool. To create the springlike opening between the two halves, insert a thick needle (or thin nail) between them, near the bottom and parallel to the fold. Squeeze the fold with pliers or a vise just below the needle. Remove the needle. You now have a custom wing burner that can reproduce shapes that are not found in the store-bought models.

None of these homemade devices are required to tie the flies in this book; there are commercial substitutes that will perform most of these tasks quite well. Where that is not the case, there are ways of working around the process in order to produce a similar result. For example, when a specific wing or wing case shape is not available in a readymade burner, the burner can be modified or the shape can be cut (in the case of Tyvek). If you are just experimenting with the fly-tying styles presented in these pages, I wouldn't suggest getting carried away with these devices until you are satisfied with the results of those experiments—both from a tying and a trout-catching standpoint. In this case, the end should justify the means.

HOOK STYLES

One benefit of fly fishing's current level of popularity is the development of new equipment for the fly fisher or fly tier. Inevitably, some of these things are of questionable value and may be examples of the manufacturers promoting a need rather than the other way around. But the fly-fishing industry is no different than any other in this regard, and the best of the new products do fill a need (or a want) for many of us. The tremendous growth in the quality and variety of modern fly-tying hooks is one area where I welcome the new options.

Strength, sharpness, and consistency have all substantially improved over the hooks that were the standard twenty years ago. While those with long memories may feel that the newer hooks are rather expensive, I doubt that the increase is significant. When the difference in quality is factored in, my feeling is that they are worth every penny. I would feel severely handicapped if forced to return to using the hooks of yesteryear.

As much as the improvements in quality, I appreciate the development of many new and useful hook shapes. I have waited a long time for some of these configurations to appear, and they have helped to fulfill designs that I have struggled to produce without them. Some of the flies in this book are barely possible without the newer hook styles, while a few still await the introduction of hooks (or hook shanks, in the case of two-part flies) that will make them more convenient or economical to produce.

The new shapes offer new possibilities, but they present new problems as well. The radically curved hooks can complicate the tying process because either the hook or the vise must be repositioned in order to avoid crowding or to prevent materials from slipping around the bend. And many downward curved shanks are difficult to weight properly without the finished fly rolling over on its back when fished (see chapter 4 for more about this). This disadvantage can be turned to an advantage when the intent is to produce an inverted fly, but if that is not the goal, the result can be disappointing.

I am an inveterate hook mangler. In the past, I have felt no compunction about tweaking, straightening, cutting, or bending hooks to my purpose, and I have broken thousands of them over the years. I still bend (and break) hooks, but fortunately, the new shapes and styles have gone a long way toward alleviating the desire to engage in this wicked exercise. In fact, the quality of the newer hooks is so high that when I do decide to subject them to some form of abuse, I almost feel remorse.

FEATHERS AND FUR

The quintessential tying materials, fur and feathers, have probably been a part of fly construction long before Aelian described Macedonian fly-fishing practices in the second or third century C.E. (depending upon the source you read). To this day, there are some fly tiers who are of the opinion that these and other natural materials remain the only ones worthy of consideration. I respect this point of view, just as I can appreciate those who fish only with split-cane rods. But even among such purists, compromises are often made; few are so pure that they tie with silk thread instead of nylon or polyester or fish with silkworm gut leaders and braided silk fly lines rather than modern synthetics. Someone once said that art, like morality, consists of drawing the line somewhere. Exactly where that delineation should be drawn is not for me to say; I can only share my own preferences and prejudices and leave the tough part to you.

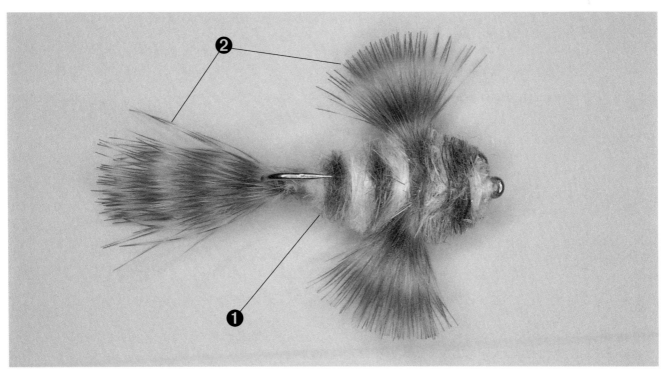

The Basic Bottomfish is a simple baitfish imitation constructed with two natural materials: (1) rabbit fur dubbing, (2) marabou (grizzly).

Some of my patterns are made mostly of natural materials, some exclusively of synthetics, and others freely combine both. I look for materials that can accomplish the desired effect. Whenever that effect can be variously achieved, I defer to the trout for the final selection. In my experience, their tastes seem to be rather eclectic. I can respect that, too.

When compared with tiers that specialize in classic patterns, my use of feathers is limited, and the feathers are easy to obtain. I still use rooster hackle on some of my dry flies, though far less often than is typical. Because of this limited use, I have come to favor the packaged microsaddles for most of my hackled dry-fly work. Some consider these expensive, but unless you can utilize most of the hackles on a dry-fly neck, it is probably false economy to compare the two on a price-per-hackle basis. I have accumulated a sizable pile of partially plucked necks that I have no hope of denuding anytime soon. Another reason that I am increasingly fond of the long saddle hackles is that they can often be wrapped without the use of hackle pliers; I have never found a pair of hackle pliers that wouldn't slip, break hackle, or generally get in my way, and I consider them irritating.

Speaking of irritations, I have a love/hate affair with partridge "hackle" (breast feathers). I love the suggestive effect of these finely barred feathers, and use them more than any other for soft-hackled flies and the legs or tails on nymphs. They can be purchased loose in packages or on the skin. This is the hate part. The packaged loose feathers typically contain a much higher percentage of unusable feathers than useable, again leaving me quite a collection of unwanted plumage. I use enough of these feathers to make the purchase of the skins practical, but

the quality seems to have declined considerably in recent years. I resent paying top dollar for birds that look like they strayed unsportingly close to the business end of a shotgun, or were mangled by a deranged housecat prior to packaging. Mottled hen hackle is sometimes recommended as a substitute, but the fibers of hen hackle do not separate the way partridge does, and they seldom display the fine barring that makes partridge so attractive. The only solution I have—and it is mitigation, at best—relies on the fact that most of the soft-hackles I tie are tiny. The "hackling" technique I use is nontraditional, but it makes maximum use of the few good feathers I find (see the Soft-Hackle Pupa in chapter 6 for details).

There are some feathers that I use because I have not found an entirely acceptable synthetic substitute. These are the soft, downy or maraboulike feathers that come from a variety of sources. Whether traditional marabou, the chicken feather equivalent (sometimes marketed as Chickabou), or the similar fluff that is found at the base of many neck or breast feathers (commonly called flue), these feathers have a supple movement that greatly enhances the lifelike qualities of many flies. Standard applications include marabou streamers, leech imitations, and countless Wooly Bugger variations. I use them to imitate the tails and fins of certain baitfish and the plumose gills of burrowing mayfly nymphs. Similarly, ostrich or rhea herl, while slightly less supple than marabou, provides a superior way of imitating the tails of large swimming or burrowing mayfly nymphs. In this application, the added strength of the herl is an advantage. Many new synthetic fibers have appeared on the market that promise maraboulike movement, but in my experience they fail to fully deliver. I have experimented

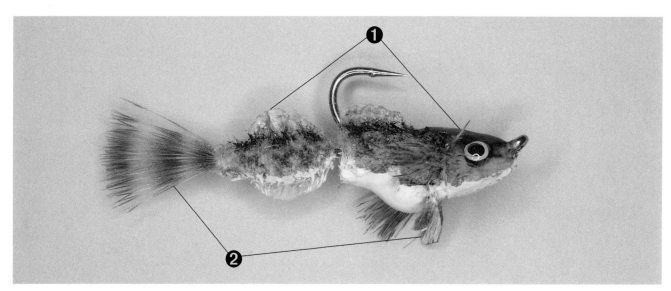

The Wiggling Hardheaded Bottomfish is a complex baitfish imitation made from two natural materials manipulated in unnatural ways: (1) rabbit fur dubbing, (2) marabou (grizzly).

with synthetic alternatives for all of these uses (combed-out nylon thread is the closest I have come to matching the movement), but I keep coming back to the feathers for their unique characteristics.

Fur is another traditional material that I use extensively for constructing flies. The majority of the flies in this book have dubbed bodies, and many of these incorporate natural fur, either alone or mixed with synthetic fibers (such as Antron). Rabbit fur is a staple for dubbing all but the smallest of flies (where fine beaver fur is a more agreeable option). Rabbit is readily available and comes in a vast array of natural and dyed colors, either on the skin or packaged as loose dubbing material. While rabbit is most often used as a wet dubbing, it is quite acceptable for dry flies when a modern floatant is applied.

There are a number of other natural furs that can be used for dubbing nymphs and wet flies. Beaver, muskrat, mole, mink, Australian opossum, and even the wiry Angora goat have applications, but it is hard to beat the versatility of rabbit. It dubs neatly, can be picked out to form a variety of shapes, and can be mixed with synthetics to add sparkling highlights. For practical purposes, I consider rabbit mixed with Antron and many of the other synthetic or natural/synthetic dubbing blends to be interchangeable on most wet, nymph, or emerger patterns, but rabbit remains my preferred natural fur.

Natural fur and feathers have always had a place in fly tying, and perhaps they always will. If you have an intransigent affection for critter coverings as fly-construction materials, then feel free to make appropriate substitutions as you read the descriptions in these pages. With a few exceptions, natural materials can be made to perform most of the tasks required to duplicate these flies—at least in the spirit of their design, if not the precise detail of their construction. Patterns that take advantage of reflective or flashy synthetics are the only instances where substituting traditional natural material becomes problematic. Bright synthetic fibers like Antron have become standards for imitating the reflective bubbles of gas surrounding emerging insects. One could, however, tie emerger patterns with the duller natural materials, and coat them with fluorocarbon powder or a commercial dry-fly preparation like Frog's Fanny. This application causes the fly to retain actual air bubbles rather than imitating them, but I'm not sure where this falls in the natural ethic. Flashy baitfish imitations present similar issues. I have heard of a bold European tier who uses eel skins and other fish skins as components of his patterns. What could be a better representation of the flashy sides of a minnow than the flashy sides of a minnow? This is certainly a natural approach, but it seems to cross the line, doesn't it?

SYNTHETIC STUFF

The variety of synthetic materials available today is almost overwhelming, with more being introduced every season. My own experimentation with such things came about through purely practical considerations. As a young tier, I seldom had all of the requisite materials for tying traditional patterns. I would scavenge scraps of found materials in an attempt to find convenient substitutes for the missing elements. Sometimes these alternatives were promising and worked their way into my present-day tying. More often, failure resulted, but I gained a better understanding of the various requirements of fly design in the process. As I accumulated more and more of the standard stuff of fly tying, the scavenging and substitution gradually declined, until I was producing traditional designs with some degree of skill.

Encounters with difficult trout that wouldn't be fooled by standard flies caused a resurgence of my experimental tying, but a longtime fishing partner motivated my renewed interest in synthetics. Jim Coyne is an amputee who lost his right arm above the elbow. We met through skiing many years ago, but when he learned of my addiction to fly fishing, he expressed an interest in relearning the sport (his grandfather was a fly fisher, and he had attempted to learn as a child). After many fits and starts, we devised the techniques and aids (foremost, a rod-holding device attached to a standard prosthetic arm) that have allowed him to become a very proficient fly angler. As Jim's own addiction grew, however, I found that I was going through a lot of flies. Purchasing commercial flies was not a satisfactory solution—Jim's belief in the effectiveness of my patterns probably exceeded my own. Teaching fly tying to a one-armed student who would be tying with his nondominant hand was the next challenge.

Fly tying can sometimes be a frustrating skill to master, but one-armed fly tying can seem like an exercise in futility. One of the first things we learned was that many patterns that were quick and easy for me to tie were almost impossible for Jim. The prosthetic arm, which was so valuable for fishing, proved to be nearly useless for tying, and we were forced to focus on methods that could work in a largely unassisted, one-handed operation. This is where synthetics came to the rescue. While they didn't make the process easy, they did offer possibilities for manipulation and management that many natural materials did not. Over time and with much (if not always patient) practice, Jim became a competent fly tier. Today, he can tie all of the simpler patterns in this book, as well as many of the more difficult ones (either as depicted or modified in ways that he finds more agreeable). He is the best one-armed fly fisher and fly tier I know. That he is also the only one I know only slightly diminishes his accomplishments.

Through this long-term interaction, most of the patterns that I had tied almost exclusively from natural materials were modified to incorporate the more manageable synthetics. I overcame my former resistance to these newer materials as I devised ways to produce flies that were as imitative and aesthetically pleasing as the more conventional flies had been. The impression that flies made with synthetic materials were clumsy and cartoonish faded as I began to view the new materials as something more than mere shortcuts. My eventual conversion to the new or revised designs was sealed by the approval of trout after trout.

While I continue to experiment with almost any material that shows promise, the commercial synthetics that I use most frequently fall into the increasingly broad category of synthetic fibers. Fibers like polypropylene yarn, Antron, Z-Lon, and Hi-Vis have found wide application in my tying. In some instances, these fibers are virtually interchangeable; in others, they are used for their specific characteristics. Bodies, overbodies, underbodies, shucks, wings, wing cases, legs, tails, and fins can all be produced through the creative use of these extremely versatile fibers. It is conceivable that one could tie all kinds of flies using these fibers and little else. I have come about as close to this as I care to with some of the synthetic baitfish imitations demonstrated in chapter 8, but I think the greatest impact these fibers have had on my tying is reflected in some of the dry-fly designs.

Dry flies that feature burnt poly wings have become something of a signature style in my tying. These wings

evolved as an attempt to duplicate the imitative silhouette of wings that were cut or burnt from breast feathers or webby hen hackle. During my natural tying phase, I favored these feather wings for my most accurate dry-fly imitations. They did have some drawbacks, however. Finding the right feathers with appropriate colors and markings was difficult. Their relative fragility and an occasional tendency to spin the tippet when cast compromised their effectiveness. And they were rather time-consuming to prepare and attach properly. My first attempts to produce a synthetic substitute were quite crude, but I kept experimenting and eventually discovered the tricks that perfected the process (see chapter 4). To my delight, the new wings solved the problems presented by the feathered versions. The burnt poly wings could be colored or marked to match most any natural wing; they were quite durable and so flexible that tippet spin was eliminated. Once the technique was mastered, they required less time to prepare and attach. Above all, they passed muster with critical trout.

In addition to these fibers, many other synthetic materials have wound their way into my tying. Synthetic flash materials, various synthetic dubbing blends, closed-cell foam, half-round vinyl lacing, nylon monofilament, and molded plastic eyes all have applications in the flies found in these pages. I am not very rigid about the use of these things. I seldom find that only one brand of material will suffice for the construction of a particular fly, and usually can make do with whatever is at hand or available. This is a good attitude to have with regard to synthetics because they can disappear from the marketplace about as easily as they appear. But neither do I consider myself strictly a modernist in my approach to material selection. New materials must prove themselves to me and to the trout before they find a place on the flies that I trust. Through experimentation, I have found some modern materials that I dislike or reject as fads. You will become aware of some of these opinions as we proceed; but don't let me stifle your creativity. I've been wrong before. I'm working on that.

PAPER AND THREAD

One material that I use on many of my nymph ties would certainly qualify for inclusion in the category of synthetics. The reason that I have chosen to address it in a separate section is that I doubt that you'll find it in your favorite fly shop. This is not because I am the only tier to use it; instead, it seems to be a material in search of a marketing strategy. Probably the fact that you can get your hands on a lifetime supply for next-to-nothing has something to do with this. If you have ever received one of those "untearable" envelopes through the mail,

The Synthetic Compara-dun is a simple mayfly dun imitation made entirely with synthetic materials: (1) poly dry-fly dubbing, (2) Z-Lon fibers, (3) Micro Fibetts.

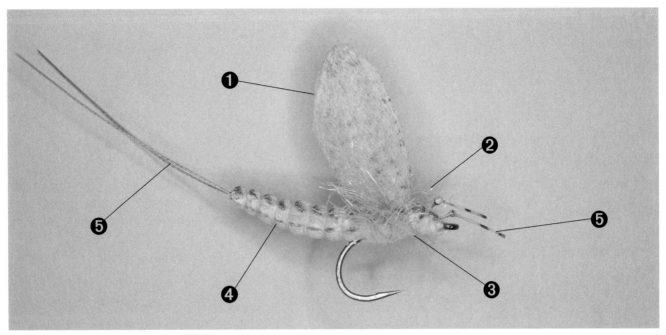

The Extended Burnt Poly-Wing Drake is a complex mayfly dun imitation tied with synthetic materials: (1) burnt poly yarn, (2) Hi-Vis fibers, (3) poly dry-fly dubbing, (4) foam strips, (5) monofilament.

you were well on your way to acquiring that supply. The material is a plastic paper known as Tyvek. Aside from envelopes, it is produced on huge rolls as a vapor-barrier for wrapping houses, but I can't recommend this as a source unless you are planning to supply the entire fly-tying industry. My own lifetime supply came in the form of waterproof score-sheets and souvenir bibs used for recreational ski racing.

Tyvek is extremely strong and can be shaped with scissors or used in a burner. I like it for making accurate reproductions of mayfly and stonefly wing cases, but it is not limited to this. I have seen (and tied) flies that, except for a dubbed underbody, were constructed entirely of Tyvek. Paul Schmookler was probably the first to make such extensive use of plastic paper in fly tying, and though I never met Paul, some of my stonefly nymphs reflect his influence (chapter 7). Some of the effects that can be achieved with Tyvek are stunning, and their appearance belies the relative ease with which those effects are produced. This is not to say that no skill is required, because Tyvek is the rough equivalent of an artist's canvas; but only the most intricate patterns require much in the way of draftsmanship.

Another readily available material that I use extensively in my tying is thread. Of course, we all use thread for tying, but I'm not referring to its usual function. One of the best ways I have found for making legs, tails, and antennae is with threads of all sorts. In addition to fly-tying thread, I use rod-winding thread and many different types of sewing thread for these purposes. This

predilection dates back to my earliest effort at fly tying. The first fly I ever tied was an attempt to reproduce a Muddler Minnow (then a relatively new pattern) using nothing but sewing thread swiped from my mother's sewing kit. It was the only material I could find. The fly was a hideous disaster, resembling nothing so much as a ball of dryer lint; but I have continued to use the material (with much improved results) to this day.

Legs, tails, and antennae are typically imitated with various feathers. On some patterns of more recent vintage, strands of rubber are substituted. Each of these has its advantages and I use them, but neither has proven as satisfactory as thread for many applications. Feathers have a classical appeal but are frequently so fragile that flies can be stripped of these delicate features through ordinary use or the gnawing of a good fish or two. I have little use for flies that are so frail that one is afraid to show them to a fish (for fear it might ruin all the hard work). Even the enticingly active rubber legs have the annoying habit of deteriorating in the fly box and becoming brittle. Thread is both strong and supple, and, properly tied, can have plenty of appropriate movement in the water. It can also be colored, marked, and manipulated in ways that offer a level of imitation that is often superior to either of the more conventional techniques.

The use of paper and thread is one of the distinguishing characteristics of my personal fly-tying style. I do not contend that these materials are the ultimate answer to anything—they are just one answer to some of the things

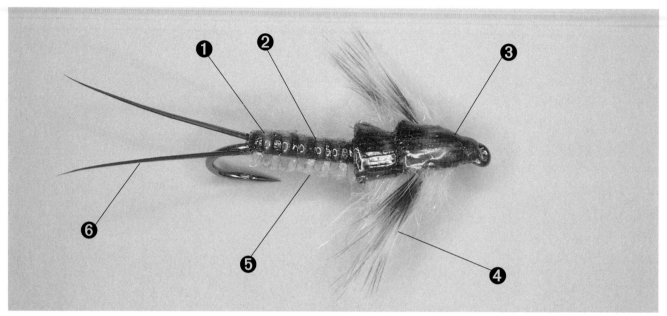

The Standard Stone is a fairly simple stonefly nymph imitation tied with a mix of natural and synthetic materials: (1) poly yarn, (2) V-Rib, (3) mottled wing-quill strips, (4) grizzly soft-hackle fibers, (5) rabbit fur dubbing, (6) goose biots.

that have troubled my tying over the years. For me, problem solving is part of the fascination of fly tying.

COATINGS

It will sound silly, but a minor reason that I am enthusiastic about the modern fly-tying adhesives is that I no longer have to send my wife in search of a bottle of Sally Hansen's Hard-as-Nails. I know I should be secure enough not to let things like this bother me, but more than once as a young, unmarried fly tier I had uncomfortable moments at the drugstore checkout counter or while nervously pacing an unfamiliar aisle looking for the damned bottle. In one embarrassingly memorable instance, my awkward explanation that "I tie flies" only seemed to heighten the suspicion with which I was viewed. Give me a manly bottle of Flexament that I can purchase without apprehension.

There are three modern adhesives that generally satisfy all of my tying needs: Flexament (a rubbery goo, similar to vinyl cement), Zap-A-Gap (a superior form of cyanoacrylate "super" glue), and Duro's 5-Minute Epoxy (a standard for fly-tying applications). All three can usually be found in the fly-tying section of a well-stocked fly shop, although Zap-A-Gap and the epoxy may also be found in hardware or hobby stores. There is some amount of overlap in the use of these glues, but they also have very specific functions. I have become quite attached (sometimes literally) to all of them.

Flexament is perhaps the most versatile of the three, and that versatility is greatly enhanced by purchasing the companion bottle of thinner that is almost always

available where it is sold. Not only does this allow the consistency to be adjusted (it tends to thicken), but it also facilitates the creation of a thinned version of the stuff for lighter applications. I use another small bottle to hold this batch, mixed to a one-to-one ratio. As its name implies, Flexament is an extremely flexible, yet durable, adhesive coating. It admirably performs the usual service as head cement, or as a reinforcing covering for feathers or fibers, but I value it most as a coating on thread legs, tails, and antennae. I formerly used the aforementioned nail polish for this purpose, which was unsatisfactory in many ways (initial stiffness, followed by cracking and peeling). As soon as I tried Flexament, I abandoned that practice forever.

When coating thread, I usually apply Flexament with my fingers (there are tidier alternatives—see chapter 4), but for other applications I like to use a brush. I dedicate an inexpensive (or discarded) artist's brush for this purpose. After use, I don't bother to clean this brush with thinner; instead, I simply wipe the excess from the bristles with a paper towel. The bristles will be glued together because of this, but, due to the flexibility of the cement, the brush will remain serviceable.

Zap-A-Gap is another wonder adhesive that has gained widespread acceptance in fly tying. In addition to some more specialized applications (see chapter 4), I routinely use it in place of conventional head cement. Its bond is so tenacious that after the rest of the fly has been rendered in shreds the head wraps will still be firmly in place. This may be overkill and probably makes whip-finishing redundant, but this glue is so useful for so many things that I can easily forgive this overzealous adhesion. It does take some getting used to, however, and can even be a bit intimidating at first. The positive qualities can quickly turn overwhelmingly negative if misapplied—there is slim margin for error and mistakes are unlikely to be forgiven. Because of this, precise control of the application is a must.

My method is to place a generous drop of the adhesive on a metal lid or scrap of aluminum foil. Wetting the tip of a bodkin in the tiny puddle provides pinpoint accuracy and makes the application quite manageable. The working time of the puddle of Zap-A-Gap is ten minutes or longer, so there is plenty of time to make several applications or to glue a number of finished flies. When the applications are completed the hardened residue can be scraped from the bodkin with a knife or scissors. If the application is less critical, a wooden toothpick can be used instead of the bodkin. If you are unsteady or accident-prone, the tip of a toothpick can also be placed in eye of the hook to prevent excess or misplaced adhesive from sealing the eye shut. Be sure to remove the toothpick before the glue sets, or the remedy may prove to be worse than the disease.

There are many brands and types of cyanoacrylate adhesive on the market, and I have used most of them with some measure of success. Many of them leave a disagreeable amount of residual haze on surrounding materials, and some do not seem to be waterproof in the long term. Zap-A-Gap is the best I have used, and I am not alone in holding that opinion (Dick Talleur acknowledges being bestowed with the title of Mr. Zap-A-Gap). I generally use only the thick formula, which is the most controllable and tends to stay where you put it, rather than migrating to other parts of the fly. Once you become accustomed to using it, this remarkable glue becomes a versatile and trusted tool and a means of repairing mistakes rather than a way of creating them.

Five-minute epoxy is the last of this trio of adhesive aids, and the one that has the narrowest application in my tying. I prefer epoxy when a higher build (or thickness) is desired in order to add a dimensional quality to the coating. I use epoxy primarily as a coating for the wing cases of nymph patterns and for covering the heads of some baitfish imitations. Neither of these is an unusual application today, but both have early precedents in my tying.

I have a small box of flies, retained for the sake of reminiscence, that represents my development as a fly tier. Two timeworn patterns from that box, each more than thirty years old, reflect my early experiments with epoxy. One is an attempt to imitate a slate drake *(Isonychia)* nymph. The wing case and abdomen are coated

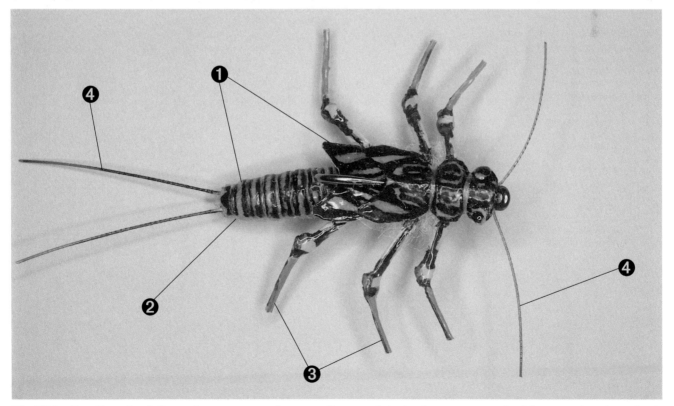

The Wriggling Paperback Stone is a very complex stonefly nymph imitation constructed with natural and synthetic materials: (1) shaped Tyvek paper, (2) rabbit fur dubbing, (3) coated sewing thread, (4) monofilament.

with epoxy. This fly was not notable for its success, but in it I see the antecedent of my current, and very successful, imitation of that same insect. The other fly is a more conventional bucktail streamer that sports an epoxy-coated head. I saved this fly in memory of an amazing small-mouth bass. That fish weighed nearly seven pounds, and it took the bucktail during a solitary float trip on the Susquehanna River in the summer of 1972—shortly after the devastating floodwaters of Hurricane Agnes had receded. I can still feel the pull of that powerful bass, just as I can recall an image of the tangled debris of trees and houses suspended more than thirty feet above my head, as I floated beneath the Susquehanna bridges.

The epoxy that I used on those flies was a slow-curing type, the hardener and amber-hued resin squeezed from sticky metal tubes gleaned from my father's workbench. I doubt that the five-minute variety was available then, and the long drying period was sufficient to limit my enthusiasm for epoxied flies. In contrast, the epoxy that I use now comes in a convenient, double-syringe container (eliminating the sticky tube problem) and dries clear in a fraction of the time. The container makes it easy to dispense equal amounts, which I mix on a scrap of paper and apply with a toothpick. I can usually coat four or five finished flies from the same batch, but because of the short working time, the procedure must be well managed. I line up the flies by pushing the hooks into the edge of a flat piece of Styrofoam prior to mixing the epoxy. Once mixed, you must work quickly and carefully to coat more than a couple of flies, and being overly ambitious is usually not rewarded. At any rate, once the toothpick trails a string of epoxy, it's time to stop and mix a fresh batch.

There are substitutes for all of these adhesives, and I only mention my preferences so that you will be familiar with what I'm using on these flies. In particular, some tiers dislike working with epoxy, and there are some new products that claim to do the same job. I don't have enough experience with these new options to make recommendations, but I do know that several coats of thick Flexament make a good alternative in most cases. And for many years I made do with little more than the dreaded nail polish I mentioned at the opening of this section—it's really pretty good stuff.

Adhesive coatings used in fly construction are Zap-A-Gap cyanoacrylate adhesive and Dave's Flexament and Thinner (top, left to right) *and Devcon five-minute epoxy* (bottom).

Two flies from the archives, demonstrating my early experiments with epoxy. The nymph was an abject failure, but the bucktail captured an enormous smallmouth bass.

COLORING

Fly tiers tend toward a preoccupation with color, often going to extreme measures to procure a particular shade of material. As witness, I'd point to the bizarre requirements for two traditional classics: The pinkish-tan body of the original Hendrickson was made from the urine-stained belly fur of a red fox vixen, and the Tup's Indispensable was so named because a body material was obtained from the indispensable part of a tup—a male sheep, or ram. I'm not sure that such fetishism about color is entirely justifiable, but that can be said about so much in our sport. I am sure that our attention to the exact nuance of color often exceeds that of most trout. We no longer debate whether trout see color—that question has been resolved to the satisfaction of nearly everyone. But we can certainly debate how important it is to them in a given situation. I am no less guilty than others of trying to match the colors I see, but I recognize that I do it to please myself more often than to please the trout. Nevertheless, I do believe that sometimes color can be a key factor in a trout's acceptance of a fly (or natural prey), and even that, in rare instances, it is the only factor. So this is a better-safe-than-sorry situation, and while it may not make a difference, it doesn't hurt either.

Dyeing is probably the earliest method that fly tiers used to alter the color of tying materials, and some antique fishing texts contained fascinating recipes concocted to satisfy the tier's urge to mimic nature's palette. I merely purchase a packet of Rit dye, and although I may mix the colors to achieve the desired result, that's about as exotic as the process becomes. I have a small, inexpensive saucepan that I reserve for dyeing purposes only (a wise practice). I put enough water into the pan to cover the material to be dyed and heat it on the stove. Then I sprinkle the dye crystals slowly into water until the color looks about right and test the result with a sample of the material. After the dyeing is completed, I rinse the material in clean water and lay it out to dry on paper towels. Some tiers set the color with white vinegar either during or after dyeing, but I have seldom found this to be necessary.

When I am dyeing material in a range of colors or shades, I often use the same dye bath for the entire process, starting with the lightest color and darkening or altering the bath as I go. Dyeing is the only good way I know to permanently color the monofilament that I use on some of my patterns, and the single bath sequence works well for this. I usually start with yellow and proceed through a range of golden browns, olive-browns,

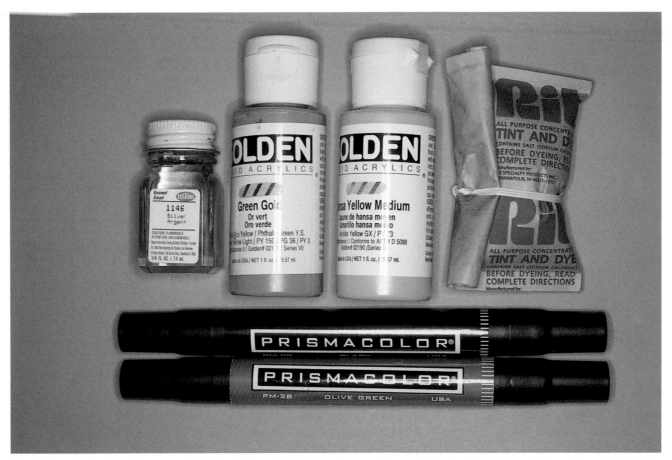

Tools for coloring fly-tying materials. Top (left to right): *Testor's metallic model paint, Golden liquid acrylic paint, Rit dye. Bottom: Prismacolor permanent markers.*

and dark browns. Many similar sequences can be devised—tan through grayish browns to black is another simple and useful progression.

Coloring with permanent marking pens is a popular technique that is quicker and far more versatile than dyeing. Some of the colors imparted by permanent marker are slightly less permanent than those delivered by most dyes and may fade with use or through the action of some dry-fly preparations. But this is of little consequence, as they are easily replenished should the fly survive long enough to need it. The great virtue of these pens is that they can be used to reproduce markings and shadings that are otherwise difficult (or even impossible) to duplicate. On some materials the markers may tend to bleed or spread, on others they will not. Test when you are unsure, and apply a coating (such as thin Flexament) before using the marker on materials that promote bleeding. Many brands of permanent markers are available, but the double-ended (fine point and broad) Prismacolor art markers are a favorite of many tiers. Fly shops often stock a basic selection of these, but if you need a color that is not carried, craft and art supply stores usually have an extensive display of these or similar markers.

In order to spare you having to make the discovery for yourself, I'll warn you that some adhesive coatings will react with the ink. The solvents in nail polish, Flexament, and other head cements are also solvents of the marker color. Using the marker over the thoroughly dried coating rather than the reverse will eliminate bleeding. If you need to apply the cement over the marker, a thickened coat (less solvent) applied in a single stroke will minimize the tendency to bleed. A more startling reaction occurs between a few colors of ink and cyanoacrylate adhesive. Never use these super glues over yellow or yellow-based markers unless you want that part of the fly to turn a brilliant red. Less often, some of these adhesives will turn brown ink to a bluish shade. Again, using the marker over the glue is a solution.

The last medium that I use for coloring is paint. While this seems straightforward enough, paint has never achieved widespread use in fly-tying except for the construction of cork or foam bass bugs. In his classic book, *Nymphs*, Ernest Schwiebert prescribed painting the undersides or underbodies of some of his remarkable patterns, but neither the practice nor the flies became popular. I doubt that he was terribly upset about this, for it meant that the effectiveness of those flies would never be diminished by overuse.

The paint that I prefer for most applications is artist's acrylic. Years ago, artists impatient with the tedious drying time required by oil paint turned to acrylic in order to achieve dramatic impasto brushstrokes without the fuss and smell of oil. This is essentially a plastic paint that can be thinned with water. You can also clean your brushes or wipe up mistakes with water, provided that you don't wait too long. Acrylic paint functions as both a coloring and a coating and is flexible and waterproof when dry. It can be found in art or craft stores, either in the conventional metal tubes or as liquid acrylic in plastic bottles (I like the liquid).

The other paints that have occasional or specialized use in my tying are enamel and lacquer model paints. I sometimes use the metallic silver or gold enamel to put a bright accent on a baitfish pattern, but metallic acrylics are also available and do the same job. I also have a very specific application for a spray lacquer, Testor's Dull Cote. There are some baitfish patterns (see the Hardheaded Bottomfish series in chapter 8) where an epoxy coating is used to shape the head, but the shine of epoxy is incongruous with the dull coloring of the materials. I spray a small amount of the Dull Cote into the plastic spray-can lid and apply to the head with a brush. The result is a compatible matte finish.

There you have it—an overview of the tools and materials that I employ to make the flies found within these pages. In the next chapter, I will demonstrate some of the specific techniques that turn the materials into flies. I should caution that this is not a basic text on fly tying. If you are new to the craft of tying, I highly recommend that you read one of the excellent manuals available or view tying videos to familiarize yourself with the fundamentals. And I recommend practice, without which it's all just words and pictures.

Fly tying can be as basic or as elaborate as one cares to make it, and the former often leads to the latter. It is driven as much by the enthralling activities of handicraft and invention as it is by the desire to beguile the trout. At the moment when the creation is accepted by the fish, the fly-tying cycle is complete and so, too, is the satisfaction of an old and honorable urge.

CHAPTER FOUR

Tying Tricks and Techniques

Surely the trout fisherman who is proficient at both angling and fly tying will be much better prepared to meet the challenge of our heavily fished streams today.

—GEORGE HARVEY, *A SIMPLIFIED COURSE IN FLY TYING*

I've heard it said many times that one cannot learn fly tying from books, yet that is how I've done it. Except for the generous writings of many fine tiers, I remain an untutored amateur. But there is truth in what is said about books (or even videos), for no matter how well the words and pictures are assembled, one can only develop the feel of the thing by doing. Becoming an accomplished fly tier won't get you to Carnegie Hall, but the rule for arriving at either place is still the same—practice, practice, practice. And if you have the opportunity to get hands-on instruction from a more experienced tier, don't pass it up. I had no access to other tiers when I was young, but you should feel no obligation to follow my example—there's no need to learn the hard way.

I gathered the basics of fly tying from a twenty-two-page booklet written by George Harvey. In it, the great Penn State angling professor covered the construction of wet flies, dry flies, streamers, and even bass bugs. This was an unvarnished presentation of the fundamentals of traditional tying, but it served me well. Inside the back cover of the booklet was a copy of Charles Wetzel's "Trout Stream Insect Emergence Tables," which was annotated with my earliest observations of the aquatic insects found on Cumberland Valley streams—including my original record of the *Hexagenia* hatches on the Yellow Breeches. There is no date to be found anywhere in its pages (it was reprinted from a previous serial publication in the *Pennsylvania Angler*), but the fact that it contains no mention of nymphs is an indication of its age.

My interest in nymphs and much of my style of tying them came from another source.

We all tend to measure our accomplishments against the standard of those we admire, and fly tying is no different. The tier that influenced my tying style more than any other also hailed from Pennsylvania. Chauncy Lively was a remarkable and highly original fly tier. His work is somewhat under-appreciated today, mostly because few of his patterns are commercially available. Some would say that this is due to the relative complexity of his designs. I have no doubt that this is true, but I consider that an indictment against the popular trend toward the quick-and-easy rather than a valid criticism of Chauncy's work.

For an eager young Pennsylvania fly tier in the 1960s, Chauncy's fly-tying column in the *Pennsylvania Angler* was about the only source of new ideas and accurate imitations to be found. I didn't have the materials or the skills to copy his patterns, but I marveled at them and aspired to tie such flies. Chauncy's flies, especially his nymph patterns, seemed to capture the exact essence of the thing imitated and always did so in novel and interesting ways. The work of many other tiers has inspired me over the years, from the uncompromising accuracy of Ernest Schwiebert to the magical illusions of Gary La-Fontaine, but Chauncy Lively set the standard.

The flies that are presented in this book are forms of self-expression, a personalized representation of the things I believe and the things I enjoy. They are an homage to difficult trout and their prey. They are not intended to have universal appeal—to trout or to fly fishers. Few have any commercial potential, and none are likely to become classics. But, in my opinion, that is what gives them their value in pressured water situations. You see, the problem with popular patterns is that everybody uses them.

Above all, these flies are fishing tools. A few of the few fly fishers that have seen some of the more elaborate patterns expressed surprise that I actually fish with them, but I told them that these flies were designed to be fished—and they are. Some of the flies are easy to tie, and others are difficult, even for me. Many of the flies use standard construction techniques, and some borrow from or build upon the ideas of others. Some incorporate original ideas and techniques that you will not have seen elsewhere. But, their real significance, I think, is less in the details of their construction than in the tactics they represent. They are not part of any "school" of fly design; they are part of a strategy. And that strategy revolves around the demands of pressured water.

In this chapter, I will describe and demonstrate some of the techniques that are used repeatedly in the construction of the flies to follow. The pages of a book are precious commodities (especially for an unknown author), and I have chosen not to waste any with needless repetition of the same procedures. Some of these methods may already be familiar, while others, like the construction of burnt poly wings, will be new. Mostly, I want to give you a chance to understand the reasoning behind the techniques and perhaps to experiment with them before we set about the task of turning them into full-blown flies.

BALANCE, BALLAST, AND WEIGHT

The posture or attitude of a fly as it drifts or moves in the water is a critical aspect of accurate imitation, and I am relentless in my pursuit of ways to accomplish this. Without attention to this element of fly design, many of the embellishments we add to a fly to make it more appealing can be wasted effort. What is the purpose of wing cases, color separation, and other imitative details if we hide them from the trout they are intended to fool?

I should get something out of the way that I know places me in the minority of fly tiers today. If you are a follower of the trends in fly fishing, you may be disappointed to learn that none of the styles or patterns in this book incorporate beadheads. I realize that such flies are among the most popular and best-selling flies on the market and that many fly fishers swear by them. My feeling is that much of their popularity derives from the fact that many casual nymph fishers are finally able to put

their flies where the fish can find them. But that is not the reason that I reject many beadhead designs.

Take a typical beadhead fly that was tied right side up, and drop it in the water. Many will roll over and play dead. This will not prevent them from catching fish. It is much harder to tie a fly that won't catch a few fish than one that will, but I prefer to fish with flies that catch fish because of their design rather than in spite of it. The original European prototypes that I have seen were simple flies that were usually tied "in-the-round," which is a sensible design. The American practice of slapping a beadhead onto any conventional pattern is not.

While I am on the subject, let me add that the other reason I am not a fan of beadheads is that they possess a distinctive trait that, while it may have some initial attraction, can become a reliable way for educated trout to distinguish between the natural and the artificial. Take a quick glance at a page full of beadhead patterns in your favorite catalog. To me, what they imitate best are other beadheads. It takes awhile for relatively new trends like this to reach the saturation point, but I think we are there. But please, if you have success with these flies, knock yourself out.

This is not to say that I have anything against weighting—even heavily weighting—a fly. The majority of my underwater patterns are carefully weighted, and even weighting through the use of a bead is fine, if attention is paid to its effect and appearance. Nor is the rollover effect limited to just beadheads. If enough wire is wrapped on the shank of many conventional patterns, they will perform the same trick. Tying the fly upside down is one solution; bending the hook shank is another.

The technique that I use for weighting underwater flies that I want to remain upright is to bend the shank of the hook upward just ahead of the midpoint, creating a keel onto which the weighting wire is wrapped. I used to make this bend with my fingers, and still do with fine wire hooks, but a pair of wire-bending pliers works better with heavier wire. Go easy with the pressure in either case or the hook will break. Some tiers heat the hook, bend it, and then reheat before plunging the hook in water to restore the temper. I find this tedious, and it doesn't seem to reduce the incidence of broken hooks. It also can damage the finish of the hook, promoting rust. I still break a few hooks from time to time, but I consider that the cost of doing business.

After bending, the weighting wire is tied along the underside of the hook in the area of the keel and then wrapped over itself for the same length. Generally, weighting wire that is about the same diameter as the hook wire or slightly smaller works well without creating too much bulk. As soon as the nonlead alternatives came on the market, I converted to their use with no re-grets. However, .015-diameter lead-free wire is the finest I have been able to find, and I substitute copper wire for small flies. You can easily tell which I am using in the tying sequences in the following chapters because the lead-free wire is gray and the copper is red.

If you are afraid to bend hooks, you might try the swimming nymph hooks, such as the Tiemco 400T or Daiichi 1770. I like these hooks, but I use them for large

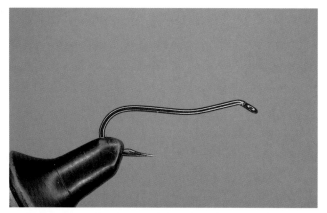

1. Bend a standard nymph hook to form a keel shape.

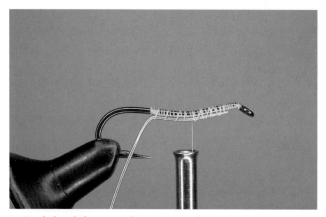

2. Lash lead-free weighting wire along the bottom of the hook shank.

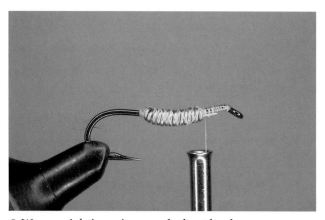

3. Wrap weighting wire over the bent hook.

dry flies or for making curved abdomens on large, two-part flies. They are fine-wire hooks and are not currently available in smaller sizes. I have recently learned that a better alternative may be available in the form of a special hook that incorporates the same bend that I produce by hand. It is called, I believe, the Oliver Edwards Natural Drift hook. I have yet to see this hook in the shops I frequent, or in catalogs for that matter, so it is probably a special order item. My only acquaintance with Mr. Edwards' work is through the few patterns reproduced in the Orvis catalog, although he has a book out. I can only assume that he shares my concerns about attaining the proper attitude of the fly in the water and that makes anything he does of interest to me.

When I want to produce a weighted nymph that rides upside down, I prefer to use slightly curved hooks like the Tiemco 200R or Daiichi 1270. These hooks are not sized the same, but either is fine for this purpose. In this case, the curve forms the keel when inverted, and the wire can be wrapped in the same manner as before except that it is tied in along the top of the curve (when the hook is in its normal, upright position in the vise). When a more flattened body is desired (such as for large

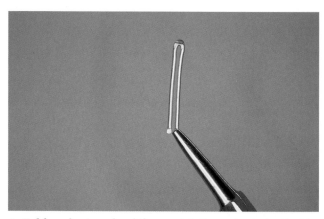

1. Fold and crimp lead-free weighting wire to be tied in.

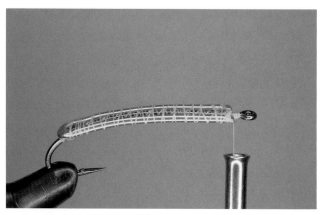

2. Attach folded wire to the top of a curved-shank hook for an inverted fly.

clinger mayfly nymphs), a doubled length of heavier weighting wire can be tied along the top of the curve. After folding the length of wire in half, I crimp the bend and the cut ends with pliers in order to smooth the transition to the hook. The doubled wire is tied around the curve of the hook, with the hook shank filling the gap between the two sides of the wire. If you have trouble with this (the gap tends to close as you wrap with thread), fix the wire to the hook with Zap-A-Gap.

With large, heavily weighted flies (such as sculpin imitations), I generally prefer an inverted tie. I use two methods for weighting these flies and sometimes combine both for very heavy flies that bump along the bottom. The first method involves twisting several strands of weighting wire together to form a thick rope and then cutting it to length and binding it to the top of the hook, which will become the bottom of the inverted fly. I position the weight toward the front of the hook in order to accentuate the action of the fly. Crimping the ends of the wire bundle will help ease the transition of the thread onto the hook shank.

The second method is, as far as I know, unique to my tying and is my answer to the foreign invasion of the beadheads and their larger alien kin, the coneheads. In this method of weighting, the weight is applied to the outside of the fly rather than under the dressing. A tin shot of the appropriate size, either round or egg-shaped, is cut in half at the slit and attached to the belly of the completed fly with Zap-A-Gap or epoxy. This weight has a very positive influence on the orientation of the fly and is hidden from view in a way that doesn't detract from

1. Cut a tin shot in half.

1. Twist lead-free weighting wire to form a wire rope.

2. Attach tin shot half to fly body with Zap-A-Gap or epoxy for an inverted fly.

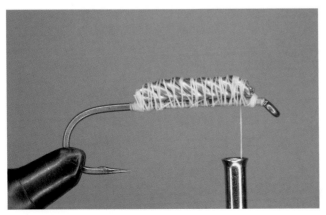

2. Tie twisted wire to the top of the hook shank for an inverted fly.

3. Paint external weight with acrylic, and coat it with either Flexament or epoxy if desired.

the appearance of the fly. I usually paint the shot with acrylic to match the belly of the fly, but this is not necessary as it rarely shows with these bottom-bouncing imitations. For the heaviest flies, I combine both methods, and the resulting fly is capable of hugging the bottom without additional assistance in deep or swift water.

By far the most difficult weighting problem is that of balancing a downward curved hook that is to remain upright during the drift. Often I will omit the weight on such flies, if they are small, and add weight to the leader in order to get them to the proper level. I ordinarily do this with small flies, whether they are weighted or not, because it is hard to get enough weight under the dressing to make much of a difference. The only effective method I have found for weighting such hooks is to use a two-part system that utilizes a buoyant material with the weight in order to overcome the tendency of these hooks to roll. Rather than achieving a rapid sink-rate, this method stabilizes an essentially unstable hook shape. A small amount of weight is wound around the rear half of the hook shank, and polypropylene yarn (or a thin strip of closed-cell foam) is tied on top of the

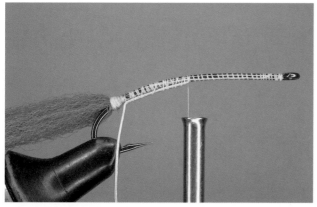

1. Balance a curved-shank hook by attaching weighting wire and poly yarn.

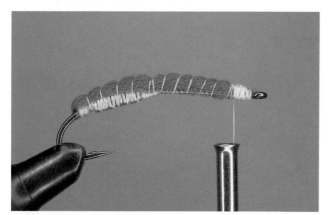

2. Wrap weighting wire over rear half of hook shank, and tie poly yarn on top.

hook as an underbody or incorporated into the dressing of the fly.

Curved-shank hooks, like beadheads, have become very popular for many modern patterns, and their seductive shapes appear to add life to the imitations they support. When thoughtfully employed, they can enhance the qualities of imitation by representing postures and forms that are not well represented by more traditional hook shapes. But, because so few of the flies that are dressed on these hooks are properly balanced, their lifelike illusion often has more appeal to us than it does to the trout. The next time you are about to be seduced by a curved or beadheaded nymph (or, heaven forbid, the combination), drop the fly in a glass of water and watch what happens. If it rolls over and dies, the seductive spell will be broken. Such flies may fool naive fish, but they are mostly an exercise in self-deception.

BODYBUILDING

Dubbing a body on a hook is one of the most ancient and basic fly-tying skills. It is also one of the most versatile. Dubbing can have a sculptural quality, and through its manipulation, any number of useful shapes and imitative elements can be represented. An extreme example of this is the Tesselated Darter pattern that is depicted in the previous chapter and at the end of the bottomfish series in chapter 8. This pattern uses two basic materials, grizzly marabou and dubbed fur, to create a very detailed and lifelike imitation of this little fish. The dubbing represents not only the head and two-part body of this baitfish, but also its dorsal and anal fins. Yet the technique that creates these elements is an amplification of a standard procedure.

The majority of the mayfly nymph patterns in chapter 5 imitate the abdomen, gills, and flattened shape of these nymphs through a simple dubbing application. A tapered covering of dubbing is wrapped over the weighting wire and then ribbed with gold wire or Krystal Flash to suggest segmentation. The dubbing is then picked or brushed out on the sides of the abdomen to suggest gills and trimmed to create the shape of the particular nymph. If appropriate or desired, the back of the abdomen can be coated with Flexament and markings can then be applied.

A variation of this process is used to mimic the broad, flattened head and tapered body of baitfish like sculpins and madtoms. A rather thick dubbing is applied over the hook and weight and brushed out to the sides of the body. The Velcro dubbing brushes described in the previous chapter make quick work of this, but a dubbing needle will suffice. The dubbing is then trimmed to match the shape of the baitfish, and a coating of Flexament is applied to the belly in order to retain the shape. On some of these flies (see the Hardheaded Bottomfish, chapter 8), a coating of five-minute epoxy is applied to the head and dulled with matte lacquer before adding eyes to the imitation. In these last flies, most of the work of refining the imitation is done after the fly is tied and removed from the vise—the actual tying process is quite simple.

If you have glanced through this book, you have already noticed that I am a huge fan of two-part, hinged flies. Salmon flies tied on articulated hooks of English manufacture are the earliest examples of this that I have encountered. It was Swisher and Richards's *Selective Trout*, however, that popularized this construction through the introduction of their wiggle nymphs—although "popularized" may be too strong a term. Despite the tremendous effectiveness of these flies, many tiers still disregard them. I doubt that I can do anything to change these attitudes, but that is good as far as my own fishing is concerned.

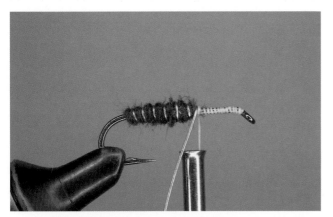

1. Rib a fur-dubbed abdomen with wire.

1. A fat tapered body of thick fur dubbing.

2. Pick or brush out dubbing on sides.

2. Aggressively brush out fur body along the sides.

3. Trim dubbing to define body shape and gills.

3. Trim brushed out fur body to an oval shape.

A few years back, I was in a Pocono fly shop and one of the patrons was asking for advice about local hatches. The proprietor mentioned the slate drakes, and the patron commented that he thought they were overrated. At this affront to one of my favorite insects, I volunteered that I had great success through much of the season with a hinged imitation of the nymphs. "Yeah, tying two flies to get one," the patron responded. "I'm not into that." Just another example of why I have learned to keep my mouth shut.

My method of constructing these flies differs slightly from the original described in *Selective Trout*, but you may want to review their method if you have any compunction about sacrificing a hook in the process. The use of two hooks for these flies makes them more expensive to build and more painful to lose. For me, the convenience and consistency of this method outweighs the added expense (and that is not something I can afford to take lightly). By all means, feel free to use a less costly hook for the rear portion, if you can find one. The main requirement for the rear hook is that it should have a straight eye.

The crucial construction detail is the hinge, which should allow free movement of the tail end of the fly through a somewhat limited range in order to avoid tangling of the segments. After assembling the tails and rear body of the fly, the hook bend is removed with diagonal wire cutters. Cover the fly with your hand as you make the cut to prevent the severed bend from flying off to parts unknown. Select a piece of monofilament to use as a connecting loop. The largest diameter that fits freely in

1. Sever the rear hook bend after completing the fly's abdomen.

2. Attach monofilament loop material to front hook, and build up dubbing spacer at rear.

4. Wrap dubbing over loop tie-down.

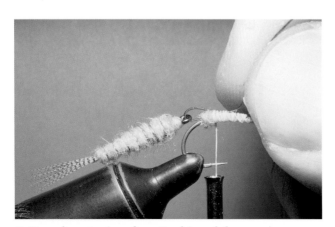

3. Draw loop to size after attaching abdomen.

5. Tie in fur hinge cover over loop.

the eye of the rear hook is generally best. Attach this firmly to the top of the front hook shank. A tiny amount of Zap-A-Gap can be applied to the wraps. Now comes the critical part.

To make an effective hinge, the mono loop must be in the vertical plane, must be sized properly, and must have a spacer between the upper and lower portions of the loop. If weighting wire will be applied to the front

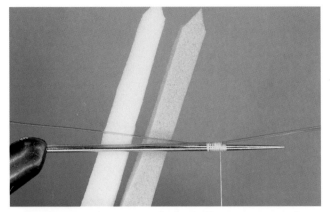

1. Attach monofilament tails to needle, and prepare foam strips to tie in.

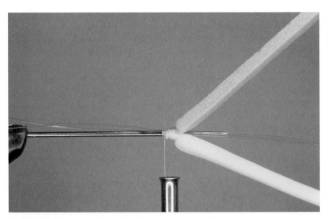

2. Tie in foam strips by tips over previous wraps.

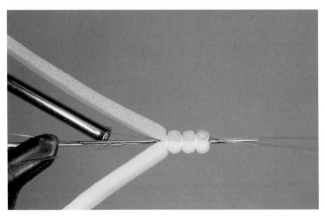

3. Slip the tying thread between the foam strips to make the true segmentation wraps.

hook, it should be wrapped over the attached mono so it can function as a spacer and then covered with thread and tight dubbing. When I weight swimming mayfly nymphs, I wrap wire on the front portion of the rear hook and the rear portion of the front hook to accentuate the hinge effect. For hinged stonefly nymphs, which are intended to wriggle as they drift along the bottom rather than swim, I concentrate weight on the front underside of the fly (using the tin shot method). Two-part baitfish imitations also have the weight concentrated toward the front. The exception is the darter pattern, which moves the weight back in order to allow the fly to assume the unique posture of these unusual fish.

If wire is not applied to the rear of the front hook, thread wraps should be built up and tight dubbing applied over the mono tie down to produce a gap between the ends of the loop. Slip the rear hook eye onto the trailing mono (be sure to check the orientation of this piece, especially on inverted ties). Bring the free end of the mono onto the top of the spacer wraps and attach it with three to six medium-tension wraps of thread. The loop should be left oversize at this point and is drawn to size by pulling on the tag end of the mono. A small loop

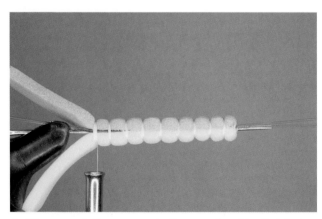

4. After completing segmentation, apply whip-finish.

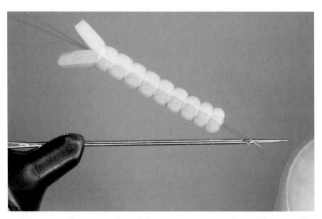

5. Remove the completed foam extension from the needle.

that still allows unencumbered movement of the rear half of the fly is the goal. Until you are practiced at sizing these loops, you may want to insert a needle into the loop to prevent it from being drawn too tight.

Now the loop can be tightly secured and the tag of mono cut off. Zap-A-Gap can be applied to the final wraps as long as care is taken not to allow any glue to stray into the hinge. The front half of the fly is ready to complete. I like to incorporate a hinge cover to enhance the illusion that the fly is one continuous body. For the stonefly nymphs, this cover is the rear wing case; with the burrowing mayfly nymphs, the flue gills conceal the hinge. For most other flies, I attach a sparse clump of matching material (poly for dries and fur or synthetic fiber for nymphs and emergers) over the hinge and trim it to meet the beginning of the rear body. Take care to place the tie-down wraps for this cover ahead of the beginning of the mono loop so that it will not interfere with the function of the hinge.

This process takes far longer to describe than it does to perform, but the devil is in the details with these flies, and I hope you will understand. In spite of the extra time and expense involved in creating these wiggling wonders, they are stunningly effective flies that will fool jaded trout in pressured water. One last bit of advice about these flies—you may be tempted to retain the rear hook intact for some imagined advantage in hooking fish. Please do not. This can ruin the action of the fly, adds no real advantage in hooking, and complicates release. These flies are so convincing that the fish take them decisively and hooking is not a problem.

While we are on the subject of extended-bodied flies, let me share a method for producing nonhinged extensions for large dry flies. Dry flies with extended bodies have been around for a long time, but their popularity has waxed and waned over the years. The look of these flies has always been appealing, but the methods of their manufacture have often been questionable. The method that I like for producing the extensions is known as needle tying, and it allows a buoyant body to be created that overcomes many of the problems encountered with other techniques (rigidity or fragility). With this technique, a sewing needle is clamped into the vise as a temporary core to support the tying, and the completed extension is slipped from the needle, leaving a flexible abdomen to be tied to the hook. I use this technique for imitations of large mayfly and stonefly adults and for accurate tail extensions on synthetic baitfish patterns, but needle tying has unlimited potential.

To begin with the insect applications, mount the needle in the vise by the eye end, and secure the tailing material (usually monofilament) toward the point of the needle with tight wraps of thread (if you find that slippage is a problem, try rubbing some beeswax on the needle before wrapping). Cut two slightly tapered strips of closed-cell foam from a sheet, and trim the narrow ends to a point. Wide strips are used to make the more flattened body of a stonefly, and slimmer strips for the rounded mayfly bodies. Bind the pointed ends of the foam strips to the needle at the forward edge of the existing wraps, tying one on top and one underneath. At this point, you could hold the strips along the needle and simply wind a tight thread rib back to the tie-off point, but I prefer to create true segmentation rather than a spiral rib.

To produce the segments, the thread is slipped between the two strips, wrapped three or four times around the foam in the same spot, slipped between the strips again, wrapped at the next segment, and so on—until the tie-off point is reached. I whip-finish by hand and use a broad loop to allow the body and tails to pass through, because the tie-off is near the vise jaws. I assume this can be accomplished with a whip-finishing tool, but I have no experience with them. If not, finishing with half hitches will suffice. When finished, grasp

1. Prepare two strands of synthetic fibers to bind to the needle.

2. Wrap thread around fibers and needle.

the foam body firmly, and pull quickly from the needle. It is now ready to be tied to the hook. While foam is used for the insect extensions in this book, buoyant hair or poly yarn can be substituted and tied in much the same manner.

I also construct synthetic baitfish tails on a needle, and this technique is very simple. Two bundles of synthetic fiber (one of the back color and one of the belly color) are laid together along the needle, bound with thread wraps that match the belly color, and whip-finished. Remove these from the needle, and coat and flatten the tail fin fibers with Flexament. When dry, the fin is trimmed to shape and colored with permanent marker to match the color of the fish's tail. The thread wraps are also coated with the cement, and the top of the wrap is colored to match the back of the baitfish. This simple, flexible, and realistic extension is now ready to be tied to the hook.

These techniques create bodies that can be used for all kinds of flies and can be modified or combined to produce effects that are pleasing in both aesthetic and fish-fooling ways. For example, the Wriggling Burnt Poly-Wing Stone found in chapter 7 combines the foam ex-

3. After completing wraps, apply whip-finish.

4. Coat, flatten, and trim tail section to shape.

tension with the hinged connection to make an accurate adult stonefly imitation that can be made to writhe on the surface—a nearly irresistible combination. Creative bodybuilding is central to successful fly making, and the possibilities are limited only by imagination.

APPENDAGES

Wraps of hackle and clumps of feathers are the traditional means of suggesting the legs of insects on most flies, and they obviously work, or the practice would not have survived so long. For fish that resist ordinary appeals, however, more can be done. Rather than just suggesting legs, they can be imitated in ways that are more accurate and more effective. This is but one of the areas where Chauncy Lively's influence is reflected in my tying; he never scrimped when it came to the legs of his imitations.

As I mentioned in the previous chapter, my favorite material for the accurate representation of legs is coated thread. Tying, rod-winding, and sewing varieties all have applications for making legs. I usually use Flexament applied with my fingers. After the application, I rub my fingertips together to remove the residue as one would with rubber cement (which is a very similar substance). For those who want a less messy method of application, a drop of the cement can be placed in the fold of a small scrap of paper, and the thread can be drawn through the fold to apply the coating. There are two versions of these legs—single-thread legs and double, knotted-thread legs. The single-thread variety is used for small flies or for slender legs. The double version is for large flies or for heavy-femured legs.

The single-thread legs take slightly more time to prepare and tie than some traditional feather applications, but they are a superior representation in many ways. I tie three strands of the coated thread to the center of the thorax location with cross wraps of tying thread. Dubbing wrapped between the legs separates them. My method is to hold the rearmost pair back along the body and dub in front of them. The next pair is then pinched back and the dubbing applied, and the process is repeated for the front pair. For the simplest or smallest flies, the only thing that remains is to cut the legs to length. This and any other finishing steps can wait until the fly is completed. I like to put a permanent bend in the legs. To do this, wipe a little Zap-A-Gap on the outer two-thirds of each leg with a dubbing needle or toothpick—be careful, because any glue that gets next to the body will ruin the action of the legs. The glue prevents the end of the thread from unraveling and provides enough stiffness at its middle to hold a bend. I make the bend with a pair of tweezers and then touch the crease with Zap-A-Gap, permanently setting the bend. The result is a leg that holds its shape yet is very flexible and will move in the water.

Double, knotted-thread legs are a bit more complicated, but on large flies they have a remarkably realistic look and feel. To make these legs, double a long length of thread and tie a series of overhand knots (half hitches) along its length. The exact distance between these knots doesn't matter; just remember that it needs to be longer than the length of a finished leg so you can tie the legs to the hook. If you err on the long side, there will be no need to measure little bug legs. Once the thread is knotted (you will need one knot for each leg, though they will be connected in pairs), slip the point of an open pair of scissors between the two threads, slide the point against a knot, and snip one thread. Do this at every other knot, then reverse the procedure and snip the opposite thread free. Done correctly, you will have connected leg pairs with a double-thread section in the middle, and a single thread projecting from each knot.

Again, this is a fairly difficult task to describe but an easy one to do. Coat the leg pairs with Flexament, or if you want to change the color, use acrylic paint. You want the coating to bind the doubled section together, so make the coating fairly thick on this section of the legs. Put the coated leg pairs on a piece of wax paper to dry (a few minutes is all that it takes).

To prepare these legs for tying to the fly, fold a leg pair in half, lining up the knots. Position the folded pair over the desired leg location on the hook. Throw a few light wraps over the leg pair. The legs can now be drawn to the proper length. Spread and position the legs with progressively tighter cross wraps. If they are a little askew, you can twist them with your fingers or tweezers near the tie-in point before adding the final wraps. Once positioned, trim the loop that protrudes from the tie-in, and because the pair is now disconnected, add drop of Zap-A-Gap. This will prevent the legs from pulling out. You can either dub around the leg bases now, or you can wait until the remaining pairs are tied in. After tying in

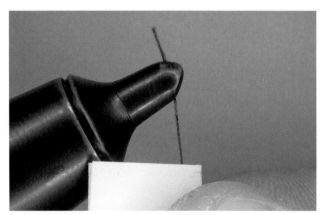

1. Apply Flexament to thread by using a folded piece of paper (an alternative to using your fingers).

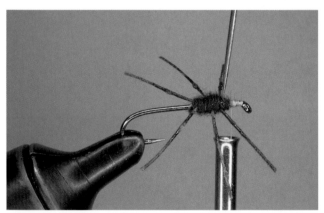

3. Separate legs by dubbing, and apply Zap-A-Gap to the outer two-thirds of each leg with a needle (in preparation for bending).

2. Attach coated-thread legs at thorax position with cross wraps.

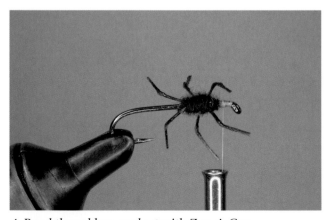

4. Bend thread legs, and set with Zap-A-Gap.

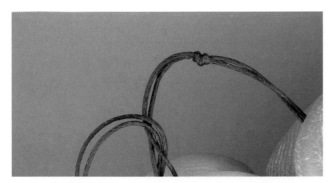

1. Tie doubled thread at intervals with overhand knots (half hitches).

2. Cut one thread free at every other knot.

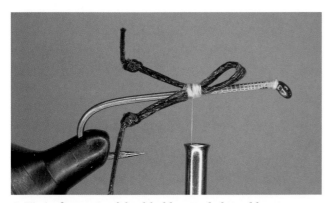

3. Tie in first pair of doubled knotted-thread legs.

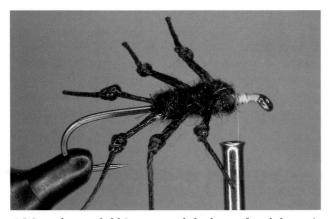

4. Wrap thorax dubbing around the base of each leg pair.

all the leg pairs, they can be trimmed to length and the ends sealed with a dab of glue.

Tying these legs is a bit more complicated than the single-thread legs, but on larger imitations they are worth the effort. And, really, they are less trouble than knotted biot legs, which have to be tied in separately, or knotted rubber legs, which can be frustrating to position correctly and are not as durable. Double, knotted-thread legs are tough, flexible, and convincing. With a little practice, the time consumed by their construction will be rewarded by the envious glances of your peers and the solid takes of "uncatchable" trout (which, of course, go hand in hand).

Coated thread is perfect for imitating other appendages, like tails or antennae. For these, there is little more involved than tying them to the hook. When I want splayed thread tails to maintain a spread position, I touch a little Zap-A-Gap to their bases with a dubbing needle. This application is opposite that of single-thread legs, but it keeps the tails separate while maintaining flexibility throughout their length.

Speaking of tails, a similar procedure is used for the monofilament tails on many of the dry-fly patterns. Commercial tailing fibers, such as Micro Fibetts, are excellent. I use them, but they are too fine to support dry flies larger than size sixteen unless they are bunched together (in which case, they tend to wick water). I use dyed mono for all but the smallest dry flies (size eighteen or under). I size the mono by the Rule of Three—divide the hook size by three to find the X designation of the mono to use for tailing. Round any fraction to the nearest whole number. This is an approximate rule, and you can increase size for two-tailed flies. Mono lacks the fine taper of the commercial tailing material, but I often cut the commercial fibers to length so this doesn't bother me. If you must have the taper, remember that the commercial tails are synthetic paintbrush bristles. You can purchase a synthetic-fiber brush with thicker bristles, break it apart, and dye bundles of the fibers to the desired colors. Not that hard really, and they do look nice.

Whichever you chose to use, please don't bother to tie the fibers or mono in separately unless you enjoy busywork. Instead, tie them in as a bunch: slide your thumbnail underneath them and against their bases and press until they flare and separate. Then take a dubbing needle dipped in a drop of Zap-A-Gap and touch it to the openings between the tails at their bases. They will now hold their positions without any loss of flexibility.

Many tiers consider tying individual appendages to be too time-consuming and settle for suggestive clumps or wraps of hackle. But individual appendages don't have to be tied in individually. If you think about it, all of the procedures I have described here are from two to six times as fast as tying individual components to the fly. The finished flies look like they are more difficult to tie than they really are, but we'll keep that little secret just between us. If our fellow fly fishers continue to suffer the impression that such flies are too much trouble to tie, we'll have the edge, won't we?

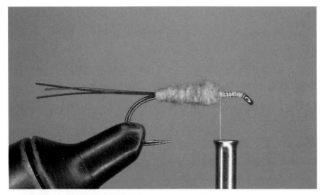

1. Tie in monofilament tails together, and apply abdomen dubbing.

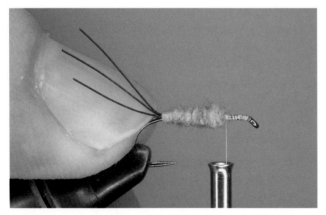

2. Separate monofilament tails by pressing a thumbnail against their bases.

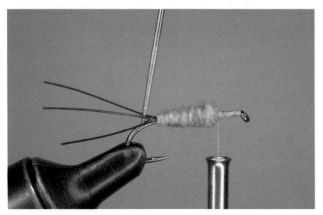

3. Fix monofilament tail positions with a little Zap-A-Gap applied with a needle.

WINGS AND WING CASES

As a young tier, wings were the bane of my existence. No aspect of fly tying was nearly so perturbing, with the possible exception of finishing off a dry-fly hackle. Of course, traditional dry flies presented a double whammy, and that may be another reason that I was attracted to nymph fishing at a tender age. In time, and through much venting and cursing, I managed to master the traditional winging techniques and was fashioning delicate little quill-slip wings and cut-hackle wings. Frustration at the vise was merely displaced to the water, however, when my carefully prepared and posted wings returned from a malicious trout's mouth mangled or rent into irreconcilable shreds. Today I prepare synthetic dry flies that have no hackle and whose wings are formed in fire, but I am not inflamed by the process. Yes, revenge long sought and carefully constructed is sweet, and my flies now return to me virtually unscathed.

Traditional dry flies are a beautiful and evocative expression of our fly-fishing heritage, but I am always amused when their construction is described as easy. The ease with which accomplished tiers produce these flies belies years of practice and, I assume, the same frustrations that attended my early attempts to tie them.

1. Tie synthetic fiber to the head of the fly.

2. Tie down forward half after reverse-dubbing the head.

Techniques mastered long ago come easily, and new skills appear daunting at first, but this is not an objective evaluation of their difficulty. Some of the wing-making methods that I introduce here may be new, but they are not difficult, only unfamiliar.

Al Troth's famous Elk Hair Caddis is one of my favorite dry flies, but stacking and manipulating loose elk hair was nearly impossible for my one-armed fishing partner. Synthetics were the solution, but Al's method of attaching the wing, which is so simple and ingenious for hollow hair, is not well suited to synthetics. Synthetic fibers are slick and do not compress like hair. When simple substitution is the only change to this pattern, the fibers in the center of the bundle tend to slip or pull out, eventually causing the collapse of the whole wing. Even an application of Zap-A-Gap, the modern fly tier's equivalent of duct tape, is not a complete success. There is so little space between the tightly bound fibers that the glue seldom penetrates to the core unless it is liberally applied to the exposed parts of the wing. This is unattractive, at best.

The solution is a method of attachment that I call the fold-over technique. A bundle of fibers that is half as thick as that desired for the finished wing is tied in at the front of the body, so that roughly equal amounts extend from either end of the wrap. Tight wraps are continued to the eye of the hook and very thin, tight dubbing is wrapped back to the original tie-in point (reverse dubbing). The forward half of the wing fibers are then folded back, and a finish wrap is made where the reverse dubbing ended. The result is a fly that looks very much like the Troth original, but the fold securely anchors the syn-

1. Align poly yarn fibers with a needle.

2. Prepare to burn fibers extending from the tip of a wing burner.

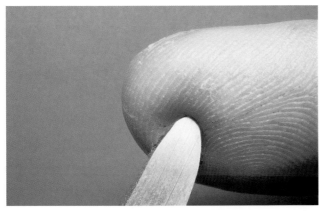

3. Roll wing burner tip against finger to connect melted bead.

4. Burnt poly wing ready for trimming.

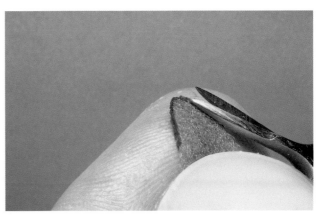

5. Trim the excess flashing with fine scissors pressed flat against the wing.

thetic fibers. There are many slight variations on this theme found in the flies of following chapters, and the technique is used on dries, wets, and nymphs.

The wing-making technique of which I am most proud is the burnt fiber wing that adorns some of my most imitative patterns. Usually made with poly yarn (but also Antron for wet flies), this wing offers an accurate profile, extreme flexibility, and remarkable durability. I have been using it for more than ten years and have yet to be disappointed by its performance. Shaping synthetic yarn in a wing-burner is the basic process, but merely placing the yarn in the burner and setting it aflame produced an unsightly mess. There was a kernel of hidden promise in the result, however, and continued experimentation culminated in the discovery of a few simple tricks that make this construction practical.

This wing was originally devised as an imitation of the closed wings of a mayfly dun. Fine-textured poly yarn is the best material for this, less because of its buoyancy than its texture and the way the melted bead that connects the fibers does not darken as much as with other synthetic fibers. There are three essential tricks for reproducing this wing effectively and consistently. The first is to make sure that the poly fibers are evenly aligned along their length. Gently stroking a dubbing needle through the fibers accomplishes this task.

Next—and this is the most critical step—the yarn must be placed in the wing burner so that the fibers only protrude from the tip of the burner. Any fibers that are exposed along the sides of the burner will melt away from the others and will not be connected. If you have trouble getting the fibers to stay in the burner without bulging out the sides, use a smaller quantity of fibers or a larger burner (each burner size can be made to shape several wing sizes).

The final step is the one that eluded me at first, and it allows a smooth, strong, and flexible bead to be formed, connecting the fibers and shaping the wing. It's quite simple, really: As soon as the protruding fibers are melted in a flame, roll the tip of the burner against your fingertip. This connects the melted fibers, and compresses the bead into a narrow strip at the top of the wing. You may have some anxiety about touching the just-melted fibers, but the wing burner's function as a heat sink dissipates the heat instantly. I have made hundreds of these wings without the slightest discomfort. If you don't trust me, you can wear a glove or roll the burner tip against another surface.

When the shaping is completed, strip away any loose fibers by holding the wing by its tip and gently stroking the fibers toward the cut end. The compression of the

bead may leave a slight edge or flashing extending to the sides of the bead, and it can be trimmed away by laying a scissors flat to the wingtip and carefully snipping the excess. Keeping the length of the fibers extending from the end of the burner to a minimum will reduce this flashing, sometimes to the point that no trimming is needed.

Tying this wing to the fly is pretty basic, but there are a few precautions that help to make a neat job. Generous headspace should be allowed; otherwise, trimming the fiber tags and dubbing a neat head will be more difficult. Pinch the wing between your fingers, and position it against the end of the body. Bring the thread loosely up and around the wing between your fingertips, and then draw it down. This procedure is known as a pinch wrap. Do this two or three times, and then check the alignment of the wing. Straighten it, if necessary, before snugging the thread for the final wraps. Grasp the tag fibers and cut them close to the wraps. Unlike the loose fiber wing described in the fold-over technique, these wing fibers are connected and are less prone to pulling free. Despite this, I like to work a little Zap-A-Gap into the cut ends for insurance. Immediately wrap over the ends before the

1. Tie in burnt poly wing at the head of the fly.

2. Apply dubbing after trimming and gluing.

glue is dry (to prevent a lump from forming), and then use a thin, tight dubbing to finish the head.

To make a downwing for an adult stonefly, a round-tipped wing burner is best. You can make do with the asymmetrical curve of a mayfly wing burner, but the poly must be offset at just the right angle, which is tricky. Otherwise, the procedure is the same, except that the wing is tied flat to the hook (which is even easier). In ad-dition, I combine the fold-over technique with the burnt poly wing for these flies. The excess poly is folded back, wrapped, and then trimmed at an angle in order to blend with the wing.

This technique can also be used to fashion adult cad-dis wings for both dry and wet imitations. I substitute Antron on the wet (diving) caddis ties. Antron tends to darken (carbonize) more than poly when melted, but it

1. Tie in burnt poly stonefly wing.

1. The first burn of the double-burn technique shapes an angular caddisfly wing.

2. Finish the wing attachment with the fold-over technique.

2. The second burn produces the angled wing tip.

3. Trim excess poly at an angle to blend with wing.

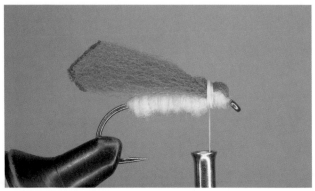

3. Tie in a double-burnt caddisfly wing with the fold-over technique.

is more reflective and less buoyant. Mayfly wing burners can be used to make caddis wings that have a rounded shape, but they can also reproduce angular caddis wings. A double-burning technique shapes this variation, eliminating the need for specific caddisfly wing burners. The wing material is inserted diagonally in the burner, and the tips are melted and pressed to create an angled edge. The wing is then repositioned in the burner so that the acute angle at the point of the edge is exposed, and it is melted and pressed again. This technique is actually more effective than using a burner with an angular shape because the point tends to make a weak spot or gap in the bead. This wing is attached in the vertical plane with the fold-over method, but two wings can also be used to create semispent dry caddis adults (see the Burnt-Poly Wing Spent Sedge, chapter 6).

Burning is also a convenient way to reproduce wing case shapes on mayfly and stonefly nymph imitations. Breast feathers are most often shaped in this manner, but my material of choice is Tyvek. This plastic paper is incredibly durable and can be colored and marked to match any nymph. To make these wing cases, cut a strip of Tyvek that is slightly wider than the burner tip. Insert the strip in the burner so that it overhangs the edge evenly, and run a flame around the edge. If the shape is deeply indented, you may have to hold the flame a little longer at the notch in order to fully shape that area. After removing the shaped wing case, apply a base color with marker, and darken the wing case tips (duplicating the darkening found on a mature nymph).

I make burners, as described in the previous chapter, for the wing case shapes and sizes I use most often, but unusual or occasionally used shapes can also be cut from Tyvek. Start by folding a strip in half and outlining one side of the shape against the fold. Carefully cut along the outline with fine, sharp scissors, and then color as desired. Sometimes I combine the two methods when the head and pronotum (shoulder) are an extension of the wing case strip (see the Inverted Clinger in chapter 5 or the Paperback Stone Nymph in chapter 7).

I think you will find that all of these techniques can be mastered with a fraction of the practice that most of us have invested in some of the more traditional techniques. Those hard-won traditional skills will always serve us well, and they are worth the investment, despite the tribulations that may have accompanied their acquisition. If they have now become easy or automatic, however, that should not deter us from adding other techniques to our repertoire. New skills and novel flies keep us one step ahead of educated trout, and that is the name of this game.

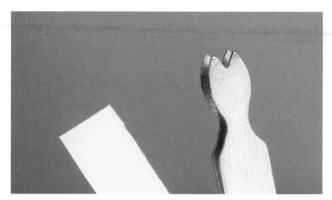

1. Tyvek strip and wing case burner.

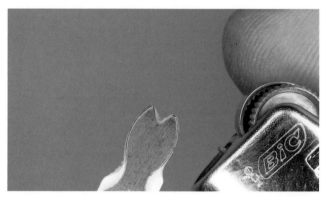

2. Burn the Tyvek strip to shape.

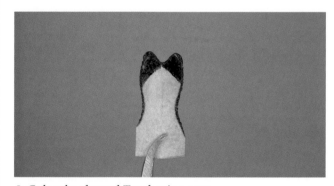

3. Color the shaped Tyvek wing case.

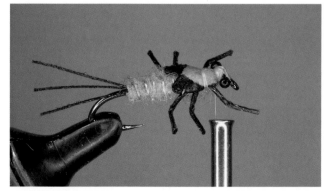

4. Attach wing case to fly with wraps fore and aft of the front leg pair.

EYES ONLY

Eyes on flies can present targets of opportunity for trout on a search-and-destroy mission, or they can be superfluous affectations. Whichever they are, I like them. They always seem to bring a pattern to life, and I'm not convinced they are as inconsequential as some believe. Mostly, I think that some tiers don't want to be bothered with the extra steps involved in adding eyes, but they don't mind if others do it for them. I think you'll find that a fly with eyes will outsell the same fly without. This is not a justification, because window-dressing always has sales appeal, but it is a curious comment on human nature.

Melted monofilament eyes are not new, but I am always surprised that some tiers don't know how to make them. Let me review the procedure and add a few refinements of my own. Cut a short length of mono, heavy mono for large eyes and thin mono for small, and place it crosswise in a pair of tweezers with tapered points. The taper allows the mono to be moved up or down to adjust the distance between the eyes. Make sure that equal amounts project from either side, and move a flame toward one end of the mono until a molten ball begins to form. Follow the ball with the flame until it just about reaches the tweezers, then move it away. Repeat on the other side. It's that simple, but things can go wrong.

If the mono catches fire, don't panic, just blow it out as it reaches the tweezers. The tweezers will act as a heat sink, but they will not stop the molten ball from wrapping around the metal if you don't retard the process. Once the mono catches fire, gas bubbles will be trapped in the ball when it cools, making it brittle. By touching the flame briefly to the ball, these bubbles will be released; though it may take a couple of tries to get them all out. As someone who has lots of experience melting P-Tex onto ski bases to repair rock gouges, I can tell you that the secret with P-Tex is to keep the flame as blue as possible during the meltdown. As soon as the flame turns yellow or orange, bubbles and carbon get into the repair, ruining the job. With mono, the idea is to get it to melt, but not to ignite—in this case, easier said than done.

The completed eyes resemble little dumbbells, and the small ones are especially tricky to tie to the hook. This is where the eye holder described in the previous chapter comes in. Pick up the eyes by pressing the

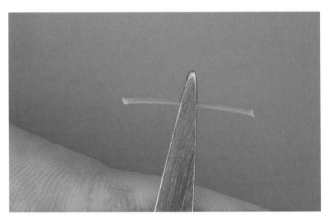

1. Position heavy monofilament in a tapered pair of tweezers.

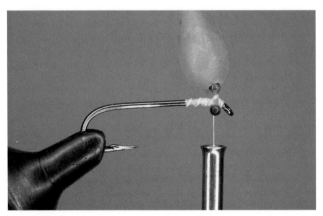

3. Use the eye holder to attach the melted mono eyes with cross wraps of thread.

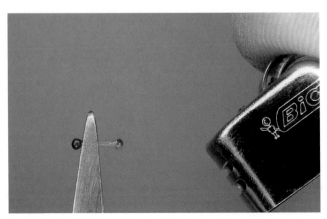

2. Melt a ball on each end of the monofilament.

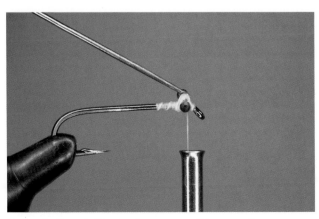

4. Apply Zap-A-Gap to the wraps with a needle.

beeswax tip onto one of the eyes, and position the eyes over the tie-in point. Use cross-wraps of thread to attach them to the hook. Add a touch of Zap-A-Gap to the wraps with a dubbing needle.

I also use two kinds of epoxy eyes on flies—one for imitating nymphs whose eyes are on the top rather than the sides of their heads, and the other for baitfish imitations where the smallest commercial eyes are too large. Making the nymph eyes is simply a matter of putting two dark spots on top of the head with a fine-tipped marker and placing a drop of five-minute epoxy on top of each spot with a toothpick. The baitfish eyes are similar except that two spots of acrylic paint form each eye.

To apply these spots, I cut the points off two round toothpicks, one near the tip and one further up the taper. The larger-tipped toothpick is used to apply the larger, colored spot, and the smaller-tipped one is used for the black pupil. Make sure the larger spot is dry before applying the center dot. When the centers are dry, apply a generous drop of five-minute epoxy over each eye, forming a clear dome.

This last epoxy-eye technique is a fine substitute for the commercial, molded eyes. For baitfish imitations with larger eyes, however, I use the molded eyes because painting dots is not my favorite pastime. The eye holder also comes in handy for this application. It allows the eyes to be removed from their backing, coated with either Zap-A-Gap or epoxy, and affixed to the fly without

1. Apply paint spot (iris) with larger diameter toothpick.

1. Apply dark spots to the head of a nymph with marker.

2. Apply paint spot (pupil) with smaller diameter toothpick.

2. Apply a small dome of five-minute epoxy over each spot with a toothpick.

3. Apply epoxy dome over each eye.

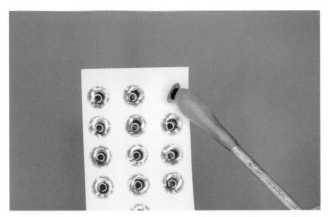

1. Remove commercial plastic eye from backing with eye holder.

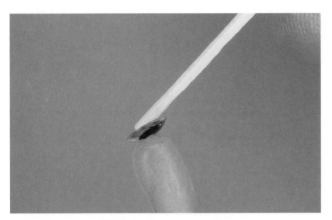

2. Apply cement (Zap-A-Gap or epoxy) to eye.

slipping around or smearing the adhesive. If you let the adhesive set up a bit before applying the eye to the fly, you won't have to hold it in position so long.

Have you ever wondered why it is that eyes are generally conceded to be a valuable addition to baitfish flies,

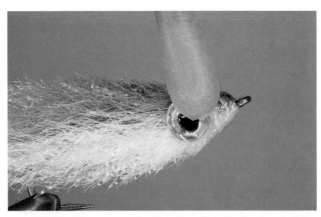

3. Position the eye on the fly's head with the eye holder.

but of no consequence on nymph imitations? Is that because we think that trout can see them on one but not on the other? Maybe, and yet baitfish flies are usually stripped quickly through the water and nymphs are usually dead-drifted. It is a tired old saw to say that trout don't count the tails on a mayfly, or that they don't wait to see if a nymph has eyes before eating it. I don't dispute the notion, but the tone is sometimes suspect, and I think it misses an important point about imitation. Many details may be inconsequential considered alone, but the cumulative effect can contribute to the overall impression. Remember the dictum that said when fish are fussy, give them less to find fault with? I take that to mean not only that less is more in some situations, but also, somewhat paradoxically, that less omitted is more convincing in others. I know that this point will glance off of the armor of the blindly biased, and I have not lost sight of my own prejudice about such matters. So, for the sake of those who will dismiss my ocular arguments, let me just repeat this about eyes on flies—I like them.

PART TWO

Flies for Pressured Water

Green drake.

Green sedge.

American salmonfly.

Rainbow Smelt.

The flies and fly-tying sequences in the following chapters are arranged in a manner that is somewhat unusual, and some explanation may help you to appreciate that arrangement. There is an important fly-tying distinction to be drawn between pattern and style. A pattern is a standard recipe for a particular fly. A style is a fly construction method or design. The Royal Wulff, Grey Ghost, and Zug Bug are patterns. The Compara-dun, Clouser Minnow, and Emergent Sparkle Pupa are styles. Duplicating a pattern is a traditional and rather restrictive approach to fly tying. Adapting a style is a more modern and open-ended approach. But neither is limited by the other. The Royal Wulff is a Wulff-style dry fly, as are the White Wulff, Gray Wulff, Grizzly Wulff, and Ausable Wulff. The Compara-dun style can be tied as a Brown Drake Compara-dun, Sulphur Compara-dun, Light Cahill Compara-dun, or Blue Quill Compara-dun, which are patterns. Patterns are subsets of styles.

The tying sequences that follow are arranged as style progressions that roughly move from easier to more difficult constructions and from general to more specific applications. Pattern recipes are included as examples of each style. To this, I have added the convention of substyles. I am not trying to create a new category, because it already exists. I would say that the Sparkle Dun is a substyle of the Compara-dun, and the Para-Wulff is a substyle of the Wulff. There is no hard and fast rule for what constitutes a substyle; it is just an organizational convenience that demonstrates a close connection between one design and another.

Because of the progressive nature of the styles and substyles, I have chosen to illustrate only what is new or different about the next fly in the sequence. A more conventional step-by-step method of illustration would require the frequent repetition of the same steps. This method allows the presentation of more styles and information in less space.

Styles and substyles are related on the basis of shared methods, and there is usually, but not always, a correlation to the degree of difficulty involved in tying related flies. To highlight the exceptions, I have employed a simple rating system. Each style or substyle is designated with the letter N, I, or A, corresponding to novice, intermediate, or advanced tying skills. Of course, this is an approximate and subjective system, but it should help to clarify the relationships between the various designs. Flies designated with an N for novice may not be easy for beginners, but experimenting with them will help the initiate to learn some of the important fundamentals. Flies designated with an A for advanced usually incorporate methods that are similar to intermediate designs, but they are more complex and time-consuming. The most difficult ties are not intended for ordinary use. Anyone attempting to fill fly boxes with such flies would soon find that there is no time left for fishing. These flies are created for very specific and highly demanding situations, and their use should be restricted to those applications.

I should also mention that there are many forms of trout prey that are not imitated by the styles, substyles, and patterns presented in the following chapters. Terrestrial insects, midges, crustaceans, and other forms can all be important at times, and I imitate and fish them. But I wanted to address the forms that tend to provoke the most focused feeding by trout in pressured waters and also the forms that provide the most consistent challenges to effective imitation. Therefore, these chapters deal exclusively with mayflies, caddisflies, stoneflies, and baitfish. I have not included imitations of the larval stage of caddisflies. Though some species drift during this stage and can create a feeding focus, the imitations of this stage are not applicable to the actual hatching activity. The forms I have selected are the most popular models for imitation by flies and are the most likely to benefit from special tying tactics in order to overcome the resistance of educated trout. If I have omitted one of your favorite categories, I apologize. Perhaps another time. . . .

For the sake of my Western counterparts or traveling anglers, I would also like to make a few comments about the adaptation of these flies for Western waters. I am an Easterner, but I have fond remembrance and great affection for every Western water I have fished (I honeymooned in the Yellowstone country, but that is another story). Despite this, I must confess that I have skied in the West far more often than I have fished there—combining the two has been a challenging, if sometimes successful, undertaking. The fly patterns found in these pages are all imitations of prey that are found in my home state of Pennsylvania. Of course, most of these are common to much of the East and the Midwest as well. A few are transcontinental species, like the little blue-winged olive *(B. tricaudatus)*, the brown drake *(E. simu-*

Yellowstone River at LeHardy Rapids: While the fly patterns presented in this book imitate primarily Eastern and Midwestern species, the tying styles can easily be adapted to imitate prey found anywhere in trout country. Local knowledge is always a valuable tool for effective imitation, but even the visiting angler can make educated guesses about which prey items are likely to be important. The character of the water in the photograph should suggest to any experienced angler that large stoneflies (Pteronarcyidae and Perlidae), clinger and crawler mayflies (Heptageniidae and Ephemerellidae), fast-water caddisflies (Rhyacophilidae, Hydropsychidae, and Brachycentridae), and fast-water baitfish (sculpins and dace) should be present.

lans), and the black dancer *(M. sepulchralis)*. The Western tier is encouraged to take advantage of the tying styles to devise imitations that match local hatches, and I have tried to suggest species that lend themselves to this adaptation. I would not presume, however, to offer patterns for insects that I don't know well, nor flies that I do not fish. Local knowledge is so valuable, and home waters are the only waters that we can claim to truly know.

On a related, but more critical note, I want to advise against accepting that hatch matching, entomology, and Latin are an encumbrance or an affectation. Contrary to the popular image of the hatch matcher as one who is bent under the burden of box upon box stuffed with so many flies that it requires an index to find the appropriate one, nothing has so simplified my fly fishing as an understanding of entomology. I rarely carry more than one medium-size box of flies and often need less. I do

have big boxes stuffed with flies, but they stay at home—a practical understanding of entomology allows me to carry only what I think I will need.

I do not want to give you the impression that I am always prepared for every hatch or for everything that happens during those hatches—I am not. But I value those times as learning experiences; they are precisely how I have accumulated those boxes of flies. After such an event, I am often occupied by tying the flies that I needed yesterday or last week. And while they are seldom of any immediate value, the next season I am better prepared, and wiser, for having been occasionally under-equipped. I am perfectly willing to live or die by the small selection I make in preparation for a day on the stream, and as time goes by, I am living better than ever.

The identification of aquatic insects is a more contentious issue. Frequent utterance of new Latin binomials is off-putting to many fly fishers. Most are content to call a little yellow stonefly just that, or a yellow sally, or them yeller bugs. Fly fishing would surely be a poorer sport if pale evening dun, white-gloved howdy, coffin fly, black dancer, and speckled peter were entirely replaced by *Ephemerella dorothea, Isonychia bicolor, Ephemera gluttulata, Mystacides sepulchralis,* and *Helicopsyche borealis.* Romantic and evocative atmosphere flows from the former, stuffy science from the latter. The downside of the romantic patois of common names is that one man's great olive-winged drake is another man's Michigan caddis. The simple truth is that, for now, the only way we can be sure we are talking about the same species is through the use of scientific names. But even this has its drawbacks.

The characteristics used by entomologists to determine species are not always the characteristics that are most important to trout or trout anglers. To compound the situation, the taxonomy of aquatic insects is undergoing a period of accelerated revision, and keeping current is a challenge. Fortunately, there are some excellent resources on the Internet that can help—just do a Web search for mayflies, caddisflies, or stoneflies and you'll be overwhelmed. But the revisions are presently so rapid that some species have changed names while I was writing this book.

Two well-known mayflies provide an example of this—the march brown (formerly *Stenonema vicarium*) and a large Eastern sulphur (formerly *Ephemerella rotunda*). Not only have the names changed, but both insects also illustrate the problem of variable morphology.

Differences in size and color often lead us to believe we are dealing with different species. From a fly-fishing standpoint, we are right to attend to such differences because they can be important to the trout we are trying to catch. Not long ago, morphological differences displayed by the march brown caused both anglers and entomologists to treat the differences as a species distinction. Anglers labeled these the march brown and the gray fox, and entomologists called them *Stenomena vicarium* and *fuscum.* Entomologists later revised this division, bringing both under the species designation *vicarium.* Very recently, another revision has changed the genus designator, so the march brown is now *Maccaffertium vicarium.* But it's still the same critter, and it still looks like two different insects at times.

March Brown: This classic Eastern mayfly acquired a new scientific designation while I was writing this book. Now listed as Maccaffertium vicarium, *its variable morphology had, at one time, convinced anglers and entomologists that it was two different species—the march brown* (Stenonema vicarium) *and the gray fox* (Stenonema fuscum). *Regardless of its current status, trout still see very different versions of this insect, and imitating those differences can still be important.*

A very similar situation affects the Eastern sulphurs. Most angling entomologies referred to *Ephemerella invaria* and *rotunda* when they discussed the large, early sulphur hatches. They are now considered to be the same species—*E. invaria.* There is another, lesser-known, Eastern sulphur, *E. septentrionalis,* which might play a role in mistaken identity. If all of this seems confusing and frustrating, that's because it is.

There is some hope on the horizon, however. Advances in the study of DNA may help to make future revisions more definitive and lasting, rather than being subject to the battle eternal between the lumpers and the splitters. An even more positive, though long-term prospect is that common names eventually become fairly standardized. When Europeans spread across the North American continent they encountered a large feline *(Felis concolor)* and called it by a dozen or more common and regional names. Today most of us recognize it as the mountain lion or cougar. Admittedly, this can be a slow process, but some entomologists are attempting to accelerate things by applying a system of logic and description—witness the recent work of Stark, Stewart, Szczytko, and Baumann, who compiled a list of common names for stoneflies. Many of these will not be familiar to anglers, but I have chosen to use them, where appropriate, in order to contribute to this process.

I have also taken the liberty of suggesting a few names for mayflies and caddisflies whose common identity is ambiguous. As anglers, we do no service to this process of standardization when we call many different insects by the same name, or worse, when we assign relatively unknown species that have no common name to an already vague and overflowing moniker. So, if we would really like to avoid using names like *Baetis tricaudatus, Attenella attenuata, Drunella cornuta,* and *Acentrella turbida,* then we need to stop referring to them all as blue-winged olives.

And finally, in this time of pressured waters, I don't want you to become discouraged about your prospects for joyous days on those waters. Despite the pressure, fly fishing continues to be a salve for the soul. While I don't like the coarsening or dumbing down of fly fishing, I am not much bothered by its popularity. All who truly love the waters and the fish are welcome to join our ranks—the more the merrier. After all, fishing pressure may complicate our sport and test our mettle, but it is hardly the pressure about which we should be most concerned. That pressure does not come from those who love trout streams.

Today, it is hard to fish on any precious wild trout stream without being conscious of the many threats that imperil its existence, and these thoughts can bring a taint of melancholy to an otherwise happy adventure. It can also be hard to imagine why such places should need protection—hard to believe that anyone could see things as beautiful as trout or trout streams and seek to destroy them. But, I suppose the sad truth is that they don't really see them—that in the oblivion of apathy or greed much beauty goes unseen and unappreciated. In the end, fly fishing is an antidote against such blindness. Fly fishing, at its best, is an active participation in the lives of wild creatures and their world. The goal of that participation is not mere exploitation, but understanding, growth, and respect. In the process, one inevitably becomes connected to the history, the traditions, and the lives of those that pursue, or have pursued, this ancient calling. Through this strange blending of human lives with the lives of fish, the lowly larvae that crawl amid the muck and detritus of streambeds become exalted things.

CHAPTER FIVE

Mayflies

Green drake.

A MATTER OF TASTE

Trout and mayflies are the classic combination—beautiful fish rising to beautiful flies. No other insect so captures the imagination of fly fishers. No other insect is more routinely imitated. The consequence of all this relentless attention is that the trout of heavily fished waters seem to recognize the standard mayfly patterns as readily as we do. Some fish display such acute disdain that the mere appearance of these frauds among the succulent mayflies seems an affront to their sensibilities—like the wino offering a swig of his Mad Dog 20/20 to wine connoisseur Robert Parker.

Such educated palates are not easily deceived, but that is the challenge. The contest promotes refinement at both ends of the line. In order to gain favor against this acquired discretion, our best efforts at preparation and presentation are required. Nothing less will do. Half measures are met by halfhearted responses. Difficult fish and demanding situations motivate fly tiers to experiment endlessly with new approaches to the classic problem of matching mayflies—skills and traditions are stretched and tested to produce flies capable of whetting the appetite of the most discerning trout. That such primitive creatures can develop such sophisticated tastes is one of the great wonders of our sport. And when our careful creations are spurned by one of these cultured beasts, we return to the vise determined rather than defeated. That, too, is a wonder of our sport.

Of course, not all trout are so difficult to satisfy. Some are gullible gluttons, responding with abandon to almost any unseasoned fly. Because of this, there is no one way of dressing mayflies that is universally appropriate. Elaborate offerings are wasted on naive trout, and bland fuzz balls insult the salmonid aesthetes. This argues for a progressive approach to fly design. The idea is to cater to the tastes of the targeted fish—serving simple down-home fare to hungry blue-collar diners and intricately prepared haute cuisine to discriminating gourmets.

The mayfly designs presented here follow just such an approach. The flies are organized into progressive sequences that proceed from the simple to the sophisticated in a series of small adjustments. The first fly in each series is a basic offering that has broad appeal. Each successive style or substyle adds a more beguiling garnish or a more exotic dressing to the previous fly design. In this way, flies can be prepared to suit the tastes of the trout and the demands of the situation. Further, these elements can be mixed and matched in ways beyond those demonstrated. This à la carte menu invites combination and experimentation. As your tying evolves along with these sequences, I encourage you to sample freely. Beyond the limitations of rigid recipes are new possibilities and opportunities for self-expression. Variety is the spice.

NYMPHS/WETS
Style 1—Poly-Case Nymph

Poly-Case Nymph: (left) *Brown Mayfly Nymph,* (right) *Olive Mayfly Nymph.*

This is a basic and unassuming nymph style, useful for a wide range of situations. Its appearance is not much different than many standard nymph ties, but the weighted, bent-hook keel, complemented by a simple poly yarn wing case, makes it very stable. A fine nymph for searching the water, it also works for a number of hatches. It is most suggestive of the classic crawlers (Hendricksons, sulphurs, pale evening duns, pale morning duns), but tied slim and small, it does well for the little swimming nymphs of Baetidae.

Tying Sequence
Begin with a 1XL or 2XL nymph hook, bent and weighted to form a keel. Attach a sparse clump of partridge or other soft hackle fibers near the bend. Tie in the ribbing wire just ahead of the tails. Dub a tapered abdomen, stopping slightly past the midpoint of the hook shank. Spiral the rib forward, tie off, and trim.

Attach a short length of poly yarn over the thorax location, wrapping the thread back to meet the dubbed abdomen. Dub forward along the thorax, leaving a generous headspace. Tie a sparse clump (about equal to the tails) of partridge or alternative feather fibers to either side at the front of the thorax for legs. Trim the stubs close to the tie down wraps, and wrap securely to the eye and back to the thorax. As an alternative, you can snip the shaft of a partridge or other soft body feather near the tip, and strip the lower flue fibers from the stem, leaving five or six fibers on either side forming a V-shape unit. Place the base of the V on top of the front of the thorax dubbing with the curve of the feather facing down. Wrap over the stem (which protrudes forward over the eye) three or four times with medium tension. Grasp the stem, and draw the feather under the wraps to create the appropriate leg length. Wrap snugly, trim the excess stem, and feather, and wrap to the eye and back. This sounds complicated, but it is not, and you may prefer it to attaching separate clumps of loose fibers.

Bring the poly yarn forward over the thorax, and wrap it snugly at the end of the thorax. Trim the excess poly, and add a drop of Zap-A-Gap to the ends, immediately wrapping over them to the eye and back. Dub a neat head with thin, tight dubbing, whip-finish, and cut the thread. Stroke a little Zap-A-Gap or head cement on the tie-off wraps and head with a dubbing needle to finish. Pick out the dubbing along the sides of the abdomen to suggest gills and trim to shape.

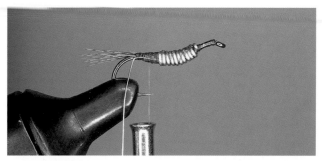

1. Attach tails and ribbing wire to bent and weighted hook.

2. Dub and rib abdomen. Tie in poly yarn.

3. Dub thorax, and tie in legs.

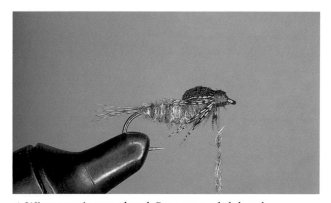

4. Wing case is completed. Prepare to dub head.

Brown Mayfly Nymph

Hook:	1XL or 2XL standard nymph, #10-22 (bent)
Thread:	brown 6/0 or 8/0
Weight:	lead-free wire or copper wire
Tails:	brown partridge fibers
Rib:	gold wire
Body:	yellowish brown to dark brown dubbing
Wing case:	dark brown or black poly yarn
Legs:	brown partridge fibers

Pattern notes: Tied in sizes 12 to 14, this is a good Hendrickson nymph imitation; in sizes 14 to 16, it works for large sulphurs or large pale morning duns; sizes 16 to 18 serve for pale evening duns or small pale morning duns.

Olive Mayfly Nymph

Hook:	1XL or 2XL standard nymph, #10-22 (bent)
Thread:	olive 6/0 or 8/0
Weight:	lead-free wire or copper wire
Tails:	olive-dyed partridge fibers
Rib:	gold wire
Body:	light olive to olive-brown dubbing
Wing case:	dark brown or black poly yarn
Legs:	olive-dyed partridge fibers

Pattern notes: Many *Ephemerella* nymphs have olive variations, but in sizes 10 to 18, this pattern also does a fair job of matching many *Drunella* nymphs (olive morning duns, Western green drakes, etc.). Sizes 16 to 22, slimly tied, work well for *Baetis* nymphs.

NYMPHS/WETS
Style 2—Thread-Legged Nymph

Thread-Legged Nymph: (left) *Little Black Quill Nymph,* (right) *Blue Quill Nymph.*

Like the first style, this nymph incorporates a weighted keel and a poly wing case. It adds flexible coated-thread legs and tails that accurately imitate the splayed posture of many drifting or pre-emergence nymphs. It is a superb style for matching small nymphs, such as species of *Baetis* (little blue-winged olives), *Paraleptophlebia* (blue quills, slate-winged mahogany duns), and *Serratella* (little black quills, little dark Hendricksons). These are important trout country nymphs from East to West, making this a particularly valuable style.

Tying Sequence

For small nymphs, I like to use a straight-eye, dry-fly hook like the Tiemco 101, but standard hooks will do. Bend and weight with copper wire. Tie two or three strands (according to species) of thin, coated thread to the tail position. Attach a fine-wire rib, and dub the abdomen and rib as before (although you can darken the top of the abdomen with a marker prior to ribbing, if that helps to suggest the coloration). Tie down the poly yarn over the thorax.

At the center of the thorax, tie in three strands of the heavier coated-thread leg material with cross wraps of thread. Pinch the hindmost leg pair back along the abdomen, and wrap dubbing over their bases. Repeat this process with each of the successive leg pairs to separate the legs and cover the abdomen.

Bring the poly forward, tie it down, and finish the nymph as before. Pick out and trim the gills. Trim the tails and legs to length. Spread the tails with your thumbnail, and set their position with Zap-A-Gap applied to their bases. If you like to bend the legs—and I do—wipe a little Zap-A-Gap on the outer two-thirds *only.* Bend them, and set the bend with another touch of the glue.

I like to coat the wing case with five-minute epoxy and darken the rear margin with marker to suggest a mature nymph. Any other markings can also be added with marker.

1. Attach thread tails and ribbing wire to bent and weighted hook.

2. Dub and rib abdomen. Tie in poly yarn. Attach coated-thread legs.

3. Separate legs by dubbing.

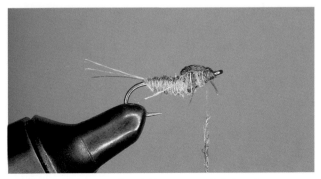

4. Wing case is completed. Prepare to dub head.

Little Black Quill Nymph (Serratella deficiens)

Hook:	Tiemco 101, #20 (bent)
Thread:	black 8/0
Weight:	fine copper wire
Tails:	three, coated tan 8/0 tying thread, black markings
Rib:	fine gold wire
Body:	grayish brown dubbing, black on top
Wing case:	black poly yarn, with white thread stripe
Legs:	coated tan 6/0 tying thread, black markings

Pattern notes: One early June morning many years ago, I first encountered a heavy hatch of these widespread and underrated mayflies on the Acid Factory stretch of the Beaverkill. Since then, I have found it on many waters, including my beloved Pocono streams. Little black quill is my name for *deficiens*, a little black-winged, black-bodied dun with pale rings on its abdomen and pale legs and tails. Other *Serratella* species (known as little dark Hendricksons) are best matched with a more brownish dressing.

Blue Quill Nymph (Paraleptophlebia adoptiva)

Hook:	Tiemco 101, #16-18 (bent)
Thread:	brown 8/0
Weight:	fine copper wire
Rib:	fine gold wire
Tails:	three, coated dark tan 8/0 tying thread
Body:	yellowish brown to reddish brown dubbing, dark on top
Wing case:	brown poly yarn, black at rear
Legs:	coated dark tan 6/0 tying thread

Pattern notes: This little Eastern and Midwestern mayfly is often the first good hatch of the season, emerging from the slower margins of the stream. Later season species *(mollis, guttata,* and *strigula)* are also important and similar. Larger (#14-16) Western species, such as *packi, heteronea,* and the transcontinental *debilis* can be significant.

NYMPHS/WETS
Substyle 2a—Thread-Legged Wet Dun/Diving Spinner

Thread-Legged Wet Dun/Diving Spinner: (left) *Slate-Winged Olive Wet Dun,* (center) *Quill Gordon Wet Dun,* (right) *Little Blue-Winged Olive Diving Spinner.*

This modernized wet fly is tied in the same manner as the previous nymph style, except that an Antron or Z-Lon wing replaces the poly wing case. Sometimes overlooked, wet adult mayfly styles have two very significant applications. One is to represent mayflies that emerge on the bottom or while in transit to the surface—a surprisingly large number of species. Mayfly emergence is not as cut-and-dried as it is often depicted. In addition to the classic underwater emergers of the *Epeorus* and *Attenella* genera, many species of *Ephemerella* and *Drunella* can also emerge before reaching the surface. The other important application is for species that crawl or dive underwater to lay their eggs—a habit of spinners in the prolific Baetidae family.

Tying Sequence
Either nymph or dry-fly hooks work well for this updated wet fly, bent as before and lightly weighted with copper wire. Attach two or three tails of coated thread or, for the little diving spinner imitations, two Micro Fibetts. Retain the wire rib or, as I prefer, substitute a strand of Krystal Flash. With Krystal Flash, or any rib except wire, it is good to wrap a tiny ball of dubbing at the rear of the hook before attaching the ribbing material. This method helps to prevent the rib from slipping off the end of the body. After dubbing the abdomen (and darkening on top, if desired), spiral the rib forward and tie off. Because there is no wing case, attach the coated-thread legs at the center of the thorax and separate with dubbing.

You can tie in the Antron or Z-Lon yarn wing conventionally at the front of the thorax, but I prefer a version of the fold-over technique for added security. Tie in a length of the wing material that is half as thick as the desired wing, and fold the forward half of the material back, wrapping tightly over the fold. Dub a neat head, whip-finish, and trim the wing, legs, and tails. Set the tails, and bend and set the legs (if desired) as with the previous style. Cement the head, and add any final markings.

1. Tie in thread tails. Dub and rib abdomen. Attach thread legs, and separate with dubbing.

2. Attach synthetic fiber wing. Prepare to dub head.

Slate-Winged Olive Wet Dun (Attenella attenuata)

Hook:	Tiemco 101, #16-18 (bent)
Thread:	olive 8/0
Weight:	fine copper wire
Tails:	three, coated olive 8/0 tying thread
Rib:	olive or pearl Krystal Flash
Body:	light or medium olive dubbing
Legs:	coated olive 6/0 tying thread or sewing thread
Wing:	medium gray Antron or Z-Lon

Pattern notes: Perhaps overrated in earlier hatch-matching texts, this underwater emerger is widespread, but only locally important in areas of the East and Midwest. They are, however, a link in a long chain of morning-emerging olive mayflies (mostly *Drunella* species) that hatch from late May through August. If they are not important in your area, please tie a yellow-bodied, pale-winged version for dusk to dark wet-fly fishing to the abundant pale evening dun *(E. dorothea)* hatches—the simplest and most effective technique I have found.

Quill Gordon Wet Dun (Epeorus pleuralis)

Hook:	1XL or 2XL standard nymph, #12-14 (bent)
Thread:	brown 8/0
Weight:	copper wire
Tails:	two, coated brownish gray 6/0 tying thread
Rib:	olive or yellow Krystal Flash
Body:	yellowish gray or olive brown dubbing, dark on back
Legs:	coated grayish or olive-brown heavy sewing thread, dark brown markings
Wing:	dark gray Antron or Z-Lon

Pattern notes: Wet-fly fishing during the Quill Gordon hatch is an old and extremely productive technique. Fish these flies deep pre-hatch and near the surface during the hatch, and you may have no need for nymphs or dries. A lighter-colored version (with a touch of pink for the females) is equally effective for the lengthy, but sporadic hatching of *E. vitreus* (yellow quill) from late May through July.

Little Blue-Winged Olive Diving Spinner (Baetis tricaudatus)

Hook:	Tiemco 101, #16-22 (bent)
Thread:	olive 8/0
Weight:	fine copper wire
Tails:	two, gray Micro Fibetts
Rib:	olive or pearl Krystal Flash
Body:	dark olive-brown dubbing with a bright olive tip
Legs:	coated olive-brown 6/0 tying thread
Wing:	clear Antron

Pattern notes: This little wet fly is effectively fished around emergent structure even when the spinner activity of this transcontinental species is not noticed. The size range for this pattern reflects the multibrooded nature of this mayfly, which becomes smaller as the season progresses. These traits, coupled with the wealth of related species, means that a pale olive to dark brown version of this fly is always a good bet—throughout the season, from East to West.

NYMPHS/WETS
Style 3—Paper-Case Crawler (I)

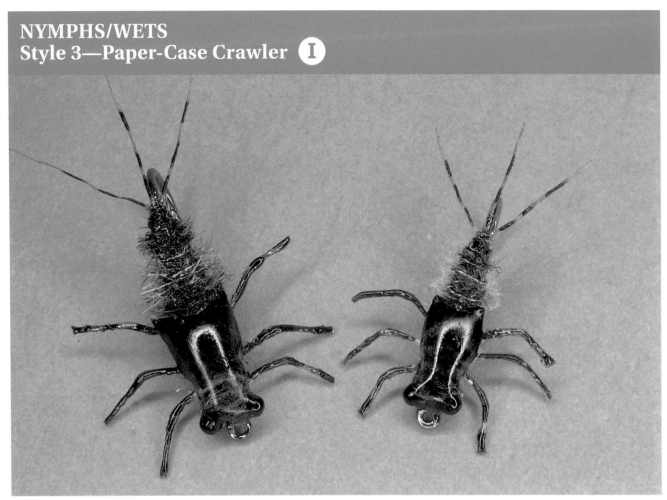

Paper-Case Crawler: (left) *Hendrickson Nymph,* (right) *Blue-Winged Sulphur Nymph.*

This is one of my all-time favorite styles for producing accurate, hatch-matching nymphs. The design imitates nymphs of the *Ephemerella* genus precisely, and for the popular Hendrickson, sulphur, or pale evening dun hatches, it is devastating. Western pale morning duns (*E. inermis, infrequens,* and relatives) would be well matched by this style. With the addition of eyes and a shaped Tyvek wing case to the assets of the preceding nymph styles, the basic nymph has now evolved into a very detailed and convincing imitation. Of course, it has become a favorite because difficult trout seem to like it as much as I do, expressing their approval with confident takes.

Tying Sequence
Start with a 1XL or 2XL nymph hook, bent and weighted. Attach a pair of melted mono eyes slightly behind the eye with cross wraps of thread, and touch a little Zap-A-Gap to the wraps. Tie in the coated thread tails and wire rib. Dub the abdomen, and darken or mark the top before ribbing. Attach the coated thread legs, and separate with thorax dubbing.

Shape a Tyvek wing case in a burner (or cut to shape), and give it a base color with marker. Darken the wing case tips. Position the wing case over the thorax, and nick the edge of the Tyvek just behind the eye position. Remove the wing case and trim the excess Tyvek ahead of the nick to a short point. Replace the wing case, and tie it down between the eyes and the front pair of legs. Trim any remaining excess from the pointed stub. I like to bring the thread underneath the hook and make two or three more wraps between the front and second pair of legs, creating a pronotum. This helps to marry the wing case to the body. Return the thread to the eyes, and apply thin dubbing around the eyes, to finish the head. Whip-finish at the hook eye or behind the mono eyes.

Pick out the abdominal gills and trim. Trim and set the legs and tails as with the previous styles. Coat the wing case and head with five-minute epoxy (or thick Flexament). Apply whatever details are desired with marker.

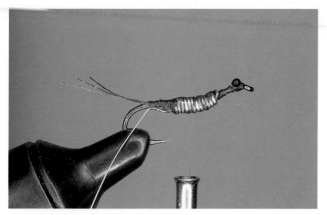

1. Attach thread tails and ribbing wire to bent, weighted hook. Tie in melted mono eyes.

2. Dub and rib abdomen. Pick out and trim gills.

3. Attach thread legs, and separate with dubbing.

4. Tie in Tyvek wing case. Prepare to dub head.

Hendrickson Nymph (Ephemerella subvaria)

Hook:	1XL or 2XL standard nymph, #12-14 (bent)
Thread:	brown or olive 8/0
Weight:	lead-free wire
Eyes:	melted mono
Tails:	three, coated brown or olive brown 6/0 tying thread, black markings
Rib:	gold wire
Body:	reddish, grayish, or olive-brown dubbing, black markings on top
Legs:	coated brown or olive-brown heavy sewing thread, black markings
Wing case:	burnt or cut Tyvek, colored dark brown or olive-brown, black tips

Pattern notes: On a fine spring day on some streams, you'll find Quill Gordons emerging from the current tongues, blue quills and little black sedges *(C. aterrima)* around the margins, dark grannoms (*Brachycentrus* spp.) in the pockets, and Hendricksons everywhere in between. Abundant options make fly selection difficult. Let the water be your guide. When in doubt, however, fish a Hendrickson nymph. All things being equal, their larger size will usually tip the balance.

Blue-Winged Sulphur Nymph (Ephemerella invaria)

Hook: 1XL or 2XL standard nymph, #14-16 (bent)
Thread: tan or brown 8/0
Weight: lead-free wire or copper wire
Eyes: melted mono
Tails: three, coated tan or brown 6/0 tying thread
Rib: gold wire
Body: yellowish or reddish brown dubbing, dark brown markings on top
Legs: coated tan or brown sewing thread, dark brown markings
Wing case: burnt or cut Tyvek, colored and marked with brown, dark tips

Pattern notes: A week or two after the Hendricksons, late afternoon hatches of these large sulphurs (sometimes supported by their sister sulphur, *E. septentrionalis*) create reliable fishing. On streams with extremely heavy populations, the extended *invaria* hatches become progressively smaller, mimicking the pale evening dun *(E. dorothea)* activity on other streams. Whichever the species, a size 18 or even 20 version of this nymph will work for the later hatches.

NYMPHS/WETS
Substyle 3a—Paper-Case Crab Crawler Ⓘ

Paper-Case Crab Crawler: (left) *Dark Olive Morning Dun Nymph,* (right) *Olive Morning Dun Nymph.*

This adaptation of the previous style is designed to match the configuration of the genus *Drunella*. These nymphs are very similar to *Ephemerella* (they were formerly classified as the Fuscata subgroup of that genus). *Drunella* nymphs are distinguished by their broad, often serrated, front-leg femurs. This crab crawler genus creates very important hatches across the country, including my favorite, the olive morning dun *(D. cornuta)*. Other Eastern and Midwestern species of note include *longicornus, cornutella, lata,* and *walkeri*. Western species like the Western green drakes *(D. doddsi, grandis,* and subspecies) and slate-winged olives *(D. flavilinea* and relatives) are also extremely significant. Doubled knotted-thread legs provide a nice representation of this group's distinctive feature and are added to this version. Many difficult fish have succumbed to this crabby creature, and I wouldn't want to meet a tough-water *Drunella* hatch without it.

Tying Sequence
This nymph is constructed in exactly the same manner as the prior style, except that only two coated, single-thread strands are tied in behind the center of the thorax and separated with dubbing. Add the front pair using the doubled knotted-thread technique.

1. Construct nymph as before. Tie in doubled knotted-thread legs at front of thorax.

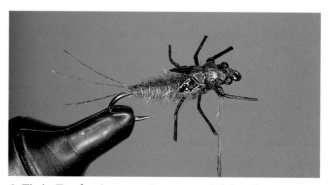

2. Tie in Tyvek wing case. Prepare to dub head.

Fold the prepared leg pair in the middle so that the knots line up. Place the folded leg pair over the front of the thorax, and wrap lightly a few times. Draw the legs to length, and secure with tight wraps. Trim off the folded loop that remains, and add a touch of Zap-A-Gap to the wraps. Dub around the legs. Proceed to tie in the wing case, and finish as with the previous style.

Olive Morning Dun Nymph **(Drunella cornuta)**

Hook:	1XL or 2XL standard nymph, #12-14 (bent)
Thread:	olive 8/0
Weight:	lead-free wire
Eyes:	melted mono
Tails:	three, coated olive 6/0 tying thread
Rib:	gold wire
Body:	tannish olive or olive-brown dubbing, dark on top
Legs:	coated olive or olive-brown heavy sewing thread (front pair doubled), sometimes marked with brown
Wing case:	burnt or cut Tyvek, colored olive or olive-brown, black tips

Pattern notes: It is hard to pick a favorite hatch, but I have spent so many fine late May or early June mornings fishing to these fast-water mayflies that they get my nod. *Hatches* was the first fly-fishing book to accurately describe the *cornuta* activity, and the authors listed no common name. Unfortunately, since that time, it has been saddled with the most common of common names, blue-winged olive. Olive morning dun is my respectful appellation. Do we really need another blue-winged olive?

Dark Olive Morning Dun Nymph **(Drunella lata)**

Hook:	1XL standard nymph or Tiemco 101, #16-18 (bent)
Thread:	olive 8/0
Weight:	copper wire
Eyes:	melted mono
Tails:	three, coated olive or brown 8/0 tying thread
Rib:	fine gold wire
Body:	olive or brown dubbing, dark on top
Legs:	bright olive or orange-brown sewing thread (front pair doubled), usually with black markings
Wing case:	burnt or cut Tyvek, colored olive with bright olive pronotum or brown (usually with rusty orange pronotum), black tips

Pattern notes: In *Hatches*, Al Caucci and Bob Nastasi dispute the presence of *lata* in Eastern streams, despite having sampled many of my Pocono home waters. But it is there. It's just that few fly fishers get up early enough on hot, July mornings to catch the hatch. Dark olive morning dun is my name for *lata*.

These olive morning dun nymphs display the broad, flattened front-leg femurs that are characteristic of the crab crawler genus, Drunella.

NYMPHS/WETS
Style 4—Inverted Clinger **I**

Inverted Clinger: (left) *Quill Gordon Nymph,* (right) *Little Yellow Quill Nymph.*

Clinger nymphs slide along the surface of rocks in their fast-water habitats, and many species emerge on the bottom or while moving toward the surface. An inverted imitation is well suited to fishing deep during the migrations that precede emergence. I use this style to imitate *Epeorus* nymphs like *pleuralis* (Quill Gordon) and *vitreus* (yellow quill, pink lady) and *Heptagenia* or *Leucrocuta* species like *L. hebe* (little yellow quill). Western species of *Epeorus, Rithrogenia, Heptagenia,* and *Nixe,* such as the Western march browns (*R. morrisoni, hageni,* and relatives), are also candidates for imitation by this style. Basically an upside-down version of style 3, this style introduces an extension of the Tyvek wing case to mimic the broad, flattened heads of these nymphs.

Tying Sequence
There's no need to bend a hook for this style. (Aren't you relieved?) Just start with a Tiemco 200R, Daiichi 1270, 1260, or something similar. Be careful, though—these hooks are only rough equivalents, and both size and shape differ from one brand to another (matching length rather than size number is the key).

Tie the weighting wire along the top of the shank, rather than underneath, as we have been doing with the right-side-up ties that incorporate the aftermarket bend. Wrap the wire over itself, and then proceed to tie in the thread tails and ribbing wire as before. Dub the abdomen and, if it is to be darkened, remember to do that on the underside. Inverted ties can be tricky if you don't pay attention. Rib the abdomen, and tie the thread legs to the thorax (no problem doing this on the top of the hook as usual). Separate the legs with dubbing.

Now, invert the hook in the vise (if you've got one of those newfangled vises, just rotate the jaws). Wrap thread to the eye, and reverse dub back to the front of the thorax. Position the wing case over the thorax, and trim the excess straight across at the eye. Round the corners to create a spade-shape head, and attach the wing case with wraps on either side of the front legs (forming the pronotum). Finishing and detailing the fly is the same as with the previous styles, except that the dorsally positioned eyes of clinger nymphs will be duplicated with two black dots topped by drops of five-minute epoxy.

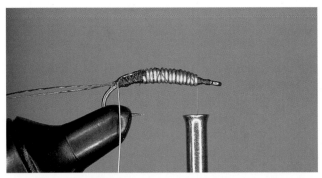

1. Attach thread tails and ribbing wire to weighted, curved-shank hook.

2. Dub and rib abdomen.

3. Tie in thread legs, and separate with dubbing. Invert hook.

4. Tie in Tyvek wing case and head. Apply dark spots to head with marker.

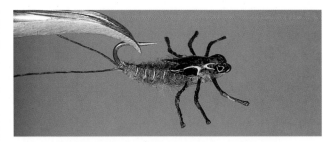

Quill Gordon Nymph (Epeorus pleuralis)

Hook:	Tiemco 200R or equivalent, #14-16
Thread:	brown 8/0
Weight:	lead-free wire
Tails:	two, coated brown or olive brown 6/0 tying thread
Rib:	gold wire
Body:	yellowish olive or olive-brown dubbing, dark on back
Legs:	coated brown or olive-brown heavy sewing thread, dark markings
Wing case:	burnt or cut Tyvek, colored brown or olive-brown, black tips
Eyes:	black dots, epoxy

Pattern notes: Generally of little value during the actual hatching, this nymph is good fished tight to the bottom a few hours or even a few days prior. It can be salvation when cold spring weather retards the hatch, forcing the stalwart angler to grub for trout. A lighter-colored version (light olive or light amber) will match the migrating nymphs of the later-season yellow quills *(E. vitreus)*.

Little Yellow Quill Nymph (Leucrocuta hebe)

Hook:	Tiemco 200R or equivalent, #18-20
Thread:	tan or brown 8/0
Weight:	copper wire
Tails:	three, coated tan or brown 8/0 tying thread
Rib:	fine gold wire
Body:	yellowish brown or grayish brown dubbing, dark on back
Legs:	coated tan or brown sewing thread, dark markings
Wing case:	burnt or cut Tyvek, mottled light or dark brown, dark tips
Eyes:	black dots, epoxy

Pattern notes: Highly underrated (in my opinion), this little mayfly follows hard on the heels of the last of the pale evening duns *(E. dorothea)*. You can be fooled into thinking that it is a continuation of that hatch, unless you capture a two-tailed dun or notice that the activity has moved to faster water. Like the earlier *dorothea* hatch, it is often preceded on the water by the unpredictable, but always enticing, yellow quills *(E. vitreus)*.

NYMPHS/WETS
Substyle 4a—Inverted Fat-Legged Clinger Ⓐ

Inverted Fat-Legged Clinger: (left) *March Brown Nymph*, (right) *Light Cahill Nymph.*

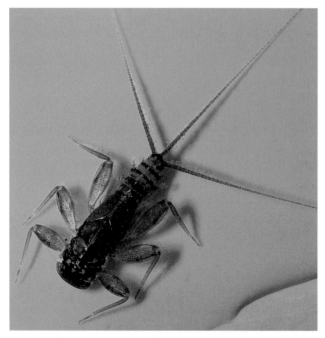

Large clinger nymphs, like this march brown, have distinctive characteristics that are difficult to imitate with conventional techniques.

The large, flattened clingers of *Maccaffertium* and *Stenacron* (march brown, light cahills, and cream cahills) have always presented imitation problems. While there are plenty of nymph patterns with march brown names, the only one I have seen that actually resembled the nymph was Chauncy Lively's March Brown Nymph. While the materials and construction methods of my version have little in common with Chauncy's fly, they share a similar appearance—that of the natural nymph. By adding doubled knotted-thread legs and a poly yarn overback to the inverted tie, a chunky, stable nymph that can be crawled over the bottom results. These nymphs are absent from Western waters, but tiers may be tempted to imitate other large clingers with this design.

Tying Sequence
Using the same curved hooks as the parent style, start by weighting this version with a doubled piece of heavy weighting wire flanking the hook shank. Tie in the tails and ribbing wire, and then invert the hook in the vise. Tie a length of poly yarn along the top of the weighted shank with the remainder extending to the rear.

Dub the abdomen, and bring the poly forward, tying it down over the thorax. Rib the abdomen tightly with the wire. Tie in the doubled knotted-thread legs, and dub over their bases, completing the thorax. Wrap thread to the eye and return with reverse dubbing. Shape and tie down the wing case as in the previous style. Pick out the gills and trim to shape. Trim and set the legs and tails. Coat the wing case, and add dorsal eyes as before. Coating the top of the abdomen with Flexament helps to keep the rib from slipping.

March Brown Nymph (Maccaffertium vicarium)

Hook:	Tiemco 200R or equivalent, #12-14
Thread:	brown 6/0 or 8/0
Weight:	heavy lead-free wire, folded
Tails:	three, coated rusty brown size A rod-winding thread or embossed mono
Rib:	gold wire
Overback:	dark amber or dark brown poly yarn
Body:	tan or grayish tan dubbing
Legs:	coated tan or dark amber heavy sewing thread (doubled), dark markings
Wing case:	burnt or cut Tyvek, mottled dark amber or dark brown, black tips
Eyes:	black spots, epoxy

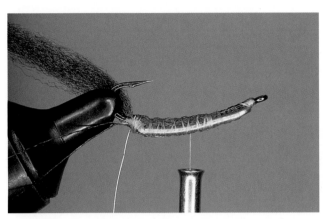

1. Attach thread tails, ribbing wire, and a poly yarn overback to an inverted, curved-shank hook weighted with folded, lead-free wire.

Pattern notes: While these hatches tend to be sparse and strung out, the fish are always on the lookout for the fat nymphs and duns. During the hatching period, drift or crawl the nymph from the current toward the shore, even if no duns are in evidence. Another tactic is to search the shallows with a tandem arrangement consisting of this nymph and a dun imitation.

Light Cahill Nymph (Stenacron interpunctatum)

Hook:	Tiemco 200R or equivalent, #14-16
Thread:	tan or brown 8/0
Weight:	heavy weighting wire, folded
Tails:	three extra long, coated light brown 6/0 tying thread or embossed mono
Rib:	gold wire
Overback:	brown poly yarn
Body:	grayish tan dubbing
Legs:	coated dark tan heavy sewing thread (doubled), brown markings
Wing case:	burnt or cut Tyvek, mottled brown, dark tips
Eyes:	black spots, epoxy

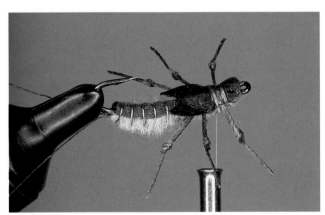

2. Dubbed abdomen and poly yarn overback ribbed with wire. Attach doubled knotted-thread legs, and dub thorax. Tie in wing case and head.

Pattern notes: While the spinners of this species are often the main event, this nymph gives you something to fish as you wait for the spinners to show. Sometimes the nymphing produces bigger fish, and the spinner fall becomes anticlimactic. During heat waves, these flies may hatch sparsely in the morning.

NYMPHS/WETS
Style 5—Wriggling Crawler Ⓐ

Wriggling Crawler: (left) *Wriggling Olive Morning Dun Nymph,* (right) *Wriggling Hendrickson Nymph.*

The first in a series of hinged imitations that build upon a Swisher and Richards legacy, this style is essentially style 3 tied in two parts. It fills a specialized niche. When *Ephemerella* or *Drunella* crawlers emerge in slow water or are flushed there by the current, they swim or struggle through the water. (*Drunella* nymphs are especially awkward and entertaining swimmers.) In these situations, a gently twitched, wriggling nymph outfishes the rigid imitations that are designed to mimic the frozen attitude of drifting nymphs. Both of these crawler genera contribute major hatches to the trout waters of the East, Midwest, and West. The tactical use of this fly, though specialized, is a winning hole card wherever these mayfly games are played.

Tying Sequence

Start with a small, straight-eye hook, and weight the forward end with copper wire. Tie in the thread tails and ribbing wire. Dub and rib the hook. Whip-finish and cement. Pick out the gills and trim to shape. Trim and set the tails. Cut the bend from the completed abdomen.

Tie the mono hinge material to a short-shank Tiemco 2488 (or 2488H), and wind a little copper wire toward the rear of the hook. Tie a pair of mono eyes be-

hind the eye of the hook, and secure everything with a little Zap-A-Gap. Dub over the rear end of the weighting wire with a small amount of thin, tight dubbing. Slip the eye of the completed abdomen onto the mono, wrap the free end of the mono on top of the front hook with a few medium-tension wraps, and draw the mono loop to size. Secure the sized loop with tight wraps, and cut off the excess mono. Touch a little Zap-A-Gap to the wraps, taking care to avoid getting the glue in the hinge.

Wrap a tiny band of tight dubbing at the back of the thorax (front hook), and tie a small tuft of dubbing material on top of the mono tie-down wraps to form a hinge cover. Trim the hinge cover to just meet the beginning of the abdomen. The front portion of the body can now be completed just as with style 3 or 3a. One note of caution about tying the smaller two-part imitations—tying too close to the bend of either hook or making too large a connecting loop can easily produce an oversize imitation. The two examples produce ten- or eleven-millimeter imitations (from the nose to the base of the tails), which is proper for these species. Frequent measuring during the construction can help accustom you the proportions required.

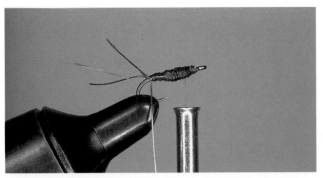

1. Attach thread tails and ribbing wire to weighted rear hook.

2. Dub and rib abdomen. Pick out and trim gills.

3. Attach abdomen to weighted front hook with mono loop. Tie in melted mono eyes.

4. Tie in hinge cover. Complete legs, thorax, and wing case as before.

Wriggling Olive Morning Dun Nymph (D. cornuta)

Hooks:	Tiemco 101, #20 (rear), and Tiemco 2488, #18 (front)
Thread:	olive 8/0
Weight:	copper wire
Tails:	three, coated olive 6/0 tying thread
Rib:	gold wire
Body:	tannish olive or olive-brown dubbing, dark on top
Eyes:	melted mono
Legs:	coated olive or olive-brown heavy sewing thread (front pair doubled)
Wing case:	burnt or cut Tyvek, colored olive or olive-brown, black tips

Pattern notes: There is a corner pool on the lower Brodheads where a short riffle drops suddenly into considerable depth. On this pattern's inaugural outing, it took fish after fish from this pool during the *cornuta* hatch, while my partner's usually effective, rigid tie took none. Since he ties two-part flies only grudgingly, he was doubly disappointed to witness the result.

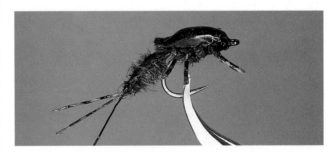

Wriggling Hendrickson Nymph (Ephemerella subvaria)

Hooks:	Tiemco 101, #20 (rear), and Tiemco 2488, #18 (front)
Thread:	brown or olive 8/0
Weight:	copper wire
Tails:	three, coated brown or olive-brown 6/0 tying thread, black markings
Rib:	gold wire
Body:	reddish, blackish, or olive-brown dubbing, black markings on top
Eyes:	melted mono
Legs:	coated brown or olive-brown heavy sewing thread, black markings
Wing case:	burnt or cut Tyvek, colored dark brown or olive-brown, black tips

Pattern notes: In pools or in long moderate runs, this version of the Hendrickson nymph can be fished with devastating effect. This pattern becomes even more of an advantage where fish are exposed to numbers of conventional nymph patterns through heavy pressure during this popular hatch. You can bet that the trout won't have seen many frauds that have the seductive action of this fly.

NYMPHS/WETS
Substyle 5a—Wriggling Swimmer Ⓐ

Wriggling Swimmer: (left) *Gray Drake Nymph,* (center) *Slate Drake Nymph,* (right) *Golden Drake Nymph.*

This Isonychia *nymph, like all large swimming nymphs, has a long abdomen, fringed tails, and conspicuous gills.*

The large swimming nymphs of the genus *Isonychia* (slate drakes) are favorites of mine for the long duration of their hatching periods and their exceptional appeal to trout. Their extended presence makes the nymph an unusually good choice for fishing the water as well as for the actual hatching activity. Other large swimmers, like *Siphlonurus* (gray drakes), and minor genera like *Siphloplecton* and *Ameletus* (great speckled olive and brown duns), can also be imitated by this style for fishing near their slow-water emergence sites. While they are not true swimmers (or true burrowers), the Eastern/Midwestern nymphs of *Anthopotamus* (golden drakes) are included because they swim to emerge and because their lateral gill structure is best represented by this style.

Tying Sequence

This is an elongated version of the prior style, and a proportionally longer rear hook matches the dimensions of these nymphs. Ostrich or rhea herl is substituted for the coated-thread tails in order to match the fringed tails of the large swimming nymphs. Another option is to tie in three strands of nylon rod-winding thread, and after fixing their position with Zap-A-Gap, to brush out the strands to simulate the feathery tails.

Because the tie demonstrated is for *Isonychia*, I am including a strand of white sewing thread on both segments to duplicate the "racing stripe" that is found (to varying degrees) on some individuals. On the rear segment, tie it in somewhere toward the rear of the abdomen, and then bring it forward and tie it off at the eye. Wind the wire rib over the stripe. On the front hook, tie the stripe on top of the hinge cover. Bring it forward, and tie it in after the wing case. Aside from the species-specific adjustments, these nymphs are constructed exactly as the Wriggling Crawler style.

While concerns about hooking ability and potential tangling of the segments are sometimes expressed about such flies, years of experience with their construction and use has dispelled such concerns. Careful attention to the proportions and construction techniques demonstrated in these pages will prevent these issues from affecting the performance of any of the hinged styles shown here or in following chapters.

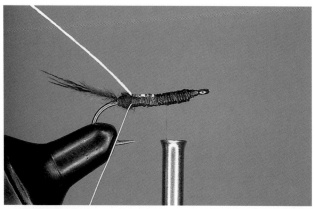

1. Attach herl-tip tails, ribbing wire, and thread stripe to weighted rear hook.

2. Dub, stripe, and rib abdomen. Pick out and trim gills.

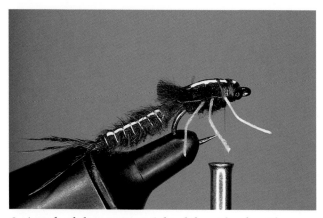

3. Attach abdomen to weighted front hook with mono loop. Tie in hinge cover and thread stripe. Complete legs, thorax, and wing case as before. Tie down thread stripe over wing case.

Gray Drake Nymph (Siphlonurus quebecensis)

Hooks:	Tiemco 101, #16 (rear), and Tiemco 2488, #16 (front)
Thread:	tan or brown 8/0
Weight:	copper wire
Tails:	three, grayish brown ostrich or rhea herl tips, dark banded (marker)
Rib:	gold wire
Body:	dark tan or grayish brown dubbing, mottled on top
Eyes:	melted mono
Legs:	coated tan heavy sewing thread, brown markings
Wing cases:	burnt or cut Tyvek, mottled brown, dark tips

Pattern notes: While not often heralded in the East, *Siphlonurus* species are widespread (Maine has about ten recognized species) and can offer fine fishing to relatively unpressured hatches in both lakes and streams. More popular hatches are found in the West and Midwest (such as the activity on the Yellowstone, Henry's Fork, and Michigan's Au Sable and Pere Marquette).

Golden Drake Nymph.

Slate Drake Nymph (Isonychia bicolor)

Hooks:	Tiemco 101, #14-16 (rear), and Tiemco 2488 or 2488H, #14-16 (front)
Thread:	dark brown or black 8/0
Weight:	copper wire
Tails:	three, grayish tan ostrich or rhea herl tips, marked with brown near the base, then black-banded in the middle, leaving a light tip (sometimes tinted orange)
Rib:	gold wire
Body:	dark reddish or blackish brown dubbing, optional white thread stripe
Eyes:	melted mono
Legs:	coated tan or light olive heavy sewing thread, black markings
Wing case:	burnt or cut Tyvek, colored dark brown, black tips

Pattern notes: On streams with heavy slate drake populations, this nymph is often my go-to fly for fishing the water. When the dark nymphal husks decorate the waterline of streamside rocks, the choice is even more obvious and rewarding. As an aside, the former species designator *sadleri* is now considered synonymous with *bicolor,* thus ending the polite dispute found in angling entomologies about which species' stripe ended where. Apparently, it is a variable trait.

Golden Drake Nymph (Anthopotamus distinctus)

Hooks:	Tiemco 101, #14-16 (rear), and Tiemco 2488 or 2488H, #14-16 (front)
Thread:	tan or brown 8/0
Weight:	copper wire
Tails:	three, light brown ostrich or rhea herl tips, dark banded
Rib:	gold wire
Body:	yellowish or reddish brown dubbing, dark mottled on top
Eyes:	melted mono
Legs:	coated tan or amber heavy sewing thread (doubled), brown markings
Wing case:	burnt or cut Tyvek, mottled brown, dark tips

Pattern notes: Because golden drakes inhabit the slower, warmer reaches of trout streams, the challenge is in locating stretches that are still hospitable for trout in midsummer. I have found them on such famous and diverse trout streams as the Yellow Breeches, Esopus, Beaverkill, and Delaware River. On some waters, these beautiful flies are found emerging alongside the equally beautiful yellow drakes *(E. varia)* or yellow hex *(H. rigida)*. Hinged nymph imitations are extremely effective for all three species.

NYMPHS/WETS
Substyle 5b—Wriggling Burrower Ⓐ

Wriggling Burrower: (left) *Brown Drake Nymph,* (center) *Yellow Hex Nymph,* (right) *White Fly Nymph.*

Large, burrowing mayflies create some of the most fa-mous and anticipated hatches of the season. Some-times the fishing to the duns and spinners doesn't live up to expectations, but the nymphs are a more reliable, though underutilized, opportunity. Big *Ephemera* (green, brown, and yellow drakes) and giant *Hexagenia* or *Litobrancha* (giant Michigan mayfly, yellow hex, dark hex, and dark green drake) nymphs are tempting

Large burrowing nymphs, such as this yellow Hex nymph (H. rigida), *swim to the surface to emerge and display plumose, dorsally-held gills. These traits require special methods in order to create convincing imitations.*

mouthfuls for the biggest trout. Sadly, few of these big flies are important in the West, but the giant Michigan mayfly *(H. limbata)* and brown drake *(E. simulans)* are transcontinental in distribution. The unusual white flies *(Ephoron* spp.) can create truly blizzardlike hatches on waters in the East, Midwest, and West.

Tying Sequence

This variation on the hinged nymph theme uses a swim-ming nymph hook like the Tiemco 400T or Daiichi 1770 for the rear segment of the larger flies. The 400T has a deeper curve in the shank, and I like to ease it a bit with my fingers before tying. On the largest imitations, a less expensive alternative is to bend an Aberdeen bait hook (seldom available smaller than size 10 or 12). These pat-terns continue the use of ostrich or rhea herl for tails be-cause burrowing nymphs also have fringed tails. Tails of brushed nylon rod-winding thread can be substituted.

All of the burrowing nymphs have plumose gills that are held dorsally, and the flue-clump gills of the Wrig-gling Burrower provide a more accurate and more mo-bile representation than the lateral gills found on most nymph ties. The flue fibers replace the hinge cover used in the previous hinged patterns.

The poly yarn wing case and doubled knotted-thread legs return in this version. They demonstrate how elements from earlier styles can be mixed and matched throughout these progressions to create variations that are not depicted, but implied. The doubled knotted-thread legs mimic the flanged legs of burrowers. The sequence of this fly's construction matches that of the others except that you tie in the poly yarn before the legs and the thorax dubbing, bringing it forward over the thorax, and tie it in by the wraps that form the pronotum.

Burrowing nymphs sport tusks of various sizes and shapes. I used to imitate these by tying the tip of a goose biot on either side of the hook eye. Then I remembered something I had read (I believe it was an article by Ernest Schwiebert) about the original purpose of the turned-up eye on English dry-fly hooks. It was to imitate the heads of mayfly duns. I realized that the straight eye on these imitations made a fair suggestion of the tusks, so I omitted the biots—a convenient rationalization of an inconsequential matter. Add the biots if you like; the fish won't care.

1. Attach herl tip tails to weighted rear hook. Dub, rib, and mark abdomen.

2. Attach abdomen with mono loop to weighted front hook. Attach melted mono eyes, flue-fiber hinge cover, and poly yarn.

3. Attach doubled knotted-thread legs, and dub thorax. Tie down poly yarn wing case.

Brown Drake Nymph (Ephemera simulans)

Hooks:	Daiichi 1770, #14-16 (rear), and Tiemco 2488 or 2488H, #14-16 (front)
Thread:	tan or brown 8/0
Weight:	copper wire
Tails:	three, brown ostrich or rhea herl tips
Rib:	gold wire
Body:	yellowish tan or yellowish brown dubbing, marked with brown
Eyes:	melted mono
Gills:	grayish tan flue fibers
Wing case:	light brown poly yarn, mottled brown, black at rear
Legs:	coated amber heavy sewing thread (doubled), brown marks

Pattern notes: The hatching period of brown drakes in streams is typically very short, making this hatch notoriously difficult to time. On Pine Creek or the Delaware River, it lasts about three days in a given location. On the Delaware, it coincides with the green drake (E. guttulata), rendering it insignificant. In lakes, however, it can be another story. On Skaneateles Lake in New York, for example, it can hatch for two or three weeks before it is replaced by the yellow hex (H. rigida)—creating a bonanza of burrowers that lasts for about two months.

Yellow Hex Nymph (Hexagenia rigida)

Hooks: Daiichi 1770, #8-12 (rear), and Tiemco 2488
             or 2488H, #8-12 (front)
Thread: tan 6/0 or 8/0
Weight: lead-free wire or copper wire
Tails: three, grayish brown ostrich or rhea herl tips
Rib: gold wire
Body: yellowish tan dubbing, marked with brown
Eyes: melted mono
Gills: brownish gray flue fibers
Wing case: light brown poly yarn, brown marks, dark at rear
Legs: coated tan heavy sewing thread (doubled), amber
             marks

Pattern notes: Some of the Finger Lakes in New York and Great
Lakes have tremendous hatches of this giant mayfly. Perhaps because their territories and hatches overlap, *rigida* is often mistaken for the better-known *H. limbata*, the giant Michigan mayfly.
Unless I miss my layman's-eye guess, the lighter-colored *Hexagenia* that I found hatching in the Yellow Breeches more than thirty
years ago is probably *rigida* (I've never keyed it out). This imitation is terrific when drifted, retrieved, or even very slowly trolled
(in lakes) prior to the hatch.

White Fly Nymph (Ephoron leukon)

Hooks: Tiemco 101, #14-16 (rear, bent), and Tiemco 2488,
             #16-18 (front)
Thread: white 8/0
Weight: copper wire
Tails: white ostrich herl tips
Rib: gold wire
Body: dirty white dubbing (abdomen), pale orange
             dubbing (thorax)
Eyes: melted mono
Gills: grayish white flue fibers
Wing case: tan poly yarn, colored amber, brown at rear
Legs: coated cream sewing thread (doubled), tan marks

Pattern notes: The white fly hatch on the Yellow Breeches is
justly famous, but these strange mayflies hatch on many streams
throughout the East and Midwest. Its sister species, *E. album*,
overlaps in the Midwest and extends into the West, creating
hatches in the Yellowstone/Missouri drainage. I find the prehatch
nymphing far more relaxing and sometimes more productive than
the insane frenzy that ensues when the snowstorm of white flies
is driven upstream.

ADULTS/EMERGERS
Style 1—Synthetic Compara-dun

Synthetic Compara-dun: (left) *Olive Dun/Spinner,* (right) *Brown Dun/Spinner.*

This first dry-fly style is a fly of many fathers. Its roots are in the old Haystack, made famous by Fran Betters—one Ausable legend fostered by another. From there it was reborn as the Compara-dun, Al Caucci's immortal brainchild. This synthetic incarnation was introduced to me by John Betts, the modern master of synthetic designs, through the instructions originally packaged with Z-Lon. It is a simple but incredibly versatile style, remarkable for its ability to imitate duns and spinners, up wings and spent wings—often with a single pattern. More visible, durable, and easier to tie than the deer-hair version, this all-purpose dry fly honors its distinguished lineage.

Tying Sequence

This style begins with a standard dry-fly hook (down-eye or straight-eye, fine or extra-fine wire). After covering the shank with a layer of thread, dub a tiny ball at the rear of the hook. Tie Micro Fibetts onto either side of this ball. The number of these filaments is determined by the size of the hook; one on each side for size 20 or smaller, two or three for sizes 16 to 18, and four or five for sizes 12 to 14. Attach a ribbing thread ahead of the tails.

Advance the thread to a point about a quarter of the shank length from the eye, and wrap the Z-Lon yarn on top of the shank. Again, the amount depends on the size, and the number of tails on a side work pretty well as a guide (one piece for size 20 down, two or three for sizes 16 to 18, etc.). Antron, Hi-Vis, and poly yarn also work for this wing, but fine-denier poly yarn is only suitable for the smallest imitations (size 18 and smaller). After wrapping the wing fibers securely, trim the butts at an angle, and wrap over them.

Dub the body tightly up to the wing. Spiral the ribbing thread forward, and tie it off. Build up a little more dubbing behind the wing. Fold the wing fibers back, and wrap several times in front of them. Do not try to erect the wing with thread; that is the job of dubbing. I like to reverse dub to the wing, build up the dubbing to erect the wing, then return to the eye with very thin, tight dubbing. Whip-finish at the eye. Spread the wing fibers into a 180-degree fan, and trim the wing to resemble an upside-down U with the side fibers slightly shorter. Touch a little Zap-A-Gap to the finish wraps and up to the base of the wing to fix the fibers in position.

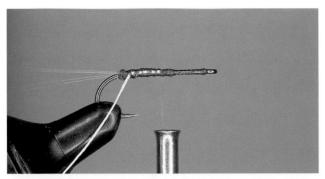

1. Split Micro Fibett tails around dubbing ball, and tie in ribbing thread.

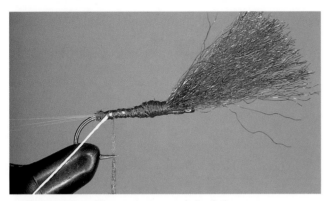

2. Tie in Z-Lon fiber. Prepare to dub abdomen.

3. Dub and rib abdomen. Build up thorax dubbing.

4. Fold back wing fibers, and build up dubbing at head.

Brown Dun/Spinner

Hook: standard dry fly, #26-10
Thread: brown 6/0 or 8/0
Tails: gray or brown Micro Fibetts
Rib: white or gray thread
Body: light brown to dark reddish brown dry-fly dubbing
Wing: dun or dark dun Z-Lon

Pattern notes: This versatile pattern is a general suggestion of many common hatches—blue quills, Hendricksons, Quill Gordons, slate drakes, and even male sulphurs or dark *Baetis* duns. It can often be made to serve double duty as a spinner imitation, making it even more useful.

Olive Dun/Spinner

Hook: standard dry fly, #26-10
Thread: olive 6/0 or 8/0
Tails: gray or olive Micro Fibetts
Rib: white or gray thread
Body: light olive to olive-brown dry-fly dubbing
Wing: dun or dark dun Z-Lon

Pattern notes: This pattern is nearly as broad in application as the brown version, representing the vast array of olive-colored flies of the *Drunella* and *Baetis* genera. Even typically brownish species may have olive variants, and I have often encountered Hendricksons and slate drakes with olive bodies.

ADULTS/EMERGERS
Substyle 1a—Inverted Synthetic Compara-dun

Inverted Synthetic Compara-dun: (left) *Trico,* (right) *Blue-Winged Sulphur.*

I often improvised this upside-down version in situ by forcibly twisting the wing to the other side of the hook—simple, and I thought I was pretty clever. Later perusal of a fly pattern compendium revealed that this mutation had not escaped the resourceful John Betts— no doubt he recognized the potential long before the idea occurred to me. This is the easiest way I know to

During popular hatches, such as the blue-winged sulphur (E. invaria), *trout see numerous dry-fly imitations. An inverted pattern can help to overcome acquired resistance to standard patterns.*

test if finicky fish are reacting to the consistent "double hernia" illusion created by a dry-fly hook reflecting in the mirrored underside of the water's surface. To avoid the possible perils of manhandling, I now tie this variation for popular hatches where constant exposure to the dry fly can generate hook shyness.

Tying Sequence
The obvious difference between this and the previous style is that the wing is tied on the underside of the hook. This works well with standard up- or straight-eye hooks until about size 20; then I like to use a large-gap, short-shank hook that is oversize in number designation. For example, the Trico *(T. stygiatus)* pattern is normally tied on a size 24 standard hook, but for the upside-down version, a Daiichi 1140 in size 20 produces the same size imitation with better hooking potential. Unlike most right-side-up dry-fly styles, there is no harm in tying the body slightly around the bend; in fact, it helps to enhance the orientation of the fly as it lands on the water.

The other difference is that I am incorporating an accurate number of Micro Fibett or monofilament tails on this version. I know, I know—trout can't count. But to say they can't see is another proposition entirely. Besides, this tailing technique is easier, so why not do it? Tie in the tails together, and then spread them with your thumbnail and fix their bases with a touch of Zap-A-Gap. You can either add a tiny wrap of dubbing over the bases before attaching the thread rib or simply place a wrap of dubbing behind the thread as you dub the body.

1. Tie in monofilament tails and thread rib. Tie Z-Lon fibers underneath the hook.

2. Invert fly. Dub and rib abdomen, and complete fly as before.

Blue-Winged Sulphur (Ephemerella invaria)

Hook:	standard dry fly, #14-16
Thread:	yellow or orange 8/0
Tails:	three, golden brown dyed mono
Rib:	white, orange, or olive thread
Body:	orange-yellow (female) or brownish yellow (male) dry-fly dubbing
Wing:	light dun Z-Lon

Pattern notes: Because this is a very reliable and popular hatch, the trout see a lot of standard imitations. This fly presents a suggestion of their prey absent the most obvious telltale of conventional dry flies. It's not always the ultimate answer, but it is useful in the process of deciphering what is.

Trico (Tricorythodes stygiatus)

Hook:	Daiichi 1140, #20
Thread:	light gray
Tails:	three, light gray Micro Fibetts, middle filament longer
Rib:	light gray thread
Body:	light grayish green (female) or olive-brown (male) dry-fly dubbing
Wing:	light dun or white Z-Lon

Pattern notes: This is my favorite Trico dun imitation, and it works for the spinners, too (darken the bodies and lengthen the tails, if you like). When the flies are thick on the surface, spoon-feed it to a steady riser with a downstream drift. Don't be too quick on the set; the British practice of saying "God save the Queen!" before tightening works, but "Hail to the Chief!" is more patriotic.

ADULTS/EMERGERS
Substyle 1b—Inverted Fluttering Spinner ①

Inverted Fluttering Spinner: (left) *Female White Fly,* (right) *Female Hendrickson Spinner.*

More complicated than the previous versions, this fly uses an inverted swimming nymph hook to mimic the characteristic posture of an egg-laying spinner. It was originally designed to match the large, dipping spinners of *Isonychia, Siphlonurus,* and *Maccaffertium.* Success with these patterns leads to imitations of medium-size species like Hendricksons and sulphurs (*Ephemerella* spp.) or white flies (*Ephoron* spp.) that infuriate trout with their aerial antics. Drifted, skittered, or dapped, this accurate, yet versatile fly represents spent, up-wing, or fluttering spinners. The inverted hook and extended front legs produce a unique look on the water that will fool trout that shun other imitations.

Tying Sequence

Unlike the application as a tail hook in the Wriggling Burrower tie, the Tiemco 400T has an edge over the Daiichi 1770 for larger versions of this fly. Its deeper belly is better for reproducing the compound curve of a flutter-ing, egg-laying spinner. However, I have not been able to find it in sizes smaller than 14 (there is a sizing difference as well—the Tiemco is longer), and the belly of the 1770 can be bent a bit more for use on smaller imitations. Poly yarn imitates the egg sac(s), and knotted mono mimics the spinner's extended front legs.

Start by tying the mono tails a little further around the rear bend than in the Inverted Synthetic Comparadun tie, and wrap a small band of dubbing over the rear tie-in point. Tie in the single or double poly yarn egg sac, and attach the ribbing thread. Advance the thread and tie the knotted-mono legs to the front half of the hook. Invert the hook in the vise, and continue to tie the remainder of the fly as with the previous version.

When it is time to erect the wing, wrap dubbing between the wing base and the leg bases. After raising the wing, hold the legs back along the body and dub the head. Finish the head, and shape the wing as before.

1. Tie in mono tails, poly yarn egg-sac(s), rib, and knotted mono legs. Prepare to attach wing fibers.

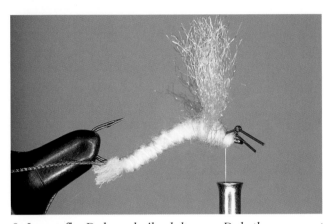

2. Invert fly. Dub and rib abdomen. Dub thorax, erect wing, and dub head.

Female White Fly (Ephoron leukon)

Hook:	Daiichi 1770, #14 (bent slightly)
Thread:	white 8/0
Tails:	three, light gray dyed mono (embossed)
Egg sacs:	yellow poly yarn (two)
Rib:	white thread
Legs:	brown dyed mono (knotted)
Body:	grayish white (abdomen, head) and pale orange (thorax) dry-fly dubbing
Wing:	white or pale gray Z-Lon or Hi-Vis

Pattern notes: The females of this unusual species don't molt into spinners, and their atrophied legs make them helpless when not in flight. While other mayflies will be found clinging to posts and screens around lights after dark, female white flies flop around on the ground. The male does molt and loses a tail in the process; hence male spinners have two tails and female egg-laying duns have three. The males have functional legs and are often seen flying with the subimago husk still clinging to their tails. As a clarification, the number of tails is confused in the white-fly text and patterns included in the recent book, *Mayflies,* by Knopp and Cormier. It is a superb book, but even in a text reviewed by entomologists, mistakes can be made.

Female Hendrickson Spinner.

Female Hendrickson Spinner (Ephemerella subvaria)

Hook:	Daiichi 1770, #16 (bent slightly)
Thread:	brown 8/0
Tails:	three, brown dyed mono (embossed)
Egg sac:	yellow poly yarn
Rib:	white or tan thread
Legs:	brown dyed mono (knotted)
Body:	rusty or dark reddish brown dry-fly dubbing
Wing:	light tan Z-Lon or Hi-Vis

Pattern notes: Hendrickson and sulphur spinners frequently drop their eggs while flying at a safe distance above the water, frustrating fly fishers and trout. One tactic that is employed with some success is to fish a tiny ball of yellow dubbing tied on a short-shank size 22 to 24 hook. Another is to incorporate this as a dropper attached to the bend of the spinner imitation.

ADULTS/EMERGERS
Style 2—Burnt Poly-Wing Dun

Burnt Poly-Wing Dun: (left) *Female Hendrickson Dun,* (right) *Dark Olive Morning Dun.*

Like a favorite child, the burnt fiber wing gets a lot of attention in my fly designs, and this application produces an easy-to-tie and realistic imitation of most mayfly duns. Lee Wulff's original hairwing dry flies were tied with a single wing to imitate the closed wings of a resting dun. But they weren't popular, so he made a rare bow to convention and tied a split-wing version—the famous Wulff we all know and love. Single wing flies have lost their stigma, but the fiber-fan legs on this style may raise some hackles among traditionalists. The fibers support and stabilize the fly and adequately imitate legs that are often obscured and distorted at their interface with the surface. As an imitation of any species of small to medium duns, this style offers a novel and accurate image to tough-water trout.

Tying Sequence

Before tying this fly, it is a good idea to review the wing-making technique described in chapter 4. With a little practice, this wing can be prepared in less time than it takes to make cut or burnt feather wings. It is more durable and won't spin when cast. Standard dry-fly hooks are fine for smaller dun imitations, but for flies in the ten to fifteen millimeter range, I prefer to use a 2X-long hook like the Tiemco 5212 or Daiichi 1280.

Tie mono tails and ribbing thread to the hook, and dub a tapered body over the rear two-thirds of the shank. After ribbing the body, secure a small amount of Hi-Vis crosswise at the front of the dubbed abdomen with cross wraps of thread—the same manner that synthetic-fiber spinner wings are typically attached. Apply a small amount of Zap-A-Gap to the wraps, and immediately follow with cross wraps of dubbing. The fiber-fan legs should be trimmed to about one-half body length (the span from leg tip to leg tip will exceed the length of the body).

Prepare a burnt poly wing, and mount it against the thorax dubbing with the pinch-wrap technique. Cut off the excess poly close to the wraps, and touch a bit of Zap-A-Gap to the cut ends. Wrap over the ends immediately after the glue has been applied, and dub the head with thin, tight dubbing. Whip-finish and cement the wraps.

1. Attach mono tails. Dub and rib abdomen.

2. Attach fiber-fan legs. Dub thorax.

3. Tie in burnt poly wing. Trim excess poly, and apply Zap-A-Gap.

4. Dub head over cement. Apply whip-finish.

Female Hendrickson Dun (Ephemerella subvaria)

Hook:	2XL dry fly, #12-14
Thread:	tan 8/0
Tails:	three, golden brown dyed mono
Rib:	white thread
Body:	pinkish tan to tannish olive dry-fly dubbing
Legs:	tan Hi-Vis, brown marks
Wing:	medium gray poly yarn (burnt)

Pattern notes: Trout sometimes seem to display a preference for the larger, lighter Hendrickson females. This may be a selection of larger prey, or it may reflect concentrations around the trout's lie. In *Caddisflies,* Gary LaFontaine relates a conversation he had with Larry Solomon (pg. 223). "The fish will stay with the one he sees the most of at first," Solomon theorized. They were discussing egg-laying caddisflies, but I think that "Solomon's Theorem" explains many instances of perceived selectivity.

Dark Olive Morning Dun (Drunella lata)

Hook:	standard dry fly, #16-18
Thread:	olive 8/0
Tails:	three, dark olive dyed mono
Rib:	light gray thread
Body:	light to medium olive dry-fly dubbing
Legs:	olive Hi-Vis
Wing:	dark gray poly yarn (burnt)

Pattern notes: In my favorite fly-fishing book, *Nymphs,* Ernest Schwiebert credits the "extremely important hatch in June" on the Brodheads to *lata,* but that activity is surely *cornuta* and its little sister species, *cornutella.* However, there are *lata* in the Brodheads and in many other Eastern and Midwestern waters—they typically hatch in July. They are part of a steady stream of morning-hatching *Drunella* olives, beginning in late May with *cornuta,* followed by *cornutella,* then by *lata,* and finally, in August, by *walkeri*—more than enough reasons to get out of bed early.

ADULTS/EMERGERS
Substyle 2a—Hackled Burnt Poly-Wing Dun

Hackled Burnt Poly-Wing Dun: (left) *Pale Evening Dun,* (right) *Pink Lady.*

If you like the burnt wing but must have hackle, this version combines the two. I designed it to imitate active, warm-weather duns. The hackle makes it easy to twitch and skitter and, when resting, matches high-riding duns that are ready for flight. Pale evening duns *(E. dorothea)*, little yellow quills *(L. hebe)*, and yellow quills and pink ladies *(E. vitreus* males and females) are prime Eastern/Midwestern warm-weather hatches, and this style is well suited to imitations of these duns. In the West, pale morning duns *(E. inermis* and *infrequens)* and slate-winged olives or "flavs" *(D. flavilinea)* are likely candidates.

Tying Sequence

This burnt-wing variation follows the procedure for the prior style until the thorax of the fly. Instead of tying the fiber-fan legs to the thorax position, tie in a dry-fly hackle. Wrap the dubbing forward to the wing position, and wind the hackle in a tight palmer wrap over the dubbing and tie off.

Prepare and mount the burnt poly wing as before, and dub and whip-finish the head of the fly. After cementing the finishing wraps, trim the hackle fibers that protrude from the bottom of the thorax flush with the dubbing. This creates a wide V-shaped notch in the hackle, which stabilizes the fly on the water. This results in what is sometimes called a thorax-style dry fly. Out of respect, however, I should add that Vince Marinaro was never very fond of the bastardization of his original design, which employed X-wraps of hackle around the thorax.

1. Tie in mono tails. Dub and rib abdomen. Tie in hackle butt.

2. Dub thorax. Palmer hackle through thorax and tie off.

3. Tie in burnt poly wing, and dub head. Trim off hackle underneath.

Pale Evening Dun (Ephemerella dorothea)

Hook:	standard dry fly, #16-20
Thread:	yellow 8/0
Tails:	three, yellow dyed mono
Rib:	white or orange thread
Body:	pale yellow or orange yellow dry-fly dubbing
Hackle:	pale ginger or cream
Wing:	cream or pale gray poly yarn (burnt, yellow-marked leading edge optional)

Pattern notes: This classic little hatch is diminished only by the late hours it keeps when the weather is hot. Just before it becomes too dark to see, you should switch to a yellow Thread-Legged Wet Dun for easier wet-fly fishing (you feel the hits, rather than trying to see them or striking at sounds). Or you can try this hatch later in the season on the West Branch of the Delaware, when you can fish it at midday.

Pink Lady (Epeorus vitreus, *female*)

Hook:	2XL dry fly, #12-14
Thread:	yellow 8/0
Tails:	two, golden brown dyed mono
Rib:	yellowish olive thread
Body:	pinkish orange, pinkish yellow, yellowish olive dry-fly dubbing (applied successively from back to front)
Hackle:	ginger variant (grizzly)
Wing:	pale gray poly yarn (burnt)

Pattern notes: This is a rather unpredictable hatch of long duration—some evenings it makes a great showing, and others . . . nothing. Nevertheless, it is one of my favorites. The capture of a four-and-a-half-pound wild brown on one of my Pocono home waters has something to do with my affection for this hatch. I performed CPR on that fish (catch, photograph, and release), but my fishing partner nearly had to administer the other CPR to me.

ADULTS/EMERGERS
Substyle 2b—Shucking Burnt Poly-Wing Dun (I)

Shucking Burnt Poly-Wing Dun: (left) *Shucking Blue Quill,* (right) *Shucking Little Blue-Winged Olive.*

Tying a clump of synthetic fibers in the place of tails is a popular way of suggesting a nymphal shuck, but a few snips of the scissors and a drop of glue can produce a far more convincing representation. The shuck on this fly has legs, tails, a dark wing case, and a translucent body, and all of this comes from tying two colors of synthetic fiber to the back of the fly. An outstanding deception that is surprisingly easy to tie, this variation adds another option for presentation to trout that are looking for a vulnerable emerger or cripple.

Tying Sequence

The body of this fly is the Burnt Poly-Wing Dun—it is the tail end that makes the difference. Begin by tying a sparse clump of synthetic yarn to the rear of a standard dry-fly hook (or 2XL for larger imitations). Antron, Z-Lon, and Hi-Vis all work fine for this purpose. Tie another, somewhat sparser and shorter dark clump on top of that.

Cut the dark clump to about one-half or one-third the length of the hook shank. Snip a few of the side fibers of the lower clump to leg-length (about two-thirds of the shank). Trim all but a few fibers (to represent the tails) from the end of the synthetic shuck, leaving the remaining fibers the length of the shank. Grasp the fibers between your fingers so that only the tails and the ends of the body fibers protrude (you may need to roll your fingers slightly to gather the fibers together). Using a dubbing needle dipped in Zap-A-Gap, glue the ends of the body fibers where they meet the tails. Be careful not to glue your fingers together, as you will need to hold the fibers until the glue sets (a few seconds). Rubbing a little wax on your fingers can help to prevent mishaps.

Dub a short band for the head of the shuck, and follow the procedure for the Burnt Poly-Wing Dun to complete the fly. Of course, hackle fanatics could follow the directions for the hackled version. You can also just tie in the two clumps of fiber, complete the rest of the fly, and then finish the shuck. This is how I do it, because I like to remove the fly from the vise for shuck shaping.

1. Attach synthetic shuck and wing case material.

2. Trim wing case and leg fibers. Glue shuck fibers, and trim tails.

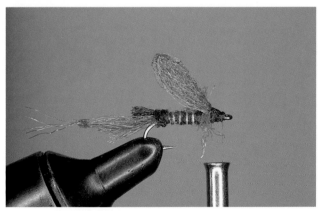

3. Complete forward half of fly as with Burnt Poly-Wing Dun.

Shucking Blue Quill (**Paraleptophlebia** *spp.*)

Hook:	standard dry fly or Tiemco 101, #16-18
Thread:	brown 8/0
Shuck:	black over brown Antron, dark brown dubbing (head)
Rib:	white thread
Body:	reddish brown dry-fly dubbing
Legs:	tan Hi-Vis
Wing:	dark gray poly yarn (burnt)

Pattern notes: Look for *Paraleptophlebia* flies to be emerging in quieter eddies and side pockets of the stream, near shore or emergent cover. Look carefully, because sparse hatches of these little flies and the quiet rises to them are easy to miss. This fly works well for both the early *(adoptiva)* and later varieties *(mollis, guttata, strigula),* but the cold-weather blue quills are more likely to have trouble evacuating their shucks.

Shucking Little Blue-Winged Olive (Baetis *spp.*)

Hook:	Tiemco 101, #16-22
Thread:	olive or brown 8/0
Shuck:	black over olive or brown Antron, dark olive or brown dubbing (head)
Rib:	white or gray thread
Body:	olive, olive-brown, or brown dry-fly dubbing
Legs:	tan, olive, or brown Hi-Vis
Wing:	light, medium, or dark gray poly yarn (burnt)

Pattern notes: *Baetis* weather (cool, overcast, drizzly) and *Baetis* water (slick, greasy-looking currents) both contribute to the trouble these ubiquitous little duns experience while escaping their shucks. The leisurely takes to the struggling duns—and to this little fly—indicate that the trout know a sure thing when they see it.

ADULTS/EMERGERS
Style 3—Burnt Poly-Wing Drake

Burnt Poly-Wing Drake: (left) *March Brown,* (right) *Yellow Drake.*

Conventional dry-fly hooks and tying styles are less convincing when applied to imitations of large mayflies, like this yellow drake.

With larger mayfly species, the problems of imitation grow as their features become more obvious. Standard hooks are problematic for large dry flies due to the weight and appearance of the excessive gap. Long-shank, fine-wire hooks are preferable, and swimming nymph hooks add a realistic curve to the long abdomen as well. A poly yarn overback is incorporated into this style. This creates an attractive, but unimportant, color separation, and its real value is to increase the buoyancy of the large body. Similarly, knotted mono legs provide imitative detail but are also used as a ploy to alter the appearance of the front of the fly. This style works well for large species like slate drakes (*Isonychia* spp.), march browns *(M. vicarium),* and brown and yellow drakes (*E. simulans* and *varia*). Western tiers could use it to devise fine Western green drake (*D. doddsi* and *grandis*) imitations.

Tying Sequence

Start with a swimming nymph hook. The Daiichi 1770 is perfect for this, but if you are using the Tiemco 400T, relieve the belly curve a bit with your fingers (also, the 400T is longer for the same number designation). Attach the mono tails (emboss them with a Leatherman pliers, if you like the look), and tie in a pair of knotted mono legs (the knots should be positioned at or just ahead of the eye of the hook). Bind a length of poly yarn to the top of the shank with the fibers extending to the rear. Wrap a small amount of dubbing at the rear, and tie in the ribbing thread (the dubbing helps to keep the rib from slipping off the end). Continue dubbing the body up to the thorax location.

Bring the poly yarn forward, and tie it down at the thorax. Cut off the excess poly, and spiral the ribbing thread tightly over the abdomen. Tie the fiber-fan legs to the thorax with cross wraps of thread, and then cement the wraps and dub around the legs.

After preparing the burnt poly wing, secure it against the thorax dubbing using pinch wraps as before. The knotted mono legs complicate the finishing process somewhat, and they will need to be held out of the way in order to trim, wrap down, and then dub over the poly wing fibers. A little dubbing should be applied behind and then in front of the legs to finish the head. Whip-finish and cement. Add markings to the wing (if appropriate) and to the top of the head (if you like) with marker.

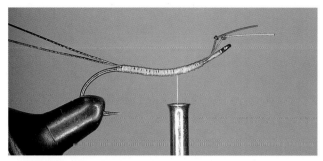

1. *Attach mono tails and knotted mono legs to a swimming nymph hook.*

2. *Tie in poly yarn overback and thread rib. Dub abdomen.*

3. *Tie down overback, and rib abdomen. Tie in fiber-fan legs, and dub thorax.*

4. *Tie in large burnt poly wing, and dub head.*

Yellow Drake (Ephemera varia)

Hook: Daiichi 1770 or equivalent, #8-12
Thread: white 6/0 or 8/0
Tails: three, brownish yellow dyed mono (embossed)
Overback: mixed brown and white poly yarn
Rib: white thread
Body: creamy or yellowish white dry-fly dubbing
Front legs: yellow dyed mono (knotted), brown marks
Rear legs: cream or tan Hi-Vis
Wing: cream or white poly yarn (burnt), brown and
             yellow marks

Pattern notes: From mid-June to early August (typically), these beautiful drakes emerge from pools and runs along the slower, warmer stretches of trout streams. They are often seen in the company of *Anthopotamus* or *Hexagenia* duns. Trout may take all of these indiscriminately (making fly selection less critical), or they may focus on whichever is more concentrated around their feeding station. The size range of *varia* duns is usually given as 13 to 16mm, but on rich limestone streams (like the Yellow Breeches) I frequently find females as large as 20mm.

March Brown (Maccaffertium vicarium)

Hook: Daiichi 1770 or equivalent, #10-12
Thread: tan 6/0 or 8/0
Tails: two, brown dyed mono (embossed)
Overback: amber or brown poly yarn
Rib: yellow or tan thread
Body: creamy or yellowish tan dry-fly dubbing
Front legs: golden brown or brown dyed mono (knotted),
             brown or black marks
Rear legs: tan Hi-Vis, brown or black marks
Wing: tan or light gray poly yarn (burnt), brown,
             or black marks

Pattern notes: These classic duns may produce concentrated hatches on some waters, but sparse, sporadic hatching is more typical. They do command the attention of the trout, however, and searching the water with this large dry is often rewarded, even when activity is spotty. They are highly variable in size and color, leading to the impression that two different species were involved (the gray fox—formerly *Stenonema fuscum*—is now considered synonymous).

ADULTS/EMERGERS
Substyle 3a—Synthetic Drake Spinner Ⓘ

Synthetic Drake Spinner: (left) *Brown Drake Spinner,* (right) *Slate Drake Spinner.*

The spinner version of the prior style, this large dry uses wings made of Hi-Vis fibers to achieve the broad impression of large spent wings. For some species, this fly can outshine the performance of the dun imitation. It is not unusual for hatches of big *Ephemera* drakes to produce better fishing during the spinner falls. *Stenonema* and *Isonychia* spinners are sometimes more important than the duns, and *Siphlonurus* spinners are by far the most fishable phase of the hatch. This spent, synthetic pattern is durable, realistic, and works for most of the larger mayfly species.

Tying Sequence
This fly is constructed the same as the previous style, except that fiber-fan wings are substituted for the fiber-fan legs (of course, the dun wing is omitted). After the tails, abdomen (including the poly overback), and knotted mono front legs are tied, attach a rather large clump of Hi-Vis fibers to the thorax with cross wraps of thread. (Sometimes I add a few strands of Krystal Flash to the underside of the wing in order to simulate the iridescence of spinner wings, but this is optional.) Apply a touch of Zap-A-Gap to the cross wraps, and dub around the wing bases. Continue to dub forward, behind, and

Tie in mono tails and knotted mono legs on swimming nymph hook. Construct overback and abdomen as before.

Tie in Hi-Vis fiber wings at thorax. Dub thorax and head.

then in front of the knotted mono legs, completing the head. Whip-finish and cement.

Hi-Vis fibers are my preference for large spinner wings because they hold their shape and have the bulk to create a broad wing. This quality can be enhanced by spreading and flattening the wing fibers and then applying a little Zap-A-Gap to their bases with a dubbing needle to fix their position. The fixed wing can then be trimmed to shape.

Slate Drake Spinner (Isonychia bicolor)

Hook:	Daiichi 1770 or equivalent, #8-12
Thread:	brown 6/0 or 8/0
Tails:	two, grayish or yellowish brown dyed mono (embossed)
Overback:	dark brown poly yarn
Rib:	dark brown or maroon thread
Body:	dark reddish brown dry-fly dubbing
Legs:	yellow dyed mono (knotted), brown marked except tips
Wing:	tan or pale gray Hi-Vis

Pattern notes: Female *Isonychia* spinners often lay their eggs while fluttering and dipping repeatedly to the water. While this activity can be challenging to imitate (see the Inverted Fluttering Spinner), eventually both the males and the females fall to the surface. Eager trout, teased by the earlier antics of the females, will be waiting to take advantage.

Brown Drake Spinner (Ephemera simulans)

Hook:	Daiichi 1770 or equivalent, #8-12
Thread:	brown 6/0 or 8/0
Tails:	three, brown dyed mono (embossed)
Overbody:	dark brown poly yarn
Rib:	yellow or tan thread
Body:	yellowish tan dry-fly dubbing (optional brown belly marks)
Legs:	brown dyed mono (knotted), black marks
Wing:	tan or pale gray Hi-Vis, brown or black marks

Pattern notes: Despite their brief hatching period in streams, brown drake spinner falls are usually concentrated affairs. Unlike some genera, where the female spinners may or may not fall to the surface after dropping their eggs, *Ephemera* females express their egg sacs all at once on the water. So, when you notice the clouds of male spinners gathering around trees and other objects near shore, you should prepare to do battle at dusk.

ADULTS/EMERGERS
Style 4—Extended Burnt Poly-Wing Drake Ⓐ

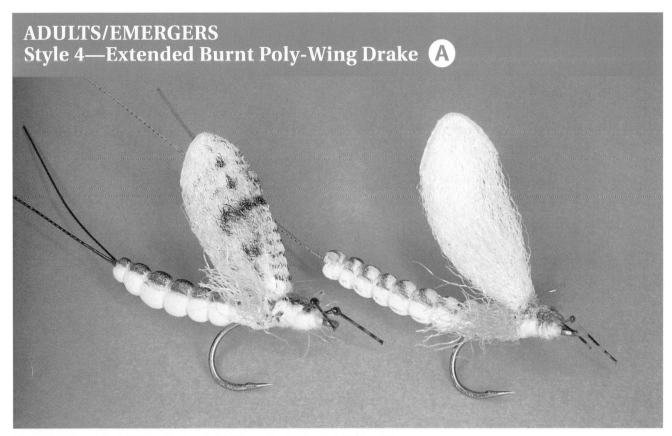

Extended Burnt Poly-Wing Drake: (left) *Green Drake,* (right) *Yellow Hex.*

The large green drakes *(E. guttulata)* and the giant mayflies of the *Hexagenia* and *Litobrancha* genera require special imitations that overcome the obvious deficiencies of standard dry flies. This is especially true on waters where these popular hatches receive steady pressure night after night. The enormous hooks required for conventional imitations (even if extra-long models are used) create flotation and appearance problems. Extended-body flies have often been devised as a possible solution, but some construction methods result in bodies that are either too stiff (like flies tied on the old fly body hooks or those with quill bodies) or too fragile (like feather or hollow hair extensions) to be truly effective. This style's needle-tied foam extension is both flexible and durable and presents a very accurate image to suspicious trout.

Tying Sequence
I recommend reviewing the needle-tying procedure described in chapter 4 before tying this fly. To construct the foam extension, clamp a needle in the vise, and tie in the tailing material (usually mono, although you can substitute coated thread) near the point. Tie in two slightly tapered and pointed strips of foam over the tail wraps. Then fold them back along the needle, and either rib them with a tight spiral of thread or, preferably, wrap

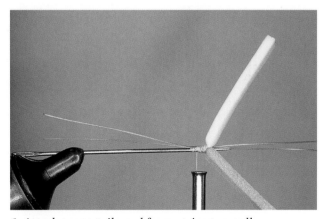

1. Attach mono tails and foam strips to needle.

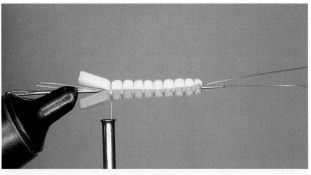

2. Complete true segmentation wraps, and apply whip-finish.

them with a true segmentation technique. In this technique, slip the thread between the foam strips, wrap it a few times, and repeat the process until you reach the tie off point. After whip-finishing near the vise jaws, remove the assembly from the needle, and attach it to an undersize, short-shank hook, such as the Tiemco 2488.

After securing the foam abdomen to the hook with thread and Zap-A-Gap, tie in the knotted-mono front legs, fiber-fan rear legs, and burnt poly wing in the same manner as the Burnt Poly-Wing Drake style. After you are done, any markings you want can be applied with markers.

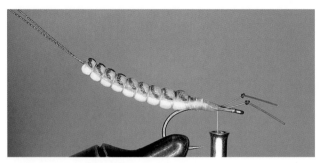

3. Secure completed foam abdomen to front hook, and tie in knotted mono legs.

4. Finish large burnt poly wing, fiber fan legs, and dubbing as with Burnt Poly-Wing Drake.

Yellow Hex.

Green Drake (Ephemera guttulata)

Hook:	Tiemco 2488, #10-12
Thread:	white or yellow, 6/0 or 8/0
Tails:	three, dark brown or black dyed mono (embossed)
Abdomen:	brown or olive-brown dry-fly foam over cream or pale yellow foam
Front legs:	brown dyed mono (knotted), black marks
Thorax:	cream or pale yellow dry-fly dubbing, brown or black marks
Rear legs:	tan Hi-Vis
Wing:	cream or tan poly yarn (burnt), black, brown, and pale yellow or olive marks

Pattern notes: One of the most beautiful and famous mayfly hatches, Eastern green drakes present special problems for imitation in all stages—nymph, dun, and spinner. They make for extremely challenging fishing on pressured waters. It is hard to predict which stage will produce the best fishing, although you might try hedging your bets with a tandem nymph/dun arrangement early and a dun/spinner setup later. Once you determine the trout's preference, you can unencumber your casting by removing the extra fly.

Yellow Hex (Hexagenia rigida)

Hook:	Tiemco 2488, #8-12
Thread:	yellow 6/0 or 8/0
Tails:	two, gold dyed mono (embossed)
Abdomen:	yellowish tan dry-fly foam over pale yellow foam, brown marks
Front legs:	gold dyed mono (knotted), brown marks
Thorax:	pale yellow dry-fly dubbing, tan and brown marks
Rear legs:	tan or yellow Hi-Vis
Wing:	pale yellow or tan poly yarn (burnt), yellow marks

Pattern notes: I have enjoyed many fine nights fishing this midsummer hatch on Skaneateles Lake in New York. On that lake, it follows an earlier June hatch of brown drakes (E. simulans). The transition from one hatch to the other usually falls around the Fourth of July holiday. While not as well known as H. limbata, it is probably more common in the East and is a lesser complement to hatches of its more famous relative in the Midwest. In addition to the Finger Lakes, it produces fine fishing on some lakes in the Adirondacks, as well as in Maine and eastern Canada.

ADULTS/EMERGERS
Substyle 4a—Extended Synthetic Drake Spinner Ⓐ

Extended Synthetic Drake Spinner: (left) *Dark Hex Spinner,* (right) *Coffin Fly.*

The spinners of large *Ephemera, Hexagenia,* and *Lito-branccha* species present the same problems for imitation as the duns, and this version of the previous style was designed to address them. It uses the foam extended body in conjunction with the broad Hi-Vis wing from the Synthetic Drake Spinner. Some fly fishers feel that translucency can be an important consideration in the construction of spinner bodies, although this certainly depends upon the prevailing light conditions under which trout view the body. Substituting translucent Ethafoam packing sheets for the standard dry-fly foam creates a remarkably effective simulation when translucency is a concern. This material is hard to color, however, and marker color (if needed) must be covered with Flexament or it will rub off.

Tying Sequence
Assemble the tails and abdomen on a needle just as with the previous style (again, details of this procedure are found in the previous chapter). When completed, attach the extension to a Tiemco 2488 or similar hook. Tie the knotted-mono front legs to the hook. As with the Synthetic Drake Spinner, a bundle of Hi-Vis fibers replace the fiber-fan legs of the prior style. However, I like to include a short poly yarn overback on the thorax, and you should tie this in before attaching the wing material. After securing the wing material with cross wraps and Zap-A-Gap, bring the poly forward between the wings, and tie it down in front of them. This is certainly optional, because anything that you do to imitate the back of a dry fly is of no consequence to the trout.

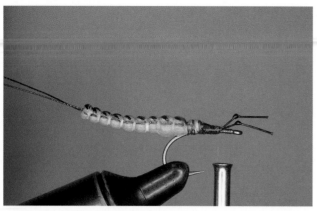

1. Construct foam abdomen as before and secure to hook. Tie in knotted monofilament legs.

2. Attach poly yarn and Hi-Vis fiber at thorax. Dub thorax, bring poly yarn forward, and tie it down. Prepare to dub head.

Coffin Fly.

Dark Hex Spinner (Hexagenia atrocaudata)

Hook:	Tiemco 2488, #10-12
Thread:	tan or brown, 6/0 or 8/0
Tails:	two, dark brown or black dyed mono (embossed)
Abdomen:	grayish brown dry-fly foam, over dark tan foam, black marks
Legs:	dark brown dyed mono (knotted), black marks
Thorax:	dark tan dry-fly dubbing, brown marks
Overback:	brown poly yarn, black marks
Wing:	mixed tan and gray Hi-Vis

Pattern notes: This is the darker, later-hatching *Hexagenia* on the Yellow Breeches. Local fly fishers mistakenly refer to them as brown drakes. They are also called big slate drakes in some texts, but I think the name dark Hex avoids confusion with *Isonychia* species, which they do not resemble. Allentown's famous Little Lehigh hosts a nice hatch of *atrocaudata*, but you should fish a stretch outside of the special regulation sections (which close to fishing an hour after sunset) in order to take best advantage of the spinners, which fall at dark.

Coffin Fly (Ephemera guttulata)

Hook:	Tiemco 2488, #10-12
Thread:	white or yellow, 6/0 or 8/0
Tails:	three, brown or golden brown dyed mono (embossed)
Abdomen:	white or pale yellow dry-fly foam (or uncolored Ethafoam), black marks
Legs:	brown dyed mono (knotted), black marks
Thorax:	cream or pale yellow dry-fly dubbing, black marks
Overback:	dark brown poly yarn
Wing:	mixed tan and white Hi-Vis, black marks

Pattern notes: Many green drake aficionados claim that the spinners are the most reliable stage of this spectacular hatch. But then, they are dry-fly fanatics, and I would give the edge to the nymph for a longer and less-frenzied fishing opportunity. To each his or her own—I would have to admit that, no matter which phase you prefer, it can be feast or famine with these big bugs.

ADULTS/EMERGERS
Style 5—Half-and-Half Mayfly Emerger Ⓘ

Half-and-Half Mayfly Emerger: (left) *Olive Morning Dun Emerger,* (right) *Hendrickson Emerger.*

I used to tie this two-part style on hooks like the Tiemco 200R, but then I saw Harold McMillan's novel Vertical Emerger, and I knew he had a better idea. I thought I had explored all the possibilities for using swimming nymph hooks, but this one escaped me, even though I had the ingredients in another form. Right tie, wrong hooks—thanks, Harold! This fly is a combination of two previous styles tied on the same hook—the Poly-Case Nymph and the Burnt Poly-Wing Dun. Does it imitate an emerger? A stillborn dun? Or does it merely present an image of the nymph and of the dun and allow the trout to take its pick? I think it serves all of these functions at various times and for various fish.

Tying Sequence
Start by placing a swimming nymph hook (keep in mind the size differences between different brands) in the vise, right side up, and tie the tails, weighting wire, and ribbing wire to the rear. Dub and rib the abdomen of the nymph, and then invert the hook. Tie in the poly yarn, dub the thorax, and add the feather-fiber legs (remember that there are two ways to do this—see the Poly-Case Nymph). Pull the poly yarn over the thorax, tie it down, and trim the excess. Dub the head of the nymph.

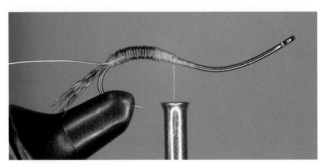

1. Tie in tails and ribbing wire on swimming nymph hook with rear portion weighted.

2. Invert hook. Complete nymph tie as with Poly-Case Nymph style.

Now proceed to construct the dun half of the fly. Dub and rib the dun's abdomen; tie in the fiber-fan legs, and ████ ██████ ████ ███████ █ █████ ████ ████ ███ mount it against the thorax dubbing. To ensure that the wing will not interfere with hooking, it should not reach the point of the hook when compressed to the rear. Dub the head; whip-finish and cement.

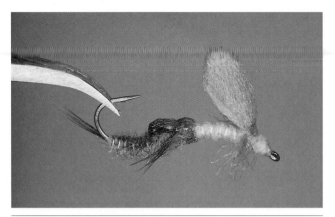

3. Dub and rib dun abdomen. Tie in fiber-fan legs, and dub thorax.

4. Tie in burnt poly wing, and dub head.

Olive Morning Dun Emerger (Drunella cornuta)

Hook:	Tiemco 400T, #12
Thread:	olive 8/0
Tails:	olive hen-hackle fibers
Nymph rib:	gold wire
Nymph body:	olive or olive-brown dubbing, dark on top
Wing case:	dark olive or brown poly yarn, black at rear
Nymph legs:	olive hen hackle fibers
Dun rib:	white thread
Dun body:	light olive dry-fly dubbing
Dun legs:	tan or light olive Hi-Vis
Wing:	gray poly yarn (burnt)

Pattern notes: An extremely important Eastern/Midwestern mayfly, *cornuta* hatches remain unknown to many fly fishers. Their morning emergence occurs on days when many anglers are looking for sulphurs, march browns, green drakes, and others during evening hours, allowing *cornuta* to hide in plain sight. The trout, however, know them well because there is little else to compete for their attention on late May and early June mornings. But the word is getting out, pressure is increasing, and this fly can offer another look during emergence.

Hendrickson Emerger.

Hendrickson Emerger (Ephemerella subvaria)

Hook:	Tiemco 400T, #12
Thread:	tan 8/0
Tails:	brown or olive dyed partridge fibers
Nymph rib:	gold wire
Nymph body:	reddish, grayish, or olive-brown dubbing, black markings on top
Wing case:	dark brown poly yarn, black at rear
Nymph legs:	brown or olive dyed partridge fibers
Dun rib:	white thread
Dun body:	pinkish tan to tannish olive dry-fly dubbing
Dun legs:	tan Hi-Vis, brown marks
Wing:	gray poly yarn (burnt)

Pattern notes: Cold weather, dry-fly pressure, and concentrations around a trout's lie can all be reasons for trout to focus their feeding on emergers. All of these can apply to the spring Hendrickson hatch. Watching to see if the duns on the surface are actually the target of rises is always a good idea, but sometimes, even when they are, educated trout may ignore standard imitations of the duns. Whichever the situation, this fly is a good trick to keep up your sleeve.

ADULTS/EMERGERS
Style 6—Wriggling Half-and-Half Mayfly Emerger Ⓐ

Wriggling Half-and-Half Mayfly Emerger: (left) *Brown Drake Emerger,* (right) *Yellow Hex Emerger.*

Another example of combining two of the previous styles into one fly, this two-part style adds attractive movement. By incorporating a hinge into the half-and-half concept, the fly can reproduce the struggle of an emerging mayfly in a way that some trout find irresistible. The parent styles—the Wriggling Burrower and the Burnt Poly-Wing Drake—are both simplified somewhat in this combo version. For the nymph component, eliminate the melted mono eyes, and replace the doubled knotted-thread legs with a clump of feather fibers. On the dun end, leave off the poly yarn overback and, of course, the mono tails. This fly is designed to mimic the large, struggling emergers of *Ephemera, Hexagenia,* and *Litobrancha,* and at times it outperforms either the nymph or the dun. This is especially true when large trout cruise big water looking for a target of opportunity. The subsurface half of this fly is visible from a much greater distance underwater than a dun imitation, and the motion attracts the trout's attention.

Tying Sequence
Start by tying the abdomen of the nymph on a swimming nymph hook (or bend an Aberdeen bait hook for the largest versions). This is tied like the rear half of the Wriggling Burrower except that you do not need weighting wire, and you replace the wire rib with a strand of Krystal Flash. When complete, cut the bend from the hook, and mount a Tiemco 200R or Daiichi 1270 in the vise. Attach the mono hinge material, making sure to dub a tight little band over the rear of the tie-down wraps to create a spacer between the sides of the mono loop. Proceed to attach the abdomen as with the previous hinged styles.

Tie in the flue-fiber gills and the poly yarn wing case just ahead of the mono loop. Dub the thorax of the nymph partway, and tie in the feather clump legs on either side. Add a little more dubbing in front of the legs. Then bring the poly yarn forward, and tie it down. Trim the excess poly, apply Zap-A-Gap to the ends, and dub the head of the nymph.

For the dun portion, begin by tying the knotted-mono front legs to the hook. Then attach the thread rib in front of the nymph, and dub the abdomen of the dun. After ribbing, tie in the fiber-fan rear legs, and dub around them. Secure the burnt poly wing to the front of the thorax, and complete the head in the same manner as the Burnt Poly-Wing Drake.

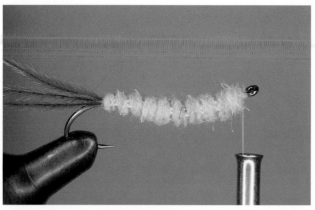

1. Tie in herl-tip tails on unweighted swimming nymph hook. Dub and rib abdomen.

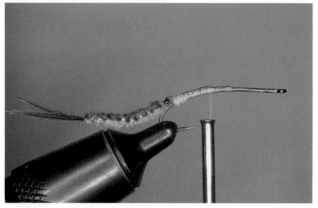

2. Attach completed abdomen to front, curved-shank hook with mono loop.

3. Apply flue-fiber hinge cover, poly yarn wing case, soft-hackle legs, and thorax dubbing to complete nymph portion of fly.

4. Construct dun portion of fly like Burnt Poly-Wing Drake, but omit poly yarn overback.

Brown Drake Emerger (Ephemera simulans)

Hooks:	Daiichi 1270, #14-16 (rear), and Daiichi 1770, #12-14 (front)
Thread:	brown 6/0 or 8/0
Tails:	three, brown ostrich or rhea herl tips
Nymph rib:	yellow or orange Krystal Flash
Nymph body:	yellowish tan or yellowish brown dubbing, brown marks
Gills:	grayish tan flue fibers
Wing case:	brown poly yarn, black at rear
Nymph legs:	brown-mottled hen pheasant fibers
Front dun legs:	light brown dyed mono, black marks
Dun rib:	yellow or tan thread
Dun body:	yellowish tan dry-fly dubbing, brown marks
Rear dun legs:	tan Hi-Vis
Wing:	tan or pale gray poly yarn (burnt), brown and black marks

Pattern notes: Because my most reliable brown drake encounters occur in lakes, this pattern is especially useful when rises begin to appear on the surface. Cruising trout, feeding into the wind (if it's breezy), make long, repetitive circuits through the emergence zones. Casting this fly into a cruiser's path and giving it an occasional twitch is more effective than hoping the fish will choose your dun imitation from among the many naturals resting sedately on the surface.

Yellow Hex Emerger (Hexagenia rigida)

Hooks:	Daiichi 1770, #8-10 (rear), and Daiichi 1270, #6-8 (front)
Thread:	yellow or tan, 6/0
Tails:	three, grayish brown ostrich or rhea herl tips
Nymph rib:	yellow Krystal Flash
Nymph body:	yellowish tan dubbing, brown marks
Gills:	brownish gray flue fibers
Wing case:	light brown poly yarn, brown at rear
Nymph legs:	mottled brown hen pheasant fibers
Front dun legs:	gold dyed mono, brown marks
Dun rib:	yellow thread
Dun body:	pale yellow dry-fly dubbing, brown marks
Rear dun legs:	tan or yellow Hi-Vis
Wing:	pale yellow or tan poly yarn (burnt), yellow marks

Pattern notes: A full-blown *Hexagenia* hatch is an amazing spectacle. A few big duns begin to appear on the surface and, before long, the water is covered with duns and their castoff nymphal shucks. I have witnessed Hex hatches so explosive that it seemed the fish could fill their bellies to bursting in a matter of minutes. This is a bewildering turn of events, and one is left to contemplate a suddenly silent surface alone in the darkness. Fortunately, most nights offer a little more time to fish, but a pattern that gets noticed is certainly an asset.

CHAPTER SIX

Sedges

Green sedge.

SECOND FIDDLE AS AN IMPORTANT INSTRUMENT

Sedges get no respect. Rodney Dangerfield would empathize. These unpretentious insects receive little of the adulation that is heaped upon the prima donna mayfly. Early angling entomologies often treated this significant insect with passing references and dismissive pronouncements. Purist's prejudice as well as simple misunderstanding promoted this inconsiderate evaluation. Some important sedge (or caddisfly) species were ignored because they were poor models for imitation by traditional dry flies. Others were disregarded because their activities or the trout's responses to them were misinterpreted. Fortunately for the fly fisher (perhaps unfortunately for the trout), this is changing—surely, if slowly.

A breakthrough came with Gary LaFontaine's *Caddisflies*. Although it echoed a few of the insights appearing in the earlier works of Schwiebert, Wright, and Solomon, it was a virtuoso performance that established a new standard for the interpretation of this underrated insect. A better understanding of the process of caddisfly emergence and the significance of their pupal (pharate adult) stage has helped to inspire attention and success. With that has come a belated trend toward grudging respect. Formerly relegated to a supporting role in the streamside symphony, some caddisflies are finally com-

ing into their own. When the first-chair mayflies fail to produce, the second-fiddle sedges can be appreciated for the masterful players they truly are.

Be that as it may, popular copies of caddisflies are underwhelming compared to the scores of innovative compositions that mimic mayflies. On famous and well-fished waters where caddisflies assume center stage (such as California's lower Sacramento River), local fly tiers are rapidly bringing sedge imitations into the limelight. But there is much to do before the sedges are as appreciated and applauded as most mayflies.

For the average fly fisher, the nod of recognition given the caddisfly is often represented by several Elk Hair Caddis patterns and a few soft-hackled wets tucked into the backup corner of a fly box. I have great respect for these simple and productive flies. One is a true modern classic and the other is a timeless design with an ancient pedigree. Both are first-rate suggestive styles for searching the water, but neither comes close to coping successfully with all of the diversity and complexity of caddisfly hatches. They do, however, offer a tried-and-true theme around which to orchestrate a progression of caddisfly variations. And that is what we'll do.

PUPAE
Style 1—Soft-Hackle Pupa

Soft-Hackle Pupa: (left) *Little Yellow Pupa,* (right) *Little Black Pupa.*

Soft-hackled wets have been catching trout here and in Europe for hundreds of years. They can be tied in most any size and be made to imitate many kinds of trout prey, from emerging mayflies and caddisflies to midges and scuds. As hatch-matching imitations, I mostly use them in small sizes to represent tiny sedges like the microcaddis and other miniature varieties. The inclusion of modern materials such as Krystal Flash and Antron dubbing is suggestive of the sparkling veil of gas bubbles that surrounds emerging caddis. Because of the small sizes I favor, the technique for hackling this style is not traditional, but it is easy and makes good use of feathers (usually partridge) that are not always well suited to tiny flies. This simple style provides all that is needed in such tiny imitations and has the added advantage of also serving as an imitation of emerging midges.

Tying Sequence
Standard dry-fly hooks work well for this style, although in the smallest sizes I often use a straight-eye hook like the Tiemco 101. I usually don't weight these flies because

they are often fished in the surface film. You can use fine copper wire for a more positive sink rate, but weight on the leader is a more effective way of fishing them deep. Rather than searching for the tiny partridge feathers required for hackling these flies in the conventional manner, I use larger, well-marked feathers and strip a sufficient number of fibers from the stem in a place where the tips are relatively even. I tie these to the top of the hook with the tips pointing forward over the eye.

Because you rib the fly with Krystal Flash, wrap a small amount of Antron dubbing (or an Antron blend) at the rear before attaching the ribbing strand. Dub the shank to the thorax position, rib it, and wind a dark bit of dubbing for the thorax. Fold back the soft-hackle fibers along the hook, and distribute the fibers around the hook with a slight rolling action of the fingertips. While holding the fibers in position, wrap a neat head over their bases. After whip-finishing and cementing the head, brush out the body dubbing slightly with the tip of a small Velcro dubbing brush. (A dubbing needle works for this, but be careful not to tear the Krystal Flash rib.)

1. Tie in soft-hackle fibers projecting forward over the eye of the hook.

2. Start dubbing, and tie in Krystal Flash rib.

3. Dub and rib the abdomen. Apply dark thorax dubbing.

4. Fold back soft-hackle fibers, distribute them around hook, and secure with head wraps.

Little Yellow Pupa

Hook:	standard dry fly, #18-26
Thread:	brown 8/0 or 12/0
Hackle:	brown partridge fibers
Rib:	yellow Krystal Flash
Body:	Antron dubbing, yellow to yellowish brown (abdomen) and brown (thorax)

Pattern notes: This fly covers a vast range of little yellowish-bodied species of such diverse genera as *Hydroptila, Oxytheria, Nyctiophylax, Polycentropus, Neureclipsus,* and *Psychomyia.* These little buggers tax my identification skills to the max, and this is one instance when I use the size and color method—if it's tiny and has a yellowish body, I use this fly.

Little Black Pupa

Hook:	standard dry fly, #18-26
Thread:	black 8/0 or 12/0
Hackle:	black hen hackle or dark partridge fibers
Rib:	pearl Krystal Flash
Body:	Antron dubbing, blackish brown (abdomen) and black (thorax)

Pattern notes: I use this imitation for tiny dark members of *Leucrotrichia, Lype, Chimarra* and, about as often, for imitating dark midges. The little black sedge, *Chimarra aterrima,* is the hatch I meet most frequently (there are also yellow-bodied *Chimarra* species). They crawl out of the water to emerge, so the imitation should be fished along the bottom near the edges of the stream or around emergent cover. I can always tell when I'm standing in a *Chimarra* emergence site because the freshly emerged adults decorate my waders above the waterline.

PUPAE
Substyle 1a—Antron-Wing Soft-Hackle Pupa

Antron-Wing Soft-Hackle Pupa: (left) *Early Smoky Wing Sedge Pupa,* (right) *Weenom Pupa.*

For somewhat larger pupal imitations, adding a more suggestive shape and a little imitative detail helps to enhance the illusion. A curved caddis pupa hook, like the Daiichi 1150, 1140, or the equivalent, provides the shape. These have a slight offset bend, and I like to straighten them to prevent spinning when retrieved. Antron fiber wing cases add the detail, and the dark thorax dubbing of the previous style (which suggested dark wing cases) is moved to the front to imitate the shaggy head of a pupa. This version can be used as a simple representation of a great many caddis species, but I like it for smallish genera like *Apatania, Micrasema,* and *Cheumatopsyche.* The little Western weedy-water sedge *(Amiocentrus aspilus)* is another good prospect for Western tiers.

Tying Sequence
Begin by tying the soft-hackle fibers to the front of the hook and wrapping the thread to the rear, ending partway around the bend of the hook (it can help to tip the front of the hook down while working around the bend). Wrap the little tag of dubbing that keeps the rib from slipping (especially important with this shape of hook). Attach the ribbing strand, and then dub and rib the body. Because the Antron fiber wing cases may interfere with brushing out the body upon completion, I like to do it before they are tied in.

Rather than tying in separate clumps of Antron fibers for the wing cases, I wrap a thin length of fibers to the near side of the thorax position and then fold the forward end of the bundle along the other side, wrapping over the fold. I trim them at an angle to suggest the wing case shape. To complete the fly, I fold back the soft-hackle fibers, secure with thread, and wrap a dubbing head before whip-finishing and cementing.

1. Tie soft-hackle fibers forward on caddis pupa hook. Dub, rib, and brush out abdomen.

2. Tie in, fold, and trim Antron wing case.

3. Fold back soft-hackle fibers, distribute them around hook, and tie them down. Dub head.

Early Smoky Wing Sedge Pupa (Apatania incerta)

Hook:	Daiichi 1150, #16-18
Thread:	brown or black 8/0
Hackle:	dark grayish brown hen or turkey fibers
Rib:	pearl Krystal Flash
Body:	grayish brown Antron dubbing
Wing cases:	black Antron yarn
Head:	blackish brown dubbing

Pattern notes: I have been surprised by hatches of this little early-season sedge when I was expecting to encounter hatches of Quill Gordons, Hendricksons, or blue quills—just another lesson learned about underestimating caddisflies. Woodland streams in north-central Pennsylvania have good hatches of *incerta,* as do many similar waters farther north. Western species of *Apatania* may also be significant.

Weenom Pupa (Micrasema *spp.*)

Hook:	Daiichi 1150, #16-20
Thread:	brown 8/0
Hackle:	dark brown partridge or dark dun hen-hackle fibers
Rib:	olive or green Krystal Flash
Body:	bright to dark green Antron dubbing
Wing cases:	black Antron yarn
Head:	dark brown dubbing

Pattern notes: Don Baylor's excellent self-published booklet, *Pocono Hatches,* first tipped me to the identity of these miniature relatives of the grannoms. Like grannoms, some may display lateral stripes, which can be imitated by darkening the back and belly with marker. Baylor refers to them as tiny green/slate caddis, but weenom is the fanciful moniker I prefer. The little Western weedy-water sedge is similar (it used to be classified under *Micrasema*).

PUPAE
Style 2—Bubble Pupa ①

Bubble Pupa: (left) *Green Sedge Pupa,* (right) *Spotted Sedge Pupa.*

The progenitor of this style is pretty obvious—Gary LaFontaine's Deep Sparkle Pupa. It is not primarily intended for fishing deep, however, and I usually fish it in the film or slightly subsurface during an emergence. A few years back, my fishing partner "accidentally" (he says) tied some of his Sparkle Pupa patterns with clear Antron overbodies rather than the colored sparkle yarn specified by Gary. I liked the results so much that I incorporated his accident into the more detailed version that I was tying. Gary probably wouldn't approve of adding wing cases and antennae to his original, but his design has been getting a lot of play, and I needed an imitative edge. I use this style to imitate medium-size species that emerge on the surface.

Tying Sequence

I tie this style on a Tiemco 101 (for reasons I'll share in a later style), but standard dry-fly hooks work just fine. You tie two lengths of Antron yarn to the rear of the hook but apply them differently than in the LaFontaine original. The darker strands will form a dark overback, and the clear strands will create the overbody or bubble. Wrap a little Antron dubbing (or Antron blend) at the base of these strands, and attach the Krystal Flash rib. Dub the

rest of the abdomen, and bring the dark overback strands forward and tie them down. Cut off the excess, and wrap the rib over the abdomen and overback.

Run a dubbing needle through the clear Antron strands to separate them, and then bring the material forward to form the bubble. Wrap loosely over the strands at the forward end of the abdomen to hold them in place, then distribute the fibers around the hook with your fingers or a dubbing needle. This overbody is a little tighter and sparser than the LaFontaine fly, and don't be concerned if there are some gaps between the strands (there should be). Once positioned, wrap tightly over the clear strands, trim the excess, and touch a little Zap-A-Gap to the wraps.

Tie and trim the Antron yarn wing cases the same as with the previous style, and attach the partridge legs over them. You can tie these in as separate clumps or with the V-feather technique (backtrack to the Poly-Case Nymph if you need a refresher). Dub the head almost to the eye. Position two wood-duck or mallard flank fibers (or two coated threads) over top of the body, and tie them in next to the eye. Fold the stubs of the fibers back, wrap over them, and cut off the remains (this is done to prevent the antennae from pulling out). Whip-finish and cement.

1. Attach dark and clear Antron to hook.

2. Dub abdomen. Bring dark Antron forward, tie it down, and rib it.

3. Bring clear Antron forward, and distribute it around hook. Tie in and trim Antron wing cases. Tie soft-hackle fibers on either side.

4. Dub head, and tie in flank-feather antennae.

Green Sedge Pupa (Rhyacophila *spp.*)

Hook:	Tiemco 101, #12-16
Thread:	brown 8/0
Overbody:	clear Antron yarn
Overback:	dark green Antron yarn
Rib:	olive or green Krystal Flash
Body:	bright olive or green Antron dubbing
Wing cases:	black or dark brown Antron yarn
Legs:	dark brown partridge fibers
Head:	dark brown dubbing
Antennae:	bronze mallard flank fibers

Pattern notes: Of all caddisfly genera, *Rhyacophila* is among the most important for fly fishers. Part of its significance is attributable to the availability of the free-living larvae, sometimes known as green rock worms. The emerging pupa and egg-laying adults are also very important, and there are green caddis hatches throughout the country. Eastern species like *fuscula, carolina,* and *torva* are common and widespread, but with over a hundred North American species, this pattern is nearly universal in its application. In smaller sizes (16 to 18), this pattern will cover green-bodied *Cheumatopsyche* species as well.

Spotted Sedge Pupa
(Hydropsyche *and* Ceratopsyche *spp.)*

Hook:	Tiemco 101, #12-16
Thread:	brown 8/0
Overbody:	clear Antron yarn
Overback:	brown Antron yarn
Rib:	yellow or orange Krystal Flash
Body:	yellow, greenish yellow, brownish yellow, or grayish tan Antron dubbing
Wing cases:	brown or dark brown Antron yarn
Legs:	brown or dark brown partridge fibers
Head:	brown or dark brown dubbing
Antennae:	lemon wood-duck or bronze mallard flank fibers

Pattern notes: No caddisflies are more important for fly fishers than the members of the *Hydropsyche* and *Ceratopsyche* genera, and the body colors listed for this pattern reflect the large number of significant species. Spotted sedges, also known as tan caddis, cinnamon caddis, and brown-mottled caddis, generate abundant hatching activity from April through October all across the country. *Ceratopsyche* is a recent revision, and such well-known Eastern and Midwestern species as *bronta, slossonae, alternans, sparna,* and *morosa* are now listed under this genus name.

PUPAE
Style 3—Dry Pupa Ⓘ

Dry Pupa: (left) *Long Horn Sedge Pupa,* (right) *Medium Evening Sedge Pupa.*

Not all caddisflies emerge on the surface of the water; some crawl out to emerge, and a few swim or skate across the surface to reach the shore before shedding their pupal shuck. I often carry a pocket-size nymph seine to check for mature nymphs (dark wing cases) or to learn about populations in new waters. It is a good way to sample mayfly nymphs (especially the fast-water dwellers), but emerging caddis pupae are hard to intercept. When one does get caught in the net, it is a sure sign that a hatch is underway. Usually, such pupae lay inert or pulsating in place, but on one occasion, a dark little specimen got up and scampered across the net and into the water. I had never seen this before, and that athletic individual helped solve a summertime puzzle that had frustrated me for quite some time. This style is my solution. Since that time, I have become aware of three genera that display this method of emergence—*Glossosoma, Oecetis,* and *Dolophilodes.* They belong to different families, and there are probably other genera that emerge this way.

Tying Sequence

I like a straight-eye dry-fly hook for this style because it seems to keep the fly from diving when twitched or skated. Tie a length of poly yarn to the top of the hook shank with the fibers extending to the rear. Wrap a little dry-fly dubbing to the rear, and tie in the Krystal Flash rib. Dub and then rib the rest of the abdomen, and attach two Micro Fibetts to the front for antennae.

Bring the poly yarn over top of the abdomen, and tie it down where the dubbing ends. Divide the remaining yarn in two, and fold the sections back along the sides. Wrap over the folds to form two buoyant wing cases. Trim the wing cases to length and tie several Micro Fibetts over each wing case for legs. Sometimes I will substitute a dry-fly hackle for the legs if a higher-riding pattern is advantageous. Wind this conventionally, and trim the bottom hackle fibers straight across for stability. Wrap the head with dry-fly dubbing, then fold the antennae back, and tie them down with thread. Whip-finish and cement.

1. Tie in poly yarn. Dub and rib abdomen. Tie Micro Fibetts at front.

2. Bring poly yarn forward, tie it down, and divide it. Tie wing cases back, and trim them. Tie Micro Fibetts along sides for legs.

3. Dub head, and tie antennae back.

Long Horn Sedge Pupa (Oecetis avara)

Hook:	Tiemco 101, #14-16
Thread:	tan 8/0
Overback/ wing cases:	tan poly yarn (colored ginger)
Rib:	yellow or orange Krystal Flash
Body/head:	ginger dry-fly dubbing
Legs:	ginger Micro Fibetts or dry-fly hackle
Antennae:	ginger Micro Fibetts (long)

Pattern notes: Summertime caddis hatches provide excellent, if frustrating, evening activity. On the Lehigh River in the Poconos, even when the water is fairly warm, trout feed enthusiastically each evening on an abundance of summer-emerging species. One evening, I estimated that six or seven varieties were hatching concurrently and several displayed unusual habits. *Oecetis* was one of these, and this pattern is one of the tactics for dealing with these hatches.

Medium Evening Sedge Pupa (Dolophilodes distinctus)

Hook:	Tiemco 101, #14-18
Thread:	black or brown 8/0
Overbody/ wing cases:	black or dark brown poly yarn
Rib:	black or pearl Krystal Flash
Body/head:	dark grayish brown dry-fly dubbing
Legs:	black or dark brown Micro Fibetts or dry-fly hackle
Antennae:	black or brown Micro Fibetts

Pattern notes: This was the species that ran across my seine, alerting me to their strange capabilities. It is also an important component of the midsummer evening hatches on the Lehigh and on many other trout rivers in the East and Midwest. Because of the way they emerge, they often escape the notice of anglers, but trout recognize their distinctive signature. If you find yourself in the midst of a summertime caddis hatch, and trout are pursuing a moving dry fly only to turn away at the last instant, one of the two Dry Pupa patterns may provide an answer. One or the other will usually suffice for most *Glossosoma* species as well.

PUPAE
Style 4—Deep-Drifting Pupa I

Deep-Drifting Pupa: (left) *Dark Blue Sedge Pupa,* (right) *Grannom Pupa.*

One thing that has always puzzled me about Gary La-Fontaine's Deep Sparkle Pupa is that it was intended to imitate caddis pupa as they are drifting along the bottom prior to generating the gases that help to buoy them to the surface. Why imitate the inflated bubble at that stage? Unfortunately, Gary's death has robbed us of a great author and innovator, and that question must probably go unanswered. I suppose that the sparkling overbody may have attractive rather than imitative value. The Deep-Drifting Pupa retains a little sparkle, but the emphasis is on imitating the insects as they appear along the bottom after escaping their pupation shelters. In deference to Gary, I would reiterate his comment that our fly fisher's usage of "pupa" is a misnomer—technically, that term applies to the insect contained by the pupal enclosure. The critters that we call "pupa" are sheathed or pharate adults. It's nitpicking, but such things make entomologists wag their bug-stained fingers at us.

Tying Sequence

A curved caddis pupa hook serves as the foundation for this style. The Daiichi 1150 is a good candidate, as is the Mustad C49S (which has the added advantage of not having an offset bend). If you're using an offset hook like the 1150, I recommend straightening it as we did for the Antron-Wing Soft-Hackled Pupa. Begin this fly by attaching a length of D-shape, clear vinyl overbody material (V-Rib, Nymph Rib, or the older version, Swannundaze) along the shank and extending to the rear. Add a pair of melted mono eyes to the other end with cross wraps and Zap-A-Gap.

Start a little dubbing at the rear, tie in the Krystal Flash ribbing strand, and then dub the rest of the abdomen. Rib the dubbed abdomen, then wrap the clear overbody with the rounded side outward, and tie it off at the forward end of the dubbed body. Apply a touch of Zap-A-Gap to the wraps, and darken the back of the overbody (and the belly, for grannom imitations) with marker. Tie a wide goose biot on either side of the thorax with the widest part of the taper toward the rear. Trim the rear edges of the biots at an angle to shape the wing cases. Tie in two coated threads projecting forward from the head.

Attach legs of soft-hackle fibers beside each biot wing case. Use the V-feather technique for this, or tie them in as separate clumps. Dub the thorax up to the mono eyes. Wrap the thread to the eye of the hook, and then fold the coated-thread antennae back over the body. Wrap over the fold, whip-finish, and cement the head.

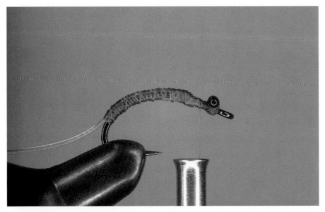

1. Attach V-Rib and melted mono eyes to caddis pupa hook.

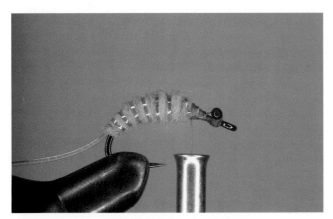

2. Dub abdomen and rib with Krystal Flash.

3. Wrap V-Rib over abdomen, and tie biot wing cases along sides. Tie thread antennae at front.

4. Tie soft-hackle fibers along sides for legs. Dub thorax, and tie antennae back.

Dark Blue Sedge Pupa (Psilotreta labida)

Hook:	Daiichi 1150 or Mustad C49S, #12-16
Thread:	brown or black 8/0
Overbody:	clear V-rib, marked dark gray on back
Eyes:	melted mono
Rib:	green or olive Krystal Flash
Body:	grayish green dubbing
Wing cases:	black goose biots
Antennae:	coated grayish brown 8/0 tying thread
Legs:	dark gray hen or turkey fibers
Thorax:	blackish brown dubbing

Pattern notes: While not represented by a large number of species, the Eastern genus *Psilotreta* does create heavy hatches that trout seem to favor. Two very similar species, *labida* and *frontalis*, overlap in range and emergence and can be matched with the same patterns. To the consternation of green drake *(E. guttulata)* addicts, dark blue sedges often hatch during the drake emergence, and their numbers may cause trout to ignore the impressive duns. This pattern becomes a valuable plan B when this occurs. If you are a die-hard green drake fanatic, you could use it as a dropper off the bend of your drake imitation, satisfying your addiction while hedging your bets.

Grannom Pupa (Brachycentrus lateralis)

Hook:	Daiichi 1150 or Tiemco 2457, #14–10
Thread:	brown 8/0
Overbody:	clear V-rib, marked dark olive on back and belly
Eyes:	melted mono
Rib:	yellow Krystal Flash
Body:	tan dubbing
Wing cases:	black goose biots
Antennae:	coated brown 8/0 tying thread
Legs:	dark brown partridge fibers
Thorax:	dark grayish brown dubbing

Pattern notes: Several *Brachycentrus* species share the name grannom or shadfly in the East and Midwest. In the West, *Brachycentrus occidentalis* is referred to as the Mother's Day caddis. There are dark and light grannoms whose adult wings range from blackish bronze to nearly white. Fairly typical of the darker grannoms, *lateralis* has light-colored lateral bands along the sides of its abdomen (this color pattern is found on many grannom pupae and adults). A variation of this pattern with green lateral stripes and a dark back and belly will help to cover other dark species.

PUPAE
Style 5—Thread-Legged Giant Pupa Ⓐ

Thread-Legged Giant Pupa: (left) *Giant Cream Pattern Wing Sedge Pupa,* (right) *Giant Red Sedge Pupa.*

Giant sedges do not create extensive fly-fishing opportunities in the East, but they require special attention in order to be accurately imitated. These caddisflies are so large that simple, suggestive patterns may not be convincing to trout that have survived many months of fly-fishing pressure. On the other hand, these hatches have the advantage of not being well known, and a good imitation can produce surprising results. This style combines coated-thread legs, shaped Tyvek wing cases, and a stabilizing, poly yarn overback to accurately imitate these caddisfly giants. On Western waters, giant orange sedges (*Dicosmoecus* spp.) are more often imitated and fished than the Eastern giants, and this style may be even more valuable for Western anglers who frequent pressured waters.

Tying Sequence

Using a curved, long-shank hook such as the Tiemco 200R or Daiichi 1270 for these big imitations creates a realistic shape without an unnecessarily large gap. The poly yarn overback on this fly allows a bit of weight to be added without the fly rolling over, but I sometimes omit the weight and rely upon tin shot or a sinking-tip line to present the fly along the bottom.

Begin by attaching two small biot tips on either side of the hook for the little tails (which are only conspicuous on large pupae). If you are adding weight, wrap wire on the rear half of the hook. Tie in a strip of clear plastic bag material and the poly yarn at the rear. (The plastic is optional, but it picks up reflections from the Krystal Flash rib and gives the imitation an iridescent glow.) Start the dubbing with a wrap or two, add the ribbing strand, and dub a fat abdomen.

Tie in two coated-thread antennae, and bring the plastic and the poly yarn forward, tying them down in the thorax area. Wind the rib forward tightly, and tie it off. Cut off the excess plastic, but leave the remaining poly projecting over the eye of the hook. Secure a pair of melted mono eyes on top, near the hook eye. Brush out the dubbing along the belly with a Velcro dubbing brush, and coat the back with Flexament.

Cut a matched pair of Tyvek wing cases, color them with marker, and coat them with Flexament. Tie these to either side of the thorax, and then attach three coated sewing-thread strands to the center of the thorax. Separate the thread legs with dubbing. Fold the remaining poly over the thorax, and secure it with a few wraps behind and in front of the legs. Trim the excess poly at an angle. Fold the coated-thread antennae back over the body, and wrap over them just behind the mono eyes. Whip finish and cement the head. I like to scrape the trailing side of the legs with a knife tip to create the feathered appearance of the legs of the natural (this works best if cotton/Dacron sewing thread is used). Add markings to the legs, if appropriate.

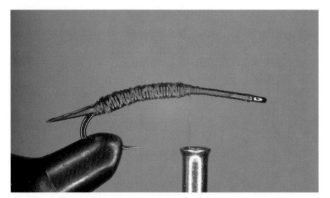

1. Tie in biot tails, and apply weight to curved-shank hook.

2. Tie in plastic strip, poly overback, and rib. Dub abdomen.

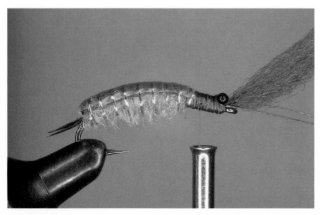

3. Tie thread antennae at front. Bring poly yarn and plastic strip forward, tie them down, and rib them. Trim plastic strip off, and attach melted mono eyes.

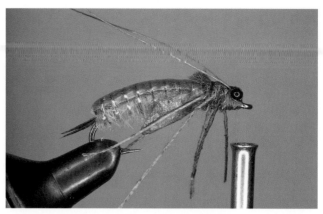

4. Tie in Tyvek wing cases and thread legs at thorax. Separate legs with thorax dubbing, and tie poly yarn down over thorax. Tie thread antennae down, and finish head.

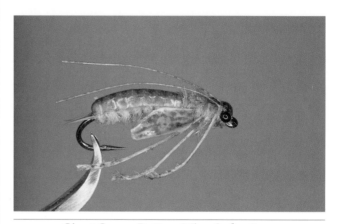

Giant Cream Pattern Wing Sedge Pupa (Hydatophylax argus)

Hook:	Daiichi 1270, #6-10
Thread:	tan 6/0
Tails:	tan goose biot tips
Weight:	copper wire
Overback:	clear plastic and tan poly yarn (darkened slightly)
Rib:	pearl Krystal Flash
Body:	tan dubbing
Antennae:	coated dark tan 6/0 tying thread
Eyes:	melted mono
Wing cases:	cut Tyvek, colored tan, light brown marks
Legs:	coated tan heavy sewing thread, light brown marks
Thorax:	dirty tan dubbing

Pattern notes: I cannot say that I have ever witnessed a heavy hatch of these sedges, but there have been times when this pattern was generously accepted by trout. I have seen the enormous, pale adults on streamside cover and suspect that many fly fishers mistake them for moths. Carry this fly, along with some stonefly nymphs, on midseason mornings when you are looking for *Drunella* mayfly hatches. These will give you other options if the morning olives fail to produce.

Giant Red Sedge Pupa (Pycnopsyche scabripennis)

Hook:	Daiichi 1270, #8-12
Thread:	brown 6/0
Tails:	reddish brown goose biot tips
Weight:	copper wire
Overback:	clear plastic and brown poly yarn
Rib:	orange Krystal Flash
Body:	rusty orange dubbing
Antennae:	coated brown 6/0 tying thread
Eyes:	melted mono
Wing cases:	cut Tyvek, colored brown, dark marks
Legs:	coated brownish orange heavy sewing thread, brown marks
Thorax:	brown dubbing

Pattern notes: This large, late-season emerger has a reputation for being malodorous and distasteful (fetid brown is an older name for this species). I can vouch for the musty aroma but will leave the question of its flavor for others to resolve. Adding ignominy to insult, the species designator, *scabripennis*, does nothing to improve its sullied reputation. Nevertheless, there are times during the late-season dearth of other insects when trout take them readily. I can only surmise that, sometimes, size does matter.

ADULTS AND EMERGERS
Style 1—Hairless Caddis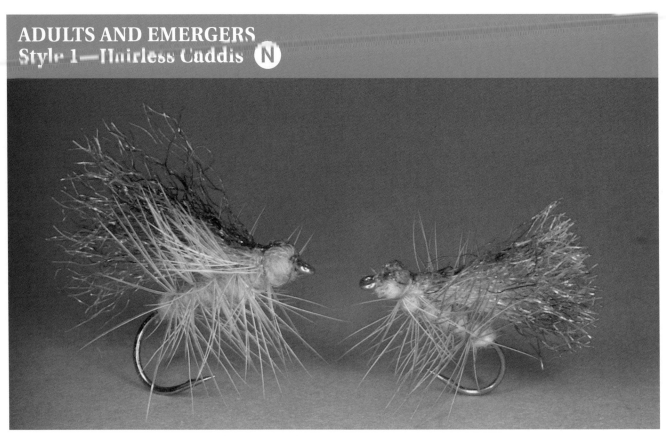

Hairless Caddis: (left) *Green Caddis,* (right) *Tan Caddis.*

Al Troth's Elk Hair Caddis is such a simple and effective style that it's almost a shame to mess with it, but this synthetic translation has some advantages, even if you're not a one-armed fly tier. The reflective synthetic wing is more visible than the elk hair version. It is also more durable and easier to keep floating after being chewed repeatedly by trout. And, yes, it is easier to tie. None of this is meant to detract from the virtues of the original, and I suspect that many who share my affection for the fly will continue to tie it just as they have before. Despite my high opinion of both versions, I seldom fish them during caddis hatches. Occasionally I'll use one as an indicator fly for presenting a damp or subsurface pattern during an emergence. On mainstem trout waters, however, the most valuable application is as a searching fly cast toward bankside cover where adult caddisflies drop to the water to drink. Where this style really shines is as an all-purpose dry fly for fishing tiny tributaries and headwater brooks. The synthetic tie will easily withstand twenty or thirty eager little trout on such waters, and a few of these flies in a thirty-five-millimeter film canister is often all I carry on tribs. In fact, I could probably get by with a single fly, if it weren't for all the damned trees.

Tying Sequence

Start with a standard dry-fly hook, and wrap a little dry-fly dubbing at the end of the shank. The Troth original uses fine gold wire to reinforce the hackle, but two refinements make that unnecessary on this version. The first is to protect the hackle stem with the little dubbing ball at the end of the hook. Second, a modern dry-fly saddle hackle attached by the butt improves durability tremendously. The traditional method of palmering a hackle required tying the hackle in by its tip so that the sharp taper of older neck hackles would place the longer fibers forward on the hook. This put the most fragile part of the stem in the place where most of the abuse occurs. The modern genetic saddles are so long and have so little taper that attaching the hackle by the butt is preferable (and easier). After the saddle hackle is tied in, dub the shank (leaving a generous head space), spiral the hackle forward over the body, and tie it off.

Ahead of the hackle, tie in a clump of synthetic fibers that is half the thickness desired for the finished wing. The free ends of the fibers should project forward and to the rear from the tie in point. Reverse-dub from the eye back to the hackle, and then fold the forward half of the wing fibers back over the body. Wrap them down with a narrow collar of thread and apply the whip-finish to the collar. Cement the collar wraps, and trim the wing fibers to length.

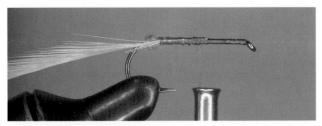

1. Start dubbing, and tie in hackle butt.

2. Dub abdomen. Palmer hackle over abdomen, and tie off.

3. Tie in Hi-Vis fibers at head so that they extend fore and aft.

4. Reverse-dub head. Fold back forward half of wing fibers, and tie down. Trim wing.

Green Caddis

Hook: standard dry fly, #8-18
Thread: brown 6/0 or 8/0
Hackle: ginger variant or grizzly saddle
Body: bright olive or green dry-fly dubbing
Wing: brown Hi-Vis (can be mottled with marker)

Pattern notes: This is a good general representation of many green-bodied caddisflies. Its virtue is suggestion rather than precise imitation, and it is a good choice for fishing shallow water under nonspecific feeding conditions. While it is based on the Elk Hair Caddis, the colors are reminiscent of an older classic, the green-bodied version of the Henryville Special tied by Ernest Schwiebert.

Tan Caddis

Hook: standard dry fly, #8-18
Thread: tan 6/0 or 8/0
Hackle: ginger or ginger variant saddle
Body: tan or yellow dry-fly dubbing
Wing: tan or light brown Hi-Vis (can be mottled with marker)

Pattern notes: This pattern is my favorite small-stream dry fly. Its colors are suggestive of the spotted sedges, although the yellow-bodied tie is also a pretty good imitation of the various little stoneflies known as yellow sallies. Both kinds of insects are common sights on small waters throughout much of the season. While specific imitation is rarely called for on these waters, I think this pattern does trigger a kind of basic recognition and is readily accepted.

ADULTS AND EMERGERS
Substyle 1a—Fluttering Sedge

Fluttering Sedge: (left) *Black Dancer,* (right) *Dark Blue Sedge.*

This is the variation on the Elk Hair Caddis theme that I tie as a match for specific caddisflies and special situations. Two activities associated with the mating and egg-laying habits of some species motivated the design. One occurs when caddisflies, such as Eastern *Psilotreta* species or the more widespread *Ceraclea* genus (which has several transcontinental species), flutter and hop on the surface during egg-laying. This is not a habit of most caddisflies, but when it happens, it demands special tactics. The other situation that this fly addresses (somewhat less successfully) is when certain species form taunting, undulating swarms near the surface. This mating dance compels infuriated trout to leap from the water in an attempt to intercept their tormentors. Genera within the Leptoceridae family routinely tease trout in this manner, and black dancers (*Mystacides* spp.) and white millers (*Nectopsyche* spp.) are found throughout trout country, in streams and in ponds. Of course, trout are not the only ones who are pixilated by this activity, and this fly is the closest I have come to a solution. I imagine that the best way to handle these aerial feeders would be to dangle this fly from the end of a fifteen-foot Spey rod. But the leapers are usually of modest size, and success with this method would be anticlimactic. My willingness to exercise tactical extremes does have some limits.

Tying Sequence

While caddisflies fly in a relatively horizontal position, a curved caddis pupa hook allows the body of this fly to assume the more vertical posture of caddisflies as they flutter to lay their eggs. The Mustad C49S is nice for this purpose because it doesn't have an offset bend. Start by applying a little wrap of dubbing well around the bend, and tie in the thread for ribbing. Continue to dub the abdomen up to the thorax location and follow with the rib. Tie the hackle in by its butt at the rear of the thorax. Attach two coated threads for antennae. Dub the thorax (sometimes this is a different color).

Wind the hackle in close wraps over the thorax and tie it off. Tie the synthetic wing material (Hi-Vis, Antron, or Z-Lon fibers) as before. Reverse-dub the head, fold the forward half of the wing to the rear, and wrap the collar. Whip-finish over the collar, and cement the head (the antennae are left to project forward). Trim the wing and antennae to length.

There is an alternative way to tie the fold-over wing when you apply hackle only over the thorax or (in the case of styles to follow) when you use fiber-fan legs. In the alternative method, tie in the wing before the hackle or legs. The wraps that hold it to the hook extend through the thorax area, and you build the thorax over it.

Complete the remainder of the fly as before. With the first method, both halves of the wing are in front of the thorax; the second method has the lower half of the wing projecting from the rear of the thorax. To illustrate, the demonstration fly is tied using the first method, and the pattern illustrations employ the second. Both techniques work fine, but if you tend to crowd the head of the fly, you may prefer the second.

1. Dub and rib abdomen with thread, and attach hackle at thorax. Tie in thread antennae, and dub thorax.

2. Palmer hackle through thorax, and tie off. Tie in wing fibers, reverse-dub head, and tie forward half of wing fibers down. Trim wing.

Black Dancer (Mystacides sepulchralis)

Hook:	Mustad C49S, #14-16
Thread:	black 8/0
Rib:	gray thread
Body:	blackish brown dry-fly dubbing
Hackle:	black or dark dun
Antennae:	coated gray 8/0 tying thread (long)
Wing:	black Hi-Vis

Pattern notes: On summer evenings, clouds of this well-named caddisfly gather over the water, and the trout try to impersonate Polaris missiles. Using the traditional hit-'em-on-the-head presentation immediately after the leap sometimes gets results, though not nearly as often as the literature suggests. A more effective technique is to join in the teasing by repeatedly presenting and withdrawing the fly about a foot or so above the launch site. After several of these feints, allow the fly to reach the trout. This tactic is far from infallible, but it usually beats the vaunted head-banging technique.

Dark Blue Sedge (Psilotreta labida)

Hook:	Mustad C49S, #12-16
Thread:	black 8/0
Rib:	gray thread
Body:	grayish green (abdomen) and gray (thorax/head) dry-fly dubbing
Hackle:	dark dun
Antennae:	coated dark gray 8/0 tying thread
Wing:	dark gray Hi-Vis

Pattern notes: Aside from disrupting stately green drake hatches, females of this species also raise a riot when laying their eggs. This is when actively fished dry flies reign over quiet, drag-free drifts, and this pattern imitates the form of these egg-layers precisely. Gary LaFontaine wrote that his nickname for this genus was the "slap-in-the-face" caddisfly. With this pattern and an active presentation, you can slap back.

ADULTS AND EMERGERS
Style 2—Synthetic Sedge

Synthetic Sedge: (left) *Little Sister Sedge,* (right) *Little Black Sedge.*

Unlike the antics of active egg layers of the *Psilotreta* genus, a few caddisfly species deposit their eggs serenely on the surface. Many others return to the surface to rest and recover after an egg-laying dive. In either case, a flush-floating fly best represents these habits. Hackled sedge imitations are good for creating or suggesting movement, but they are poor flies for matching quiet caddisflies. This relatively simple synthetic tie presents an excellent image to trout that are sipping sedate egg layers or exhausted divers. It utilizes the same fold-over wing as the previous styles and borrows the fiber-fan legs that were first introduced with the Burnt Poly-Wing Dun (in the previous chapter). Despite the association of caddisflies with slashing riseforms, many important caddisfly genera (like *Hydropsyche, Ceratopsyche, Cheumatopsyche, Rhyacophila,* and *Chimarra*) are met by quiet rises at some point in their egg-laying activities. At these times, a traditional dry-fly presentation can be effective, but traditionally hackled fly patterns won't provide an appropriate image.

Tying Sequence

Standard dry-fly hooks generally work well for this style, but I prefer the Tiemco 101 for small imitations because the straight eye doesn't interfere with the effective gap of the hook. Starting just ahead of the bend, dub and rib the body as with the previous styles, and tie the coated-thread antennae to the front. At the center of the thorax, tie the fiber-fan legs to the hook with cross wraps of thread, and cement the wraps with Zap-A-Gap. Dub around the legs to form the thorax. Attach the wing, reverse-dub the head, and tie down the forward half with the collar wraps. Whip-finish and cement as before. Trim the wing, legs, and antennae to length.

The alternative fold-over technique is also applicable to this style. You may find that, in addition to alleviating crowding at the head, this technique makes tying small flies of this style a little easier.

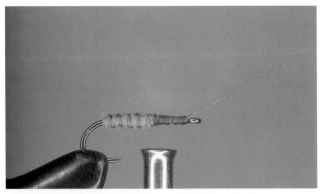

1. Dub and rib abdomen. Tie in thread antennae.

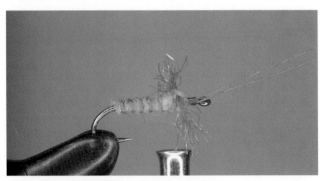

2. Tie in fiber fan legs, and dub thorax.

3. Tie in wing fibers, and reverse-dub head.

4. Fold back forward half of wing fibers, and tie them down. Trim wing.

Little Sister Sedge (Cheumatopsyche *spp.*)

Hook:	Tiemco 101, #16-18
Thread:	brown 8/0
Rib:	brown or gray thread
Body:	olive or olive-brown (abdomen) and ginger (thorax/head) dry-fly dubbing
Antennae:	coated brown 8/0 tying thread
Legs:	ginger or brown Antron or Hi-Vis
Wing:	dark brown Antron or Hi-Vis

Pattern notes: These little relatives of the spotted sedges are extremely important in their own right and create prolific hatches from East to West (and North to South). This little pattern is not intended for fishing during the emergence, but rather to match the adults during egg-laying periods (although the activities sometimes overlap). A number of species (like *campyla* and *pettiti*) are transcontinental. Most species are dark-winged with green or olive bodies, but there are also ginger- or tan-winged varieties.

Little Black Sedge (Chimarra aterrima)

Hook:	Tiemco 101, #18-20
Thread:	black 8/0
Rib:	brown or gray thread
Body:	blackish brown dry-fly dubbing, bright green tip
Antennae:	coated black 8/0 thread
Legs:	black or dark brown Antron or Hi-Vis
Wing:	black Antron or Hi-Vis

Pattern notes: The little black sedge generates subtle but significant feeding on both the Yellow Breeches and the Brodheads. Such diverse habitats reflect its wide-ranging importance in many medium-to-large Eastern and Midwestern trout streams. These secretive little sedges have the curious distinction of having been both overrated and underrated in recent fly-fishing literature. Because of their small size, dark color, and quiet demeanor, fly fishers can easily miss them or mistake their true significance during emergence or egg laying. Inspecting the underside of leaves and logs along the banks where they emerge will reveal their presence before the mating and egg laying get underway.

ADULTS AND EMERGERS
Substyle 2a— Shucking Synthetic Sedge Ⓘ

Shucking Synthetic Sedge: (left) *Shucking Weenom,* (right) *Shucking Spotted Sedge.*

Emerging caddisflies are vulnerable as they struggle in or under the surface during the evacuation of the pupal shuck. Not every caddisfly emerges successfully. During heavy hatches, those that are in the process of emerging and those that will never successfully complete the process build up to the point that trout focus exclusively on this vulnerable stage between their life in the water and their anticipated life in the air. Standard adult caddisfly imitations are often modified to reflect this stage by adding of a clump of synthetic fibers to represent the pupal shuck. The flaw in such an approach is that the submerged component of the imitation, which the trout view clearly, is less imitative than the above-water elements that are only seen at the last moment, and then are subject to distortion. But this basic approach is easily improved with a few simple alterations. This modification of the Synthetic Sedge style adds a synthetic fiber shuck that realistically reproduces the trout's underwater view of emerging or crippled caddisflies.

Tying Sequence

As a variation on the Synthetic Sedge style, this tie uses the same dry-fly hooks, either standard or straight eye. The first step in the actual tying process is to attach the Antron fiber body of the pupal shuck to the rear of the hook. You can melt or glue (Zap-A-Gap) the fiber ends together. Either is easier to do before you tie the fibers to the hook.

After attaching the translucent abdomen, tie Antron fiber wing cases along either side with the same folding technique as the Antron-Wing Soft-Hackle Pupa. Trim the fibers at an angle to suggest the wing case shape. Tie in a few longer fibers over the wing cases with the same folding method to represent legs. Apply a short band of Antron dubbing in front of the legs and wing cases to suggest the head of the pupal shuck. The remainder of the fly is the Synthetic Sedge tie with a Krystal Flash rib substituted for the thread rib on the original.

1. Tie in melted or glued Antron shuck fibers.

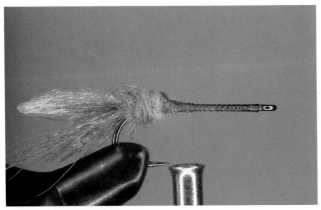

2. Tie in Antron fiber wing cases and leg fibers. Dub head of pupa.

3. Tie forward half of fly the same way as Synthetic Sedge, but rib abdomen with Krystal Flash.

Shucking Spotted Sedge.

Shucking Weenom (Micrasema *spp.*)

Hook: Tiemco 101, #16-20
Thread: brown 8/0
Pupal Shuck Half
Body: green Antron (melted or glued)
Wing cases: black Antron
Legs: dark brown or black Antron
Head: dark brown Antron dubbing
Synthetic Sedge Half
Rib: olive or green Krystal Flash
Body: green (abdomen) and brown (thorax/head) dry-fly dubbing
Antennae: coated brown 8/0 tying thread
Legs: dark brown or black Antron or Hi-Vis
Wing: black Antron or Hi-Vis

Pattern notes: I am not good at identifying the species of this genus (there are at least three in Pocono streams) and not much better at predicting when they will hatch, but I have often found trout rising steadily to them in long runs or the tails of pools. Tiny caddisflies that emerge from slick water often have a high casualty rate. When these little sedges attempt to penetrate the surface, they tend to accumulate in and under the film, making this pattern especially effective. Often mistaken for the little black sedges (*C. aterrima*), weenoms have green bodies and emerge at the surface rather than crawling out of the water.

Shucking Spotted Sedge (Hydropsyche/Ceratopsyche *spp.*)

Hook: Tiemco 101, #12-16
Thread: tan 8/0
Pupal Shuck Half
Body: pale yellow or tan Antron (melted or glued)
Wing cases: brown Antron
Legs: ginger or brown Antron
Head: ginger or brown Antron dubbing
Synthetic Sedge Half
Rib: yellow or orange Krystal Flash
Body: pale yellow or tan dry-fly dubbing
Antennae: coated tan or brown 8/0 tying thread
Legs: tan or ginger Antron or Hi-Vis
Wing: tan or ginger Antron or Hi-Vis

Pattern notes: While caddisflies may never be as popular as mayflies, the significance of *Hydropsyche* and *Ceratopsyche* hatches is hard to ignore. More flies are patterned after these caddisfly genera than any other. On pressured waters, it helps to have a few different patterns prepared to meet these hatches in order to give skeptical trout another look. This pattern has imitation and novelty going for it and is a worthy addition to your spotted sedge collection.

ADULTS AND EMERGERS
Style 3—Burnt Antron-Wing Diving Sedge ⓘ

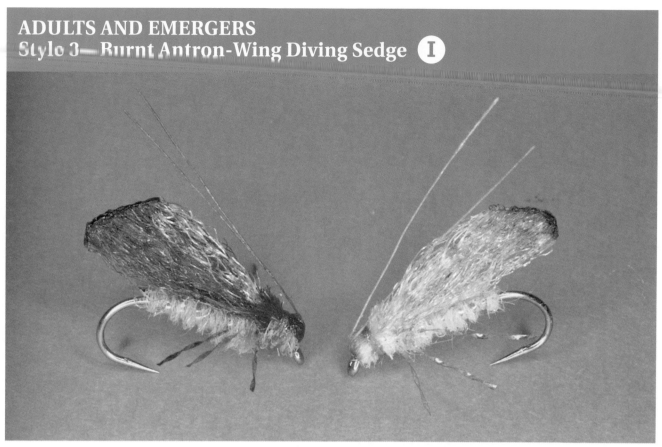

Burnt Antron-Wing Diving Sedge: (left) *Green Sedge Diver,* (right) *Spotted Sedge Diver.*

Diving underwater is the most common egg-laying method employed by caddisflies. The most widespread and significant trout-stream genera display this trait. This modern wet fly matches the appearance of these divers very well. During the heyday of the wet fly, whether the old-timers wielding their "buggy-whip" fly rods were aware of it or not (and some clearly were), periods of exceptional success with the wet were attributable to underwater insect activity being matched by the classic patterns. Modern materials allow us to do an even better job of imitating that underwater action, particularly that of diving egg-laying caddisflies. An Antron-dubbed body ribbed with Krystal Flash, a sparkling, burnt Antron fiber wing, and kicking Krystal Flash legs combine in this updated wet-fly style. This shining example proves that wet flies haven't receded into fly fishing history—they have a brilliant future.

Tying Sequence

Using a standard dry-fly hook, start the Antron dubbing near the bend, and tie in the Krystal Flash rib. Dub the abdomen, and wind the rib. Tie in two coated threads for antennae. Attach three Krystal Flash strands at the center of the thorax, and separate them with dubbing.

Shape the Antron wing in a burner. If the caddisfly wing being imitated has a rounded rear margin, you can use a mayfly wing burner. If the shape is angular, the mayfly burner will still work, but use the double burn method described in chapter 4. Secure the wing at the front of the thorax, and reverse-dub the head.

Fold the excess Antron back over the thorax, and wrap a narrow collar of thread to tie it down. Trim what remains behind the collar at an angle so it blends with the wing. Whip-finish at the collar and cement. Apply a touch of the cement (Zap-A-Gap) to the head, and hold the antennae against it until set (or you could tie the antennae down at the collar before whip-finishing). Trim the legs to length, and dab cement on their tips (though they appear to be single strands, they tend to split apart into multiple strands with hard use). Mottle the wing (if appropriate) with marker.

1. *Start dubbing, tie in rib, and dub abdomen. Tie thread antennae at front.*

2. *Rib abdomen. Tie in Krystal Flash legs at thorax, and separate with dubbing.*

3. *Tie in burnt Antron wing. Prepare to reverse-dub head.*

4. *Fold back forward half of Antron wing, tie it down, and trim off. Fix thread antennae with cement.*

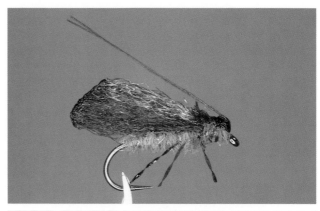

Green Sedge Diver (Rhyacophila *spp.*)

Hook:	standard dry fly, #12-16
Thread:	brown 8/0
Rib:	olive or green Krystal Flash
Body:	bright olive or green Antron dubbing
Antennae:	coated brown 8/0 thread
Legs:	brown (root beer) Krystal Flash
Wing:	mixed clear and brown Antron (burnt), mottled dark gray

Pattern notes: A traditional wet-fly swing with a few twitches sometimes works pretty well when green sedges are diving to lay eggs. More often, however, a dead drift or a swing under very slight tension works better. These sedges are fast-water flies, and even their egg-laying activity seems to be concentrated near swifter seams and edges. Because emergence and oviposition can overlap, fishing this fly in tandem with an emerger (pupa) can help to sort out which phase is more important to the trout at the time.

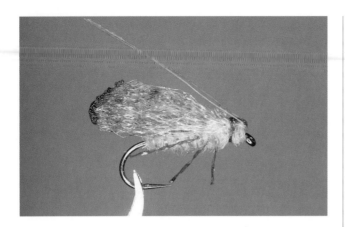

Spotted Sedge Diver
(Hydropsyche *and* Ceratopsyche *spp.)*

Hook:	standard dry-fly, #18–10
Thread:	tan 8/0
Rib:	yellow or orange Krystal Flash
Body:	yellow, tan, or ginger Antron dubbing
Antennae:	coated brown 8/0 tying thread
Legs:	orange Krystal Flash, tinted slightly brown
Wing:	mixed clear and ginger Antron, mottled brown

Pattern notes: On many streams, the dominant presence of spotted sedges throughout much of the season gives this pattern an edge as a searching fly in addition to application during the actual egg-laying period. The number of patterns devoted to these sedges reflects their importance, and one should really be equipped with a full range of imitations—deep pupa, emergers, dry and wet adults—in order to take advantage of all stages of their life cycle. The trout do.

ADULTS AND EMERGERS
Style 4—Burnt Poly-Wing Spent Sedge Ⓐ

Burnt Poly-Wing Spent Sedge: (left) *Dark Grannom,* (right) *White Miller.*

A dark grannom enjoying the interlude between emergence and egg laying. After egg laying, most will lie semispent on the surface.

This extremely accurate representation of an adult sedge is reserved for times when medium to large egg layers lay semispent on the surface. It is a rather complex tie, but when the task is to compete with a multitude of naturals on pressured water, it functions admirably. The tactic is to present it downstream, fly-first, to a steadily feeding trout (spoon-feeding). The burnt poly wings provide an accurate outline and excellent floatation on the smooth water of pools where hypercritical trout focus on the splayed adults. Although the legs, eyes, and antennae may seem like superfluous affectations under conditions that present lesser demands (and they would be), in smooth, clear water where trout endure constant fly-fishing pressure, such attention to detail often pays dividends.

Tying Sequence

You can use either standard or straight-eye dry-fly hooks for this style, although the straight-eye hooks may be better for fishing with an occasional twitch to attract the trout's attention. Dub and rib the abdomen of the fly as with previous styles. Tie in two coated-thread antennae. Attach the poly underwing fibers on top of the thorax location with the excess forward over the hook eye.

Shape two matching wings out of poly yarn in a wing burner, and mount them on either side on top of the underwing. Trim the excess poly from the burnt wings close to the thorax wraps, and apply a little Zap-A-Gap to the tie-down wraps. Wrap a pair of melted mono eyes on top of the underwing material near the eye of the hook. Attach three coated-thread legs at the center of the thorax, and separate them with thin dubbing.

Fold the forward half of the poly underwing material back over the thorax, and tie it down with a few wraps behind and in front of the legs. Cut off the excess at an angle behind the rear wraps. Whip-finish at the forward wraps, and coat the top of the head and the thorax with Zap-A-Gap or Flexament. Apply any desired accents or mottling with marker. Bend and set the thread legs as for the Thread-Legged Nymph style (chapter 5).

1. Dub and rib abdomen, and tie in thread antennae. Secure poly yarn underwing on top.

2. Tie burnt poly wings along both sides. Tie in melted mono eyes and thread legs.

3. Separate legs with thorax dubbing. Fold back forward half of poly yarn, and tie it down over thorax.

Dark Grannom (Brachycentrus spp.)

Hook:	Tiemco 101, #14-18
Thread:	brown 8/0
Rib:	dark gray or brown thread
Body:	dark gray or green (abdomen) and dark brown (thorax) dry-fly dubbing
Antennae:	coated dark brown 8/0 tying thread
Underwing:	dark gray poly yarn
Wings:	brown poly yarn (burnt), mottled dark gray
Eyes:	melted mono
Legs:	coated dark brown sewing thread

Pattern notes: Dark grannoms (such as *B. numerosus* and *lateralis* in the East and Midwest and *B. occidentalis* in the West) produce fine spring hatches for fly fishers across the country. But the egg-laying activity and its aftermath create the best dry-fly fishing. Exhausted females, most in a semispent position, cover the water. Trout become highly attuned to the appearance of these adults, and this pattern matches them precisely. A lighter version with tan wings and a light green body will match pale varieties like *B. appalachia*, which is a spring hatch, and *B. americanus*, which hatches later in the North and West.

White Miller (Nectopsyche spp.)

Hook:	Tiemco 101, #12-14
Thread:	white 8/0
Rib:	white thread
Body:	white or pale green (abdomen) and dirty white (thorax) dry-fly dubbing
Antennae:	coated white 6/0 tying thread
Underwing:	white poly yarn
Wings:	white poly yarn (burnt)
Eyes:	melted mono
Legs:	coated white or tan sewing thread

Pattern notes: These ghostly caddisflies emerge throughout the summer from the slower sections of trout streams and lakes or ponds. Their significance depends on water temperature and competition from other insects. On Skaneateles Lake, the egg laying often precedes the yellow Hex hatch, but the trout and landlocked salmon are seldom interested. I can remember idly contemplating their expiring forms while waiting for the giant mayflies to bring the fish to the surface of this exquisite Finger Lake. On the water, their triangular, semispent attitude and long antennae reminded me of a Hershey's Kiss with its little paper tag extended. (I was hungry and a little faint from the heat.)

ADULTS AND EMERGERS
Style 5—Half-And-Half Sedge Emerger ①

Half-and-Half Sedge Emerger: (left) *Spotted Sedge Emerger,* (right) *Green Sedge Emerger.*

Like the Half-and-Half Mayfly Emerger demonstrated in the previous chapter, this fly combines two previous styles into one fly. In this instance, the styles are the Antron-Wing Soft-Hackled Pupa and a stripped-down version of the Synthetic Sedge (minus the rib, legs, and antennae). Combined on an oversize caddis pupa hook, the more detailed rear half is submerged, where it is viewed clearly by the trout, and the synthetic wing holds the forward half in the film. The wing also provides visibility for tracking the fly. This design follows the same rationale as LaFontaine's Emergent Sparkle Pupa, but the rear half rides deeper, making it visible to the fish at a greater distance. It is a very effective style for imitating all caddisfly species that emerge on the surface and is surprisingly easy to tie.

Tying Sequence

Begin with an oversize Mustad C49S (or equivalent), and attach the soft-hackle fibers (pointing forward) to the middle of the hook. Dub and rib the rear half just as with the Antron-Wing Soft-Hackle Pupa, and brush out the dubbing. Fold on the Antron fiber wing cases, and wrap them in place. After trimming the wing cases, fold the soft-hackle fibers back, and distribute the fibers around the hook as you tie them down. Dub a head in front of the hackle.

1. Tie in soft-hackle fibers facing forward at middle of caddis pupa hook. Dub, rib, and brush out abdomen.

2. Tie in Antron fiber wing case along sides. Fold back soft-hackle fibers, distribute them around hook, and tie down. Dub head of pupa.

The simplified Synthetic Sedge occupies the rest of the hook. Dub the shank with dry-fly dubbing. Attach the wing fibers, and reverse-dub the head. Fold the forward half of the wing back, and wrap the collar. Whip-finish at the collar and cement. Trim the wing to length.

3. Dub adult abdomen, tie in wing fibers, and reverse-dub head.

4. Fold back forward half of wing fibers, and tie them down. Trim wing.

Green Sedge Emerger.

Spotted Sedge Emerger (Hydropsyche *and* Ceratopsyche *spp.*)

Hook: Mustad C49S, #10-12
Thread: tan 6/0 or 8/0
Hackle: brown partridge fibers
Rib: yellow or orange Krystal Flash
Pupal body: yellow, tan, or grayish tan Antron dubbing
Wing cases: brown Antron
Adult body: yellow or tan dry-fly dubbing
Wing: ginger or brown Hi-Vis

Pattern notes: Just another weapon in the arsenal of imitations I use for spotted sedge hatches, this fly is a favorite for fooling trout that are focused on the surface. These sedges usually hatch in the afternoon or evening, but I have encountered them in the morning as well. Of all the hatch-matching flies that come and go from my fly box during the season, this one (along with *Isonychia* nymph imitations) stays in the box for the longest period of time.

Green Sedge Emerger (Rhyacophila *spp.*)

Hook: Mustad C49S, #10-12
Thread: brown 6/0 or 8/0
Hackle: dark brown partridge fibers
Rib: olive or green Krystal Flash
Pupal body: bright olive or green Antron dubbing
Wing cases: black or dark brown Antron
Adult body: bright olive or green dry-fly dubbing
Wing: dark brown Hi-Vis

Pattern notes: During the fast-water emergence of green sedges, this pattern is an excellent tool for imitating their rapid escape from the pupal shuck. The combination of quickly moving water and quickly moving emergers leads to explosive rises. The violence of trout feeding in swift water is truly an awesome surprise, and one of the joys of fishing a fast-water emergence, whether sedges or mayflies, is witnessing the rush of the rise. Green sedge hatches may not be as dense as other important caddisflies, but they are a blast—literally.

ADULTS AND EMERGERS
Style 6 Wriggling Half And-Half Sedge Emerger Ⓐ

Wriggling Half-and-Half Sedge Emerger: (left) *Dark Blue Sedge Emerger,* (right) *Light Shadfly Emerger.*

OK, as the wag in the Pocono fly shop said, this really is tying two flies to get one. But the fly that results has some pretty powerful attractions. The two flies connected in this hinged dry are the Bubble Pupa (minus the dark overback) and a full-dress Synthetic Sedge with a Krystal Flash rib. This one fly not only imitates the appearance of the pupal and adult stages accurately, but it also allows you to mimic the struggle of emergence. Fly fishers sometimes fish a tandem arrangement consisting of a dry and a pupal imitation during caddisfly activity, and this style puts both in one package. So, while you may have to tie two flies, you don't have to tie two flies to your leader. Combining adult and pupa, surface and subsurface, the look and the movement, makes for a potent pair. Not enough? Here's another bonus: I mentioned in the instructions for tying the Bubble Pupa that I would give you a reason for tying that style on a straight-eye hook. If you haven't already guessed, it's a way of simplifying the tying of this style with a little recycling. When you have to retire a Bubble Pupa due to a broken bend or a mangled point, you can use it for the rear half of this fly. In which case, it's just a matter of attaching the recycled Bubble Pupa with a mono loop and tying the relatively simple Synthetic Sedge. Which would be getting two flies by tying one—or something like that.

Tying Sequence

To construct the slightly simplified Bubble Pupa, start by tying the clear Antron overbody to a Tiemco 101. Dub and rib the body. Bring the overbody fibers forward and distribute them around the hook. After tying them down, fold on the fiber wing cases and secure with wraps over the fold. Add the soft-hackle legs, and dub the head. Tie in the antennae, whip-finish, and cement. Cut off the bend of the hook.

Before commencing to tie the Synthetic Sedge component, tie a few strands of clear Antron to the rear of a Mustad C49S (to create a hinge cover that suggests gas bubbles escaping as the adult emerges), and secure the mono loop material to the shank. Wrap a little dubbing spacer to keep the loop open. Slip the pupa onto the mono, and attach the loop as with all other hinged flies. Tie in the rib, and dub the shank up to the thorax. After ribbing, use either of the folded wing methods (refer back to the Fluttering Sedge if you've forgotten) to complete the forward part of the fly. Whip-finish at the collar and cement. Trim the wing, legs, and antennae.

1. Tie in clear Antron fibers, and dub and rib abdomen. Bring Antron fibers forward, and tie down. Tie in Antron fiber wing case.

2. Tie soft-hackle fibers along sides. Dub head, and tie in flank-fiber antennae.

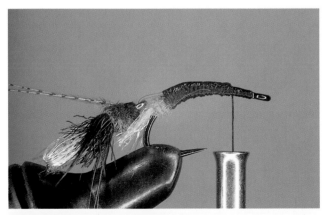

3. Tie in clear Antron hinge cover, and attach simplified Bubble Pupa to mono loop.

4. Tie the forward half of fly the same as Synthetic Sedge except for Krystal Flash rib.

Dark Blue Sedge Emerger (Psilotreta labida)

Hooks:	Tiemco 101, #12-16 (rear), and Mustad C49S, #12-16 (front)
Thread:	black 8/0

Bubble Pupa Half

Overbody:	clear Antron
Rib:	olive or green Krystal Flash
Body:	grayish green Antron dubbing
Wing cases:	black Antron
Legs:	dark gray hen-hackle fibers
Head:	blackish brown dubbing
Antennae:	bronze mallard flank fibers

Synthetic Sedge Half

Hinge cover:	clear Antron
Rib:	olive or green Krystal Flash
Body:	grayish green dry-fly dubbing
Antennae:	coated dark gray 8/0 tying thread
Legs:	dark gray or dark brown Antron or Hi-Vis
Wing:	dark gray Hi-Vis

Pattern notes: In waters that favor them, dark blue sedges can hatch in amazing concentrations. I can painfully recall a hatch on the Lehigh River, many years ago, which was truly epic in scale. Trout were tearing at the surface all around me, and a dark Elk Hair Caddis was the only match I had to offer. It fooled one small dimwitted fish. From such experiences, lessons are learned, and I no longer face these hatches so ill-equipped. This pattern, conceived with that erstwhile failure in mind, is substantial revenge for that sedge-filled evening of humiliation.

Light Shadfly Emerger (**Brachycentrus appalachia**)

Hooks: Tiemco 101, #12-14 (rear), and Mustad C49S, #12-14 (front)
Thread: tan 8/0

Bubble Pupa Half

Overbody: clear Antron
Rib: olive or yellow Krystal Flash
Body: apple green Antron dubbing
Wing cases: tan or ginger Antron
Legs: light brown partridge fibers
Head: ginger dubbing
Antennae: lemon wood-duck flank fibers

Synthetic Sedge Half

Hinge cover: clear Antron
Rib: olive or yellow Krystal Flash
Body: apple green dry-fly dubbing
Antennae: coated tan 8/0 tying thread
Legs: tan or ginger Antron or Hi-Vis
Wing: light tan Hi-Vis

Pattern notes: This light-colored grannom, also known as the apple caddis for the color of its body, is an important spring emerger on many of my favorite Pocono streams. The Delaware River also hosts good hatches (of this and just about everything else). It is found in many Eastern trout streams but is not as well publicized as such species as *numerosus, lateralis,* and *fuliginosus.* Its pale wings appear almost white at times, and the emergence coincides with white (or American) shad runs in the upper Delaware and their heralds—the white blossoms of the shadbush (serviceberry). Because of these associations, shadfly is a fitting name for this species.

CHAPTER SEVEN

Stones

American salmonfly.

NOCTURNES AND NEGLECT

When most fly-fishers set out to match the hatch, the insects involved are frequently mayflies, less frequently caddisflies, sometimes midges, but seldom stoneflies. With the exception of a few famous hatches, such as the Western salmonfly *(Pteronarcys californica),* stonefly imitations are most often fished as generic attractors. Wherever fast, boulder-strewn water coincides with the possible presence of large trout, anglers probe the pockets with large, weighted stonefly nymphs or dance a bushy, hairwing dry over the current tongues. The hope is that the large-fly/large-fish dictum will pay off in pounds of trout on the line. The popularity of this approach is testament to its success, but it only begins to tap the immense potential presented by these rock crawlers.

Why are stoneflies treated with such superficial tactics when they have such obvious big-fish appeal? The short answer, with regard to many stonefly species, is that emergence, mating, and egg laying are nocturnal activities. It's not that this is so very unusual—some caddisflies and a few mayflies also exhibit these secretive habits. The rub is that fishing after dark or before dawn will never be a popular time frame. With stoneflies, the compounding factor is that prime stonefly water—a fast, rocky reach—is the last place most anglers would like to find themselves in the dark.

The opportunities to exploit stonefly activity do exist, however, and not all species are strictly night lovers. Some large Western species (probably due to colder water temperatures at the time of emergence) and a number of smaller species do their things in the daytime. For the more photophobic varieties, late evening and early morning offer reasonable chances to catch their waxing or waning activity. On many otherwise-pounded streams, these are among the best times to encounter some truly exceptional fish. Where it is legal and prudent, however, nighttime offers the best chance to fool big fish that shun the sunlight. If you think the large-fly/large-fish approach works well in the daytime, you should see how well it works when the bugs are actually emerging or fluttering on the starlit surface.

The stonefly styles in this series of flies may help shed some light on these underutilized, unmatched hatches. Add nerve, knowledge, and secure wading skills and you'll be prepared to uncover the dark secrets of the stones. The best fish in the stream are already well acquainted with these rock-crawling wonders; you should be, too.

NYMPHS
Style 1—Standard Stone Nymph

Standard Stone Nymph: (left) *Dark Stone Nymph,* (right) *Golden Stone Nymph.*

This basic stonefly nymph imitation, while it employs a variety of materials, is about as simple a tie as can be made to reasonably suggest these important insects. Due to the weighted, keel-shaped (bent) hook, it is stable throughout the drift and can be tied to represent a number of species, from very large to rather small. It is an appropriate fly for searching broken, rock-ridden water at any time. Beyond this more common application, it is accurate enough to represent certain species during their period of emergence. This fly has also become a favorite go-to fly for deep drifting to large lake-run steelhead and brown trout. When garish attractors and egg patterns fail to turn their heads, a switch to this fly can produce. If they are exposed to extensive fishing pressure on their upriver journey, migratory fish learn to avoid the barrage of brightly-colored gewgaws that constantly bombard them. Then this more subdued and suggestive style has its innings.

Tying Sequence
Begin by bending a 2X- or 3X-long nymph hook and weighting the keel with wire. Tie in the poly yarn over-back, and attach a long, thin goose or turkey biot to either side of the shank (the poly yarn provides separation between the biots). Start a little dubbing at the rear and attach the D-shape vinyl rib.

Dub a fat abdomen; then bring the poly yarn forward, and tie it down over the thorax. Cut off the excess poly. Wind the rib over the abdomen in an open spiral, and tie it off. Prepare a wing quill strip by coloring it (if needed) and coating it with Flexament.

Tie the prepared strip over the thorax, with the thicker end forward. Dub the rear half of the thorax. Fold the quill strip over a needle so that the folded rear edge is slightly behind the thorax dubbing. Tie the strip down just ahead of the thorax dubbing; then fold the remaining strip to the rear, wrapping over the fold. Dub about half of the remaining thorax space, and tie a generous clump of soft-hackle fibers to either side for legs. Dub the rest of the thorax. Once again, fold the quill strip over a needle, forming the second wing case. Tie it down and cut off the excess. Wrap a fat thread head and whip-finish. Coat the back of the abdomen, the wing cases, and the head with Flexament.

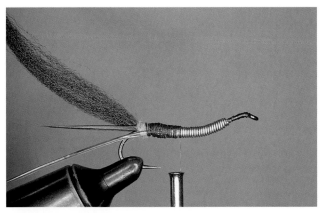

1. *Attach poly yarn overback and biot tails to weighted, bent hook. Start dubbing, and tie in V-Rib.*

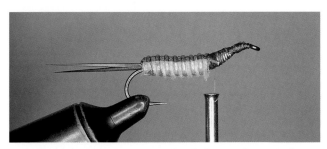

2. *Dub abdomen. Bring overback forward, tie it down, and rib it.*

3. *Tie in wing quill strip, and dub rear half of thorax. Fold quill strip forward, tie it down, and fold it to the rear. Tie soft-hackle fibers along sides.*

4. *Dub forward half of thorax, fold quill strip forward again, and tie off at head.*

Dark Stone Nymph

Hook:	2XL or 3XL nymph hook, #6-14
Thread:	black or brown 6/0
Weight:	lead-free wire
Overback:	black poly yarn
Tails:	black or brown biots
Rib:	black, brown, or clear V-Rib
Body:	blackish or grayish brown dubbing
Wing cases:	black or dark brown goose quill strip
Legs:	black or dark brown hen-hackle fibers

Pattern notes: In addition to being a good general-purpose nymph, this pattern is suggestive of several dark species. In the larger sizes, it resembles dark members of the Perlidae (such as *Paragnetina media*) and the Pteronarcyidae (such as *Pteronarcys dorsata*). Fishing fast-water emergence sites immediately pre-hatch (usually late evening) is an especially effective application.

Golden Stone Nymph

Hook:	2XL or 3XL nymph hook, #6-14
Thread:	brown or amber 6/0
Weight:	lead-free wire
Overback:	brown poly yarn
Tails:	brown or amber biots
Rib:	amber V-Rib
Body:	golden or amber dubbing
Wing cases:	mottled turkey tail or peacock secondary, tinted yellow or amber

Pattern notes: The more colorful members of the Perlidae family, collectively called golden stones by fly fishers, are a significant trout food from coast to coast. This pattern is generally suggestive of these nymphs. When drifted in the current tongues that envelop boulders and breaks, it works extremely well.

NYMPHS
Substyle 1a—Curling Stone Nymph Ⅰ

Curling Stone Nymph: Salmonfly Nymph.

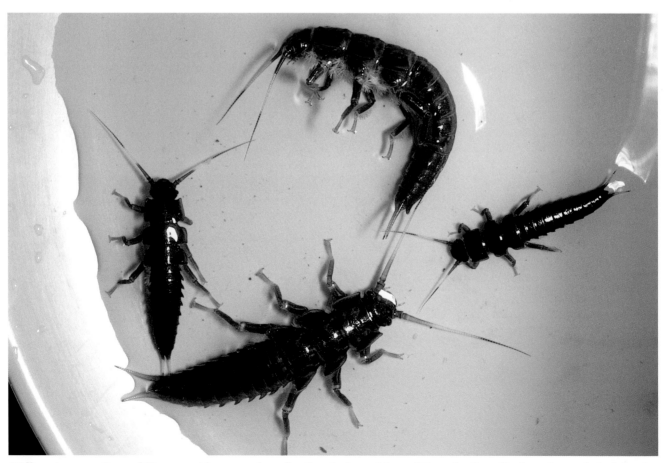

Different generations of Pterynarcidae nymphs reflecting their multiyear life cycle. One displays the curled, defensive posture that they often assume when drifting.

Stonefly nymphs of the *Pteronarcys* genus are sometimes called curlers for the defensive posture they assume in your hand. When caught by the current, they curl as they drift. Curved stonefly nymph imitations have become rather popular, but if they are heavily weighted with wire or beads, many drift upside-down. Gary LaFontaine's Natural Drift Stone was the first serious attempt to create a severely bent imitation that was stable during the drift. The weighted rear end of this fly was counterbalanced with a spun deer-hair thorax. The modification of the Standard Stone tie presented here uses poly yarn to achieve the same result. Both Gary's fly and this one will sometimes roll when retrieved (due to the radical bend of the hook), but they mimic the curling stones accurately during the drift. This style has a narrow application and is not the best choice for fishing swift, churning water, but where that water breaks into pools or long smooth runs, it is unsurpassed.

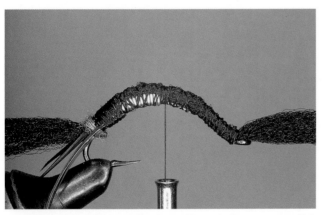

1. Attach poly yarn overback and biot tails to an English bait hook that has been weighted on its rear half. Start dubbing, and tie in V-Rib.

2. Complete nymph in the same manner as the Standard Stone, but tie in thread antennae, and tie the forward half of the poly yarn down to form a head and pronotum.

Tying Sequence

About the only hook that adequately suggests the curl of *Pteronarcys* nymphs is the Mustad 37160, sometimes described as an English bait hook. In addition to its radical curve, it also has an offset bend, which I like to straighten before tying. Aside from the hook, you need to make a few other adjustments to the Standard Stone tie to produce this imitation of the big salmonflies.

The first difference is that you apply the weighting wire only to the rear half of the hook. Another is the addition of two coated-thread antennae at the front of the hook. The most important change is that you tie down the poly yarn overback over the entire length of the hook, and the yarn extends over the front as well as the rear of the hook. Then follow the procedure for the Standard Stone. After forming the second wing case from the quill strip, dub the head, and fold the poly yarn that remains back over the thorax. Make a collar wrap in front of the legs to secure the yarn. Cut off the excess a little behind the collar, forming a pronotum. Coat the back of the nymph (including the head and pronotum) with Flexament.

Salmonfly Nymph (Pteronarcys *spp.*)

Hook:	Mustad 37160, #6-12
Thread:	black, brown, or rust 6/0
Weight:	lead-free wire
Overback:	black or dark brown poly yarn
Tails:	black or brown biots
Rib:	black, brown, or clear V-Rib
Body:	blackish brown, grayish brown, or rusty orange dubbing
Antennae:	coated black or brown 2/0 or 3/0 tying thread
Wing cases:	black or dark brown wing quill strip
Legs:	black or dark brown hen-hackle fibers

Pattern notes: The two most important species that can be matched by this pattern are the orange-accented Western salmonfly *(P. californica)* and the similar, but more somber, American salmonfly *(P. dorsata)*. The Western variety gets all the press, but *dorsata* has a much broader range, extending all the way across the continent and north to Alaska. Another possibility for imitation is the Eastern species *biloba* (sometimes listed under the genus *Allonarcys*). It usually inhabits small streams or headwaters, and the smaller versions, which represent the multiyear life cycle of these nymphs, are preferable (I dislike catching small trout on large hooks).

NYMPHS
Style 2—Paper-Case Stone Nymph Ⓘ

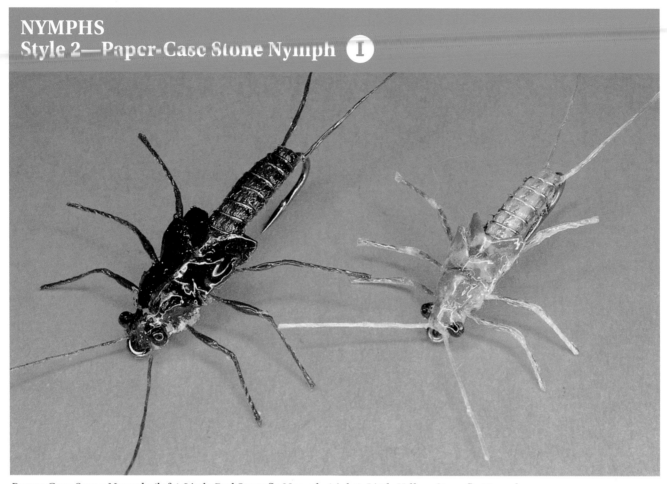

Paper-Case Stone Nymph: (left) *Little Red Stonefly Nymph,* (right) *Little Yellow Stonefly Nymph.*

Large stoneflies attract the attention of trout and trout anglers, but smaller species can also be important. Some have the advantage of being active during the daytime. The blackish or brownish nymphs of Capniidae and Taeniopterygidae, and the colorful members of Chloroperlidae and Perlodidae offer fishing opportunities that extend from late winter through summer. The early season nymphs—whose dark colors retain heat and are camouflage against rocks and bare trees—emerge as the sun warms the cold water of March and April. The later-emerging, bright green and yellow species appear when leaves fill the streamside canopy with the same colors. Even though many of these late-spring or summer stoneflies emerge after dark, the adults are often active during the day, and the nymphs can drift in heavy concentrations at sunset. At dusk, a little yellow or green nymph can be remarkably effective. These diminutive stoneflies may not be as impressive as their giant kin, but they are elegant little insects that are well worth getting to know. The Paper-Case Stone imitates these nymphs beautifully and is readily accepted by trout, even on intensely pressured streams.

Tying Sequence

A mildly curved hook shank, as found on hooks like the Tiemco 200R and Daiichi 1270, is about as far as I like to go when imitating nymphs other than members of the Pteronarcyidae. Because of the counterbalancing effect of the poly yarn overback, some weight can be added to this fly. I often omit the weight from the smallest sizes, however, choosing to weight the leader instead.

Begin by tying the poly yarn to the rear of the hook. If weight is desired, wrap wire around the rear half of the hook. Tie a coated thread along either side of the hook. Each thread will serve as both tail and antenna. Attach the ribbing wire.

Dub the abdomen. Bring the poly yarn over the body, tying it down in the thorax area. Leave the excess extended forward from the eye of the hook. Tie in a pair of melted mono eyes. Attach the coated-thread legs at the center of the thorax, and separate them with dubbing. Prepare two wing cases by cutting or burning the shapes from Tyvek. Color the wing cases, and coat them with Flexament.

Tie the first wing case to the hook between the front and middle pair of legs, and cover the tie-down wraps with thin dubbing. Attach the second wing case between the front legs and the mono eyes. Reverse-dub the head with thin dubbing. Fold the remaining poly to the rear, and tie it down, forming a narrow collar behind the mono eyes. Whip-finish at the collar, and cut off the excess, creating a pronotum as on the Curling Stone tie. Bend and set the legs (see the Thread-Legged Nymph, chapter 5). Coat the back of the fly with Flexament, and add any appropriate markings.

4. Fold back the forward half of the poly yarn, and tie it down behind and in front of forward leg pair. Trim the excess poly to form the pronotum.

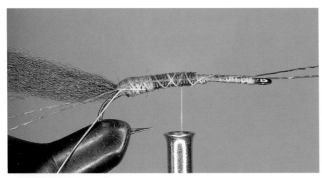

1. Tie poly yarn overback to a curved-shank hook that has been weighted on its rear half. Tie in thread for tails and antennae, and attach the ribbing wire.

2. Dub abdomen. Bring poly yarn forward, tie it down, and rib it.

Little Red Stonefly Nymph (Strophopteryx fasciata)

Hook:	Tiemco 200R, #14-16
Thread:	brown 8/0
Overback:	brown poly yarn, tinted slightly red
Weight:	copper wire (optional)
Tails/antennae:	coated reddish brown 6/0 tying thread
Rib:	gold wire
Body:	cream or yellowish tan dubbing
Eyes:	melted mono
Legs:	coated reddish brown sewing thread
Wing cases:	cut or burnt Tyvek, colored reddish brown, dark marks

Pattern notes: This early-season, Eastern hatch sometimes offers good dry-fly fishing, but the nymphing is usually more reliable. A little interlude of warm sunshine can ignite a hatch, even during the dreary, gray weather of a reluctant spring. The trout respond to the warmth and the food, and this little nymph can provide action in the face of otherwise bleak conditions.

3. Tie in thread legs, and separate with dubbing. Attach melted mono eyes at the front, and the two Tyvek wing cases down over the thorax.

Little Yellow Stonefly Nymph (Isoperla bilineata)

Hook:	Tiemco 200R, #16-18
Thread:	yellow 8/0
Overback:	yellow poly yarn, marked on sides and center with olive or brown
Weight:	copper wire (optional)
Tails/antennae:	coated yellow 6/0 tying thread
Rib:	fine gold wire
Body:	pale yellow dubbing
Eyes:	melted mono
Legs:	coated yellow sewing thread
Wing cases:	cut or burnt Tyvek, colored yellow, olive or brown marks

Pattern notes: Mud Run is a stunning little Pocono stream that flows through a rocky cut on its way to the Lehigh River. Its beauty belies its name. The tannic waters are not rich but harbor a fine population of wild brook and brown trout and a surprising variety of aquatic insects. This little nymph is one of the most common, and this pattern is one of the most consistent producers on this stream from late May through early July. The rugged charm of a mountain stream adds to the appeal of fishing this fly, and *Isoperla bilineata* has a vast range, extending from the East Coast to parts of the eastern slope of the Rocky Mountains.

NYMPHS
Style 3—Paperback Stone Nymph Ⓐ

Paperback Stone Nymph: (left) *Moltin' Stone Nymph,* (right) *Embossed Stone Nymph.*

Fast water can hide the flaws of an imitation, and opportunistic trout will snatch food from heavier flows when compelled by hunger. But trout eat most stonefly nymphs in the buffer zone of slower water that forms wherever bottom structure slows the flow. While feeding within these protected bands, they get a pretty good look at prospective prey. If concentrations of stonefly nymphs are traversing these zones as they move toward their emergence sites, trout can become quite picky about the imitations they'll accept. To further compound the situation, larger prey forms, like Perlidae nymphs, are especially easy to distinguish from frauds under these conditions. Many anglers fall into the habit of fishing generalized stonefly nymph imitations as part of shotgun-style fishing strategy. When this strategy succeeds, it is because nonspecific imitations work better when the trout are not focused on specific prey. Unfortunately, such an approach misses the bulls-eye of stonefly imitation—fishing an accurate imitation during periods of concentration and specific focus by the trout. The Paperback Stone was designed to take advantage of these situations and can be far more productive than generalized patterns that are fished in a haphazard manner.

This Perlidae nymph has just shed its skin. If exposed, it is a conspicuous target for trout.

Tying Sequence

This style uses a moderately curved hook like the Tiemco 200R or Daiichi 1270, although straight or keel-bent shanks could also be used. Tyvek is substituted for the poly yarn overback. But the counterbalance pro-

The embossed stone (P. media) is a widespread species that thrives in a surprising variety of streams due to their unusual tolerance of conditions that are not suited to other species.

vided by poly is still useful (especially on straight or curved hook shanks), and it is tied as an underbody over the weight. In order to provide a broader, more flattened base for the body of the fly, the heavy folded-wire weighting technique is also used (see chapter 4).

After securing the underbody of heavy wire and poly yarn to the shank, cut a strip of Tyvek, and color it for the overback. Taper this strip at one end, and tie that end to the rear of the hook. Tie in dyed mono or coated thread on either side for the tails and antennae. I usually use the same strand to represent both, but you can tie in finer material separately for the antennae, if you wish. Reverse-dub the abdomen so that you can use the tying thread to tie down the overback with a true segmentation wrap. To do this, make two or three wraps of thread in the same place to delineate a segment, and advance to the next segment by slipping the thread between the overback and the dubbed abdomen.

Prepare three pairs of doubled, knotted-thread legs (see chapter 4) and two Tyvek wing cases. Leave the Tyvek strip used for the forward wing case long to allow the head and pronotum of the nymph to be shaped from the same strip. Attach the rear pair of legs, and dub around them. Secure the rear wing case just ahead of the

legs. Position the forward wing case on top so that the rear edge rests in the location desired on the finished fly. Nick the edge of the Tyvek with scissors at the front and rear of pronotum location and at the front of the head (the eye of the hook). Remove the piece and make small notches at the front and rear of the pronotum on either side. Cut a short tie-down tab from the head mark forward. Use the tab to tie the front wing case strip behind the eye (and upside down).

Attach the remaining leg pairs, and dub around them. Reverse-dub the head, and fold the wing case strip to the rear. Wrap thread in the notches at the rear of the pronotum; then move the thread forward under the body, and wrap it in the forward pronotum notches. Whip-finish in the forward notches. Coat the back of the fly with Flexament, and add any additional markings. Place dark spots at the eye positions with marker, and put a dome of five-minute epoxy over each.

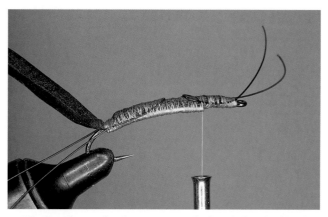

1. Tie Tyvek overback to a curved-shank hook that has been balanced with poly yarn tied over folded wire. Tie in tails and antennae.

2. Reverse-dub abdomen, and wrap the overback with the true segmentation technique.

3. Tie the first leg pair at the rear of the thorax, and apply dubbing. Tie in the rear wing case, and attach the forward wing case at the front of the hook. Attach the remaining leg pairs, and dub the thorax and head.

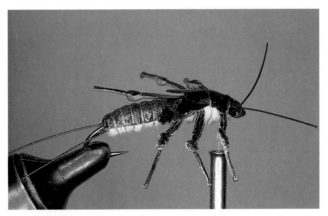

4. Fold back the forward wing case, and tie it down behind and in front of the forward leg pair.

Embossed Stone Nymph.

Moltin' Stone Nymph (Perlidae)

Hook:	Tiemco 200R, #8-12
Thread:	white or tan 6/0
Underbody:	poly yarn over heavy lead-free wire (folded)
Overback:	white Tyvek strip, tan marks
Tails/antennae:	coated white sewing thread
Body:	cream or white dubbing
Legs:	coated white heavy sewing thread (doubled), tan marks
Wing cases:	cut or burnt white Tyvek, tan marks

Pattern notes: This pattern doesn't match a particular species of Perlidae; instead, it imitates a particularly vulnerable stage in their development. At the end of each instar, these nymphs (like all nymphs) shed their skins. For a short time, they are colorless and helpless. Waving a white flag in the face of an enemy may be a plea for truce, but the trout—merciless predators that they are—are disinclined to comply. If you are fond of searching the water with stonefly nymphs, this is a pattern you really should try.

Embossed Stone Nymph (Paragnetina media)

Hook:	Tiemco 200R, #8-12
Underbody:	poly yarn over heavy lead-free wire (folded)
Overback:	Tyvek strip, colored brown or blackish brown
Tails/antennae:	dark brown dyed mono (or coated thread)
Body:	creamy tan or dirty yellow dubbing
Legs:	coated brown heavy sewing thread (doubled), dark marks
Wing cases:	cut or burnt Tyvek, colored brown, dark marks

Pattern notes: Except for a few limestone spring creeks, this common stonefly is well represented on most of the Eastern trout streams of my experience. It is also found in abundance in the Midwest, ranging north into central Canada. Its emergence typically reaches a peak sometime in June, and trout become extremely receptive to this pattern around sunset. Unless there has been a heavy rain, you cannot miss the signs of media activity—their dark husks will be adorning nearly every exposed rock along the stream.

NYMPHS
Substyle 3a—Crawling Paperback Stone Nymph Ⓐ

Crawling Paperback Stone Nymph: (left) *Beautiful Stone Nymph,* (right) *American Salmonfly Nymph.*

This imitation of large roving stonefly nymphs is a secret weapon. I don't tie or fish it that often, but when I do, I have come to expect results. It is an elaborate tie that is the product of many years of development. Before you decide that tying this fly is too much trouble, allow me to share two of the many experiences that convinced me to continue the effort.

The prototype's initiation occurred more than a decade ago on a storied section of the Brodheads. This was my one and only opportunity to fish the famous water of the Henryville Flyfishers—Ernest Schwiebert's home water. The invitation came through the good graces of my wife, who was working as a medical secretary for a doctor who was a club member. The most promising prospect for this all-too-brief evening was dry-fly action from the pale evening dun hatch. However, the section that my host suggested I fish was a rough reach of pocket water that didn't favor these duns. Nevertheless, I awaited their appearance. As dusk approached with few flies and no rises, I realized that I was

rapidly running out of time. I turned to an experimental, hinged imitation of the dark stoneflies *(P. media)* that had been hatching for about a week or so. Shortly after tying this fly to my leader, all thought of the little yellow mayflies was forgotten. Hefty brown trout hit on almost every cast, intercepting the nymph behind nearly every boulder. I can't recall the exact number that I entered in the logbook when I returned to the clubhouse, but it was more than enough to make an indelible impression. A rare opportunity, almost squandered, was salvaged by the experimental stone.

The other event was an unusual application of this fly, a few years later, on a popular Lake Ontario tributary. The salmon were running, and their steadily increasing numbers were attracting steadily increasing crowds. But I was there to catch trout, not salmon. I had fished all morning with nothing but a momentary hookup on a Standard Stone. Normally, I wouldn't risk a more complex tie on this snag-filled water, but I was desperate. On the first drift of this big hinged nymph, I hooked and

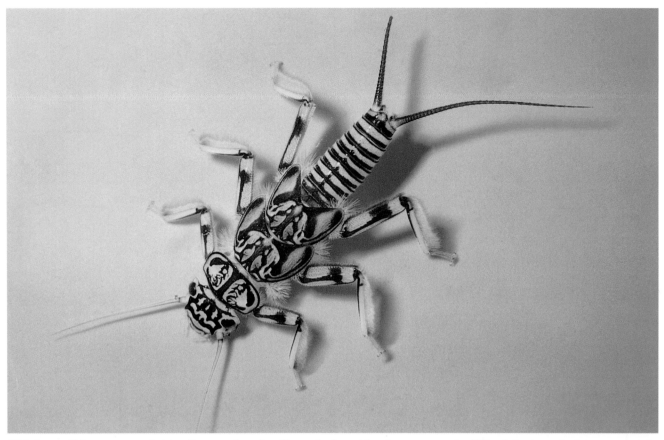

This beautiful stone nymph is well-named and well-marked, making it an extremely difficult insect to imitate accurately.

eventually landed a ten-pound summer steelhead. On the second drift, a larger steelie of about twelve pounds surrendered from the same spot. The third drift produced a nine-pound male brown, and on the fourth drift, an impetuous little twelve-inch brook trout (the only one I have caught on this river) inhaled my wriggling imitation as I was about to lift it from the water. I have caught many of the big lake-run fish over the years but have never had them respond to a fly in such an astounding way. My partner, who was snapping photos of the fish as I released them, was equally astounded (and probably a little peeved). My guess, upon reflection, was that heavy wading traffic from salmon anglers crossing the shallow riffle above me had dislodged stoneflies and delivered them to the fish. A good fly is often improved by the company it keeps.

On the other hand, this fly really is a royal pain to tie, and maybe you shouldn't bother with it. Besides, I would be severely disappointed if this fly ever became popular.

Tying Sequence

Essentially an inverted, hinged version of the Paperback Stone, this fly is designed to crawl along the bottom, wagging its tail as it goes. The rear hook is an inexpensive Aberdeen (such as the Eagle Claw 214EL), and the front hook is a standard wet-fly hook (such as the Daiichi 1530 or Tiemco 3769). Retain the folded-wire underbody to provide a flattened shape on both hooks, but add half a tin shot to the underside of the fly to orient it. Omit the poly yarn.

Assemble the wire underbody, Tyvek overback, mono tails, and dubbed abdomen in the same manner as the previous fly. There is no problem if the Aberdeen hook used for the rear segment is oversize, as long as you tie the abdomen to the appropriate length (a bit more than half the body length of the finished fly). Once you complete the abdomen and coat the back with Flexament, cut the bend from the hook.

After lashing the folded wire to the front hook, tie in the mono loop material. Build a spacer out of thread or dubbing, and then slip the rear segment onto the mono (remember that this is an inverted tie—it goes on upside down). Attach the free end of the mono to the top, draw the loop to size, and secure it with tight wraps and cement.

Invert the hook in the vise, and attach the rear pair of legs. Dub around them before tying the rear wing case in position. Tie the front wing case strip and the antennae to the front of the hook. Add the remaining leg pairs and dubbing. Tie down the front wing case strip, and finish the fly in the manner of the Paperback Stone. Brush or pick out the thorax dubbing between the legs. Cut a tin shot in half, and glue it to the front of the thorax with Zap-A-Gap or five-minute epoxy. If you like (I do), paint the shot to match the thorax and coat it with Flexament or five-minute epoxy.

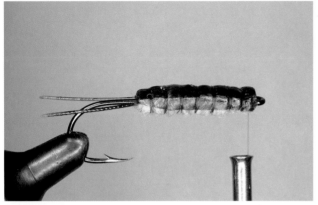

1. Attach mono tails and Tyvek overback to the rear hook, which has been weighted with folded wire. Reverse-dub the abdomen, and tie the overback down with true segmentation wraps.

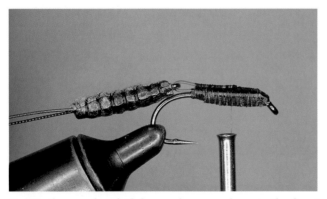

2. Attach completed abdomen by mono loop to the front hook that has been weighted with folded wire.

3. Invert fly, and complete forward half in exactly the same manner as the Paperback Stone Nymph.

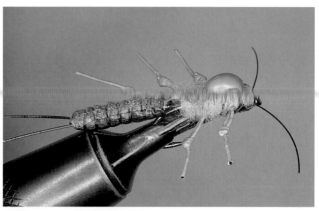

4. Glue tin shot half to the underside, and paint to match the thorax dubbing with acrylic paint, if desired.

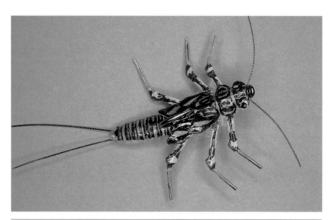

Beautiful Stone Nymph (Paragnetina immarginata)

Hooks:	Eagle Claw 214EL, #10 (rear), and Daiichi 1530, #8-10 (front)
Thread:	yellow 6/0
Underbody:	heavy lead-free wire (folded)
Overback:	Tyvek strip, colored yellow or amber, black bands
Tails:	brown or dark amber dyed mono (embossed)
Body:	pale yellow or light amber dubbing
Legs:	coated yellow or amber heavy sewing thread (doubled), black marks
Wing cases:	cut or burnt Tyvek, colored yellow or amber, black marks
Antennae:	brown or amber dyed mono (embossed)
External weight:	tin shot half (BB)

Pattern notes: Their intricate patterns and large size make Perlidae nymphs such as *immarginata* some of the most difficult insects to imitate accurately. But they have so much appeal that they warrant the extra effort. Fierce and active, these predatory nymphs are favorites of fast-water trout. While this imitation is not irresistible, there are times when it comes as close to that as I could wish. Those times usually occur around dawn, in long pocket-water stretches, on summer days.

American Salmonfly Nymph (Pteronarcys dorsata)

Hooks:	Eagle Claw 214EL, #10 (rear), and Daiichi 1530, #6-10
Thread:	brown or black 6/0
Underbody:	heavy lead-free wire (folded)
Overback:	Tyvek strip, colored brown or blackish brown
Tails:	dark brown dyed mono (embossed)
Body:	gray or grayish brown dubbing
Legs:	coated gray or brown heavy sewing thread (doubled), dark on top
Wing cases:	cut or burnt Tyvek, colored brown or blackish brown, dark marks
Antennae:	dark brown dyed mono (embossed)

External weight: tin shot half (BB or AAA)

Pattern notes: Unlike its relative, *P. biloba*, this giant stonefly seems to favor big water. And big water means big fish. Try this fly on the Yellow Breeches, where a large, but relatively unknown population hatches in June, or on Penn's Creek, or the Delaware River . . . or any of the hundreds of other streams and rivers that host these enormous nymphs. Drifting this big monster at twilight can produce monstrous fish that are not seen—or dreamed of—in the light of day.

ADULTS
Style 1—Fluttering Stone

Fluttering Stone: (left) *Little Green Stonefly,* (right) *Yellow Sally.*

Brilliant little green or yellow stoneflies fluttering in the broken sunlight are a common sight over swift, rocky streams from late spring through summer. Many of the members of Chloroperlidae and Perlodidae are active during the day, and I have frequently been surprised by their egg-laying flights. In fact, these surprises have been frequent enough to motivate me to develop a fly that matches the egg-laying posture of the females. The dipping and fluttering adults create quite a stir for such small flies, and the trout feed on them in a slashing, frenzied fashion. Smaller fish often become impatient and attempt to capture the flyers by executing extreme aerial maneuvers. I have never been able to predict when oviposition will occur with any degree of precision, but the fishing to this activity is so fast-paced and delightful that I carry this imitation whenever the possibility exists. Although I usually tie this style to represent small species, there is no reason it cannot also be tied in larger sizes (although I recommend switching to a Tiemco 200R or Daiichi 1270).

Tying Sequence
This tie is basically the Fluttering Sedge with tails. Like that fly, it uses a continuous-bend hook (such as the Mustad C49S) to suggest the nearly vertical attitude of the bodies of the egg-laying adults (unlike caddisflies, stoneflies also fly in a vertical position). Begin by tying two coated threads along the shank to serve as tails and antennae. You can attach the ribbing thread before dubbing the abdomen, as long as you remember to start the first dubbing wrap behind the thread (to prevent slippage).

In the previous chapter, I mentioned the alternative method of employing the fold-over synthetic wing. For demonstration purposes, this style will be constructed with that method, but keep in mind that they are freely interchangeable, and you should use whichever you prefer. After dubbing and ribbing the abdomen, secure the wing material with wraps from the end of the abdomen to the eye of the hook. Attach the hackle to the rear of the thorax.

Dub the thorax, and wrap the hackle over the dubbing, tying it off at the front of the dubbing. Reverse-dub the head. Fold the forward half of the wing back, securing it with a narrow collar of thread and a whip-finish. Position the tails by spreading them with your thumbnail and setting them with a touch of Zap-A-Gap at their bases (this can also be done to the antennae). I like to touch a bit of cement to the tips of the thread, to prevent them from fraying with hard use.

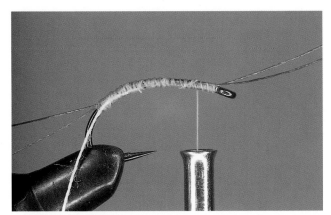

1. Attach ribbing thread and thread for tails and antennae to a caddis pupa hook.

2. Dub and rib abdomen. Tie the wing fibers down over the thorax, and attach the hackle to the rear of the thorax.

3. Dub the thorax, palmer hackle forward, and tie off. Reverse-dub head.

4. Tie down the forward half of the wing fibers, and trim wing.

Little Green Stonefly (Alloperla spp.)

Hook:	Mustad C49S, #14-16
Thread:	yellow 8/0
Tails/antennae:	coated gray 8/0 tying thread
Rib:	olive or yellow thread
Body:	bright olive or light green dry-fly dubbing
Wing:	light gray Hi-Vis
Hackle:	cream

Pattern notes: For reasons that I can't explain, I have never found the little green stoneflies (also called green or lime sallies) in the same concentrations encountered with the yellow varieties. Despite this, an imitation danced over shallow riffles or along the edges of the stream has been quite effective. On cool waters that fish well through the middle of the day, this tactic can drum up some summertime action when nothing else is happening.

*Yellow Sally (*Isoperla *spp.)*

Hook: Mustad C49S, #12-14
Thread: yellow 8/0
Tails/antennae: coated yellowish brown 6/0 tying thread
Rib: cream or yellow thread
Body: red, orange, and yellow (sequentially) or
                 all-yellow dry-fly dubbing
Wing: tan or light gray Hi-Vis
Hackle: cream or light ginger

Pattern notes: "Yellow sally" is a blanket term that fly fishers apply to any small yellow stonefly. These include yellow species of Chloroperlidae, as well as small species belonging to the Perlodidae and Perlidae families. A number of yellow sally imitations include a red butt that is described as an egg sac. Most of the stonefly egg sacs that I have seen were black, but some species of *Isoperla* do have reddish abdomens—perhaps the source of this attractive embellishment.

ADULTS
Style 2—Synthetic Stone

Synthetic Stone: (left) *Willowfly,* (right) *Snowfly.*

The cold-weather activities of the late-winter and early-spring stoneflies usually offer more measured, less frenetic dry-fly fishing than the summertime species. As a complement to this subdued egg-laying action, early-season conditions can conspire to encourage an atypical emergence on the water's surface, adding another dry-fly possibility. Rising water, which forces these stoneflies to emerge in the slower, warmer water of pools is often the cause of this anomaly. Under these circumstances, a flush-floating imitation of the adults can be more effective than a high-riding hackled fly. The Synthetic Stone is not limited to passive presentations, however, and another application of this style is to represent stonefly species that deposit their eggs by swimming across the surface, rather than fluttering above it.

Tying Sequence
A tailed version of the Synthetic Sedge, this fly can be tied on standard dry-fly hooks, but I prefer a straight-eye hook for the smaller sizes. As in the previous style, tie coated threads to the shank for tails and antennae. Then dub and rib the abdomen. This style demonstration also uses the alternative fold-over winging method, but either technique is acceptable.

After attaching the wing material, tie in a sparse clump of synthetic fibers across the shank with cross wraps of thread. Dub the thorax, and reverse-dub the head. Fold the forward half of the wing to the rear, and make the collar wraps to secure the wing. Whip-finish at the collar and cement. Set the position of the tails and antennae with Zap-A-Gap.

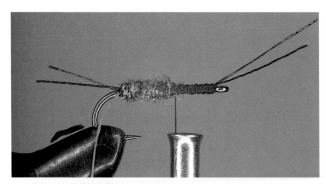

1. Tie in thread for tails and antennae. Attach rib, and dub abdomen.

2. After ribbing the abdomen, tie down wing fibers through the thorax area.

3. Tie in fiber-fan legs, and dub thorax. Reverse-dub head.

4. Fold back the forward half of the wing fibers, tie them down, and trim wing.

Willowfly (Taeniopteryx spp.)

Hook: Tiemco 101, #12-16
Thread: brown 8/0
Tails/antennae: coated brown 6/0 tying thread
Rib: gray or brown thread
Body: grayish brown dry-fly dubbing
Wing: gray Hi-Vis
Legs: gray or brown Hi-Vis

Pattern notes: *Taeniopteryx* hatches often reach their peak well before the early-season mayflies make an appearance. Under unseasonably warm late-winter or early-spring conditions, some species may have come and gone before the trout season opens. On the other hand, on streams that stay open year-round, these dark little stoneflies offer one of the best bets for preseason dry-fly action.

Snowfly (Allocapnia spp.)

Hook: Tiemco 101, #14-18
Thread: black 8/0
Tails/antennae: coated black 8/0 tying thread
Rib: gray or brown thread
Body: blackish brown dry-fly dubbing
Wing: black or gray Antron or Hi-Vis
Legs: black or brown Antron or Hi-Vis

Pattern notes: These "winter stoneflies" can be a real boon for nonskiing anglers who suffer from cabin fever. On streams that are open for winter fishing, they present the possibility of dry-fly fishing while snowbanks still surround the stream—a unique opportunity for the hopelessly addicted. A modest February thaw can produce hatches that are remarkably heavy, and revitalized trout enjoy this winter feast.

ADULTS
Style 3—Burnt Poly-Wing Stone ⓘ

Burnt Poly-Wing Stone: (left) *Early Brown Stonefly,* (right) *Freckled Stone.*

After perfecting the wing-making process that resulted in the Burnt Poly-Wing Dun, this was the next imitation to incorporate the wing. At first, I tied it as an alternative wing on the Synthetic Stone (a variation you should feel free to explore). Eventually, I added the thread legs and mono eyes that enhance this extremely accurate style. The choice to select this style over the previous one is usually based on two factors. Streams that receive heavy pressure, which consequently contain sophisticated trout, are obvious candidates for the more detailed tie. The other factor has more to do with the water type that the particular stonefly utilizes for emergence and oviposition. Slick currents or pools are situations where a more accurate representation can pay off. When both conditions are met, the choice is easy. Despite the level of detail incorporated into this fly, it is not very difficult to tie.

Tying Sequence

The first part of this fly is constructed on the same hook style and in the same manner as the Synthetic Stone. After attaching the coated thread for the tails and antennae, dub and rib the body. At the thorax, tie coated threads in place of the fiber-fan legs, and separate them with dubbing. Prepare a burnt poly wing by shaping in a

wing burner. Mayfly wing burners have an asymmetrical shape and are not the best tool for this process. It is possible to insert the poly yarn at a slight angle to compensate for the asymmetrical shape, but this is awkward and inconsistent. A better solution is either to reshape a commercial burner or to make your own (see chapter 3).

Tie in the prepared wing ahead of the front legs, and secure a pair of mono eyes on top. Cover the wraps with very thin dubbing. Fold the remainder of the poly yarn over the thorax, and tie it down with wraps behind the front legs. Apply the whip-finishing wraps in front of the legs, and trim the excess poly so that it tapers into the wing. Coat the head and pronotum, and set the legs, tails, and antennae as before.

1. Tie in thread for tails and antennae, attach rib, and dub abdomen.

2. After ribbing the abdomen, tie in thread legs at the thorax, and separate with dubbing.

3. Tie in burnt poly wing at the head, and attach melted mono eyes on top.

4. Fold back the forward portion of the wing, and tie it down behind and in front of the forward leg pair. Trim the excess poly at an angle.

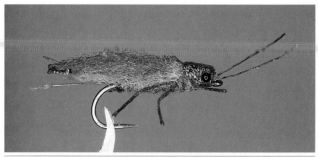

Early Brown Stonefly (Taeniopteryx nivalis)

Hook:	Tiemco 101, #14-16
Thread:	brown 8/0
Tails/antennae:	coated brown 6/0 tying thread
Rib:	gray or white thread
Body:	grayish brown dry-fly dubbing
Legs:	coated grayish brown sewing thread
Wing:	brownish gray poly yarn (burnt)
Eyes:	melted mono

Pattern notes: On limestone streams that receive a lot of preseason fly-fishing pressure, like the Yellow Breeches or Allentown's Little Lehigh, stoneflies are seldom considered by the mayfly- or midge-conscious anglers. But both streams have hatches of winter stoneflies (several species of *Taeniopteryx* and *Allocapnia* on the Breeches and *Allocapnia granulata* on the Little Lehigh). When these stoneflies bring fussy fish to the surface, an astute student of streamside entomology can have a field day with this imitation or a smaller darker version (for *Allocapnia*). The envy of adjacent anglers will be palpable, however, so tie up some extras to ease their pain.

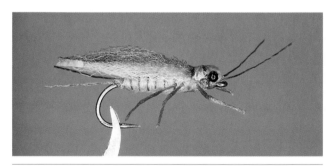

Freckled Stone (Perlesta placida)

Hook:	Tiemco 101, #14-16
Thread:	brown or yellow 8/0
Tails/antennae:	coated brown 6/0 tying thread
Rib:	brown thread
Body:	dirty yellow dry-fly dubbing
Legs:	coated yellowish brown sewing thread
Wing:	yellow poly yarn, tinted light brown except for edges
Eyes:	melted mono

Pattern notes: Called yellow sallies by most anglers, these little stoneflies are miniature members of the Perlidae family (which includes the large golden stones). Unlike most stoneflies that share this name, *P. placida* favors larger streams and rivers. They are perhaps the most common stonefly on the Yellow Breeches, where the adults can be found from June through August. Their enormous range covers eastern and central Canada and stretches south to Florida and Texas. Although they are nocturnal by habit, both the nymph and the dry can be effective around dusk.

ADULTS
Style 4—Extended Burnt Poly-Wing Stone Ⓐ

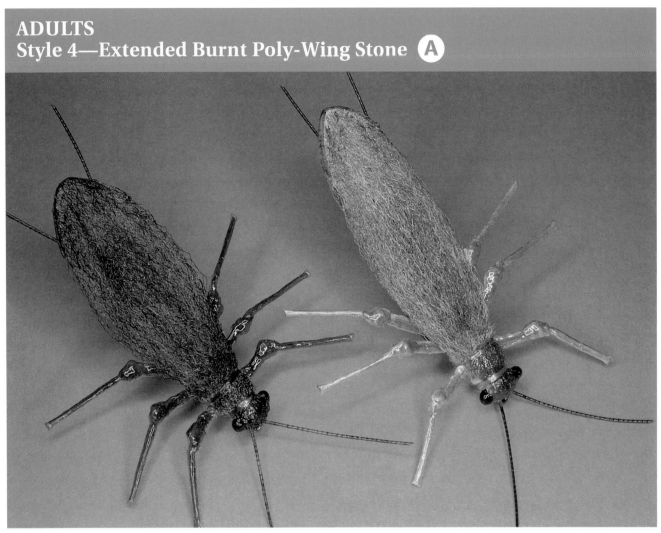

Extended Burnt Poly-Wing Stone: (left) *Embossed Stone,* (right) *Boreal Stone.*

Imitations of large adult stoneflies are standard fare in the West, where they are tied in anticipation of the premiere dry-fly extravaganzas of the season—the hatches of the Western salmonfly *(P. californica)* and the big golden stoneflies (*Calineuria californica* and *Hesperoperla pacifica*). In the East, where the big stoneflies have nocturnal habits, they are fished only by an intrepid few. The popular ties in either region tend to be heavily hackled hairwing flies. These work pretty well when actively fished in broken water. Offered as imitations of adults that are struggling in a quiet pocket behind an emergence site or on the slick water of unbroken runs, they are less convincing. Over time, heavy dry-fly pressure can also diminish the effectiveness of rough approximations. When a more precise copy of large stoneflies is required, the Extended Burnt Poly-Wing Stone excels at overcoming the resistance of critical, smooth-water trout. Use the bushy, suggestive patterns when fish are chasing active adults in fast water, but know that the biggest fish like to conserve en-

ergy, and this exacting imitation—presented quietly, with only an occasional twitch—is more suited to their temperament.

Tying Sequence
This fly uses the stonefly version of the needle-tied foam abdomen, so you may find it helpful to review the description of that process found in chapter 4. This extended body permits the use of an undersize standard dry-fly hook, rather than the larger and more obvious hooks required for conventional dressings. Cut the foam strips wider than the strips that are used for large mayfly bodies (such as the Extended Burnt Poly-Wing Drake). Another difference is that you tie the mono tails to the needle after the foam, separating the tails.

After attaching the foam strips and tails to the needle, wrap the abdomen with the true segmentation technique. When the segmentation is completed and the whip-finish is applied, remove the abdomen from the needle. Secure the extension to the hook with thread wraps and Zap-A-Gap. Tie the antennae to the front of the hook, and then attach each pair of the doubled knot-ted-thread legs, dubbing as you go.

Prepare a large burnt poly wing; then tie it to the hook ahead of the front legs. Tie a large pair of melted mono eyes on top of the wing wraps, and reverse-dub the head. Fold the excess poly back over the thorax and secure with pronotum wraps, behind and in front of the front leg pair. Whip-finish at the forward pronotum wraps. Cut the poly yarn at an angle behind the rear pronotum wraps (to blend with the wing), and coat the head and pronotum with Flexament.

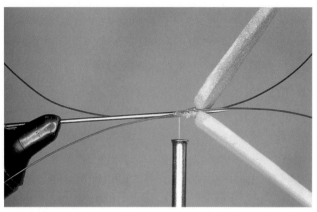

1. Attach foam strips to the needle, followed by the monofilament tails.

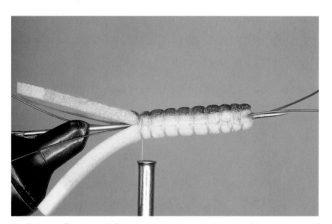

2. Wrap foam with true segmentation technique, and then apply whip-finish.

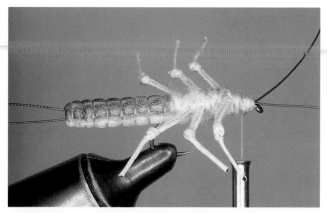

3. Secure completed abdomen to front hook, and tie in monofilament for the antennae. Tie in leg pairs, and dub thorax.

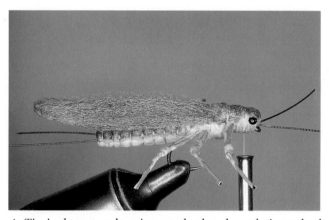

4. Tie in burnt poly wing at the head, and tie melted mono eyes on top. After dubbing the head, fold back forward half of the poly, and tie it down behind and in front of the forward leg pair. Trim the excess poly.

Embossed Stone (**Paragnetina media**)

Hook:	standard dry-fly, #10-12
Thread:	brown 6/0
Abdomen:	dark grayish brown over yellowish tan foam strips
Tails:	dark brown dyed mono (embossed)
Antennae:	dark brown dyed mono (embossed)
Legs:	coated yellowish brown heavy sewing thread (doubled), dark on top
Thorax:	yellowish tan dry-fly dubbing
Wing:	dark brownish gray poly yarn (burnt)
Eyes:	melted mono

Pattern notes: When hatches of this common stonefly reach their peak in early June, this adult imitation can offer explosive fishing at dusk or dawn. The early morning hours are probably better if pale evening dun *(E. dorothea)* or yellow quill *(E. vitreus)* hatches will be competing for the trout's attention (or yours) at dusk. Carry this pattern as an option in the evening, however, because the *dorothea* emergence is heavier on pools, and the fast-water yellow quill action is often unpredictable.

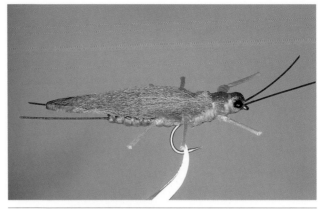

Boreal Stone (**Acroneuria lycorias**)

Hook:	standard dry fly, #10-12
Thread:	yellow or tan 6/0
Abdomen:	yellowish brown over yellow foam strips, darkened on top
Tails:	yellowish brown dyed mono (embossed)
Antennae:	brown dyed mono (embossed)
Legs:	coated brownish yellow heavy sewing thread (doubled), light brown marks
Thorax:	light yellow dry-fly dubbing
Wing:	tan poly yarn (burnt), gray and brown streaks
Eyes:	melted mono

Pattern notes: This stonefly can create extended dry-fly opportunities owing to the waters it favors. Populations are most common in cold, swift northern streams in the East, Midwest, and parts of Canada. These chilly waters allow a more gradual, spotty emergence that can last through a good part of the day. The emergence never rivals the density of Western salmonfly hatches, but it can provide exciting fishing amid boreal beauty.

ADULTS
Substyle 1a—Wriggling Burnt Poly-Wing Stone Ⓐ

Wriggling Burnt Poly-Wing Stone: (left) *Eastern Stonefly,* (right) *American Salmonfly.*

As good as the Extended Burnt Poly-Wing Stone is, I couldn't resist adding an extra enticement. Hinged dry flies are rare sights—in a fly box or on the water—and the urge to add a hinge to the previous style was uncontrollable. The fish that have seen this fly haven't exercised much restraint in response. I must say, though, that I consider it a dirty trick to expose ordinary trout to this extraordinary fly, and I do restrain myself. I learned, long ago, that one of the dangers inherent in developing extraordinary flies is that one is tempted to use them all the time. Fortunately, the time and effort invested in their construction usually serves as an adequate brake on that impulse. Overuse is a misapplication, and it's a fitting punishment when the fly is severed from the leader by a trout that could have been seduced by a lesser offering. Only the most demanding situations warrant extreme flies. Even the deadliest designs can be dulled to the point of ineffectiveness by overuse. Consider the way a

skilled hunter selects firearms—it is important to use enough gun but unsporting to use too much.

Tying Sequence
Tie the rear half of this fly in the same manner as the needle-tied extension on the previous design, except that you construct the abdomen forward on a hook (such as the Tiemco 200R or Daiichi 1270) rather than backward on a needle. This procedure is a little more awkward at the start, and a little easier to finish (the whip-finishing wraps are simplified by being at the front).

Once you complete the abdomen, cut the hook bend from the rear segment. Tie a poly yarn hinge cover slightly around the bend of the hook. I coat this with Flexament to keep it from interfering with the hinge. Attach the mono loop material on top of the hinge cover, and build up a spacer with dubbing. Slip the abdomen onto the mono, and secure and size the free end of the loop as with all previous hinged imitations.

You can now complete the forward half of the fly just like the Extended Burnt Poly-Wing Stone. After attaching the antennae, add the legs and thorax dubbing. Tie in the burnt poly wing, and affix the mono eyes on top. Fold back the extra poly, and tie it down with the pronotum wraps. Apply the whip-finish as before, trim the poly, and coat the head and pronotum with Flexament.

4. After dubbing the head, fold back forward half of the poly, and tie it down behind and in front of the forward leg pair. Trim excess poly.

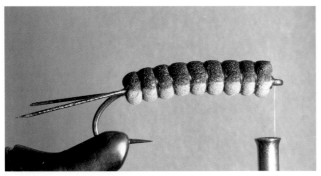

1. Tie foam strips near the bend of the rear hook, and attach monofilament tails on the sides. Wrap foam forward with the true segmentation technique, and apply whip-finish.

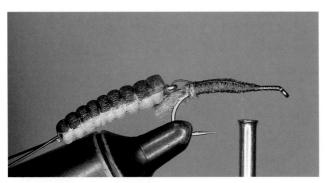

2. Tie a poly yarn hinge cover to the front hook, and attach completed abdomen with a mono loop.

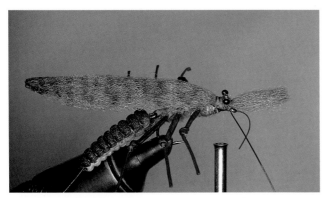

3. Tie in antennae, leg pairs, and thorax dubbing as before. Tie in burnt poly wing at the head, and wrap melted mono eyes on top.

Eastern Stonefly (Agnetina capitata)

Hooks:	Daiichi 1270, #12-14 (rear), and 2XL dry-fly, #10-12 (front)
Thread:	yellow or tan 6/0
Abdomen:	tannish yellow over light yellow foam strips, dark bars on top
Tails:	yellowish brown dyed mono (embossed)
Hinge cover:	light yellow poly yarn (coated)
Antennae:	light brown dyed mono (embossed)
Legs:	coated yellow heavy sewing thread (doubled), dark marks
Wing:	tan poly yarn (burnt), brown streaks
Eyes:	melted mono

Pattern notes: The classic Eastern creeper, *capitata* was listed in older texts under the genus names *Perla* or *Neophasganophora*. Whatever its label, it has been memorialized in everything from simple wet flies to unique nymph patterns by Preston Jennings, the Darbees, Art Flick, and Ernest Schwiebert. Imitations of the adults are less notable, but the opportunity to catch fast-water trout on the surface deserves a fly that respects this tradition. Dawn is the time, pocket water is the place, and this is the fly.

American Salmonfly (Pteronarcys dorsata)

Hooks:	Daiichi 1270, #10-12 (rear), and 2XL dry-fly, #8-10 (front)
Thread:	brown or rusty orange 0/0
Abdomen:	dark grayish brown over grayish tan foam strips
Tails:	dark brown dyed mono (embossed)
Hinge cover:	grayish tan poly yarn
Antennae:	dark brown dyed mono (embossed)
Legs:	coated grayish brown heavy sewing thread (doubled), dark on top with light brown or rusty orange accents (acrylic paint)
Wing:	grayish brown poly yarn (burnt), dark mottling
Eyes:	melted mono

Pattern notes: Even though this fly is effective during the nocturnal egg-laying activity, there are just too many hazards after dark to risk losing the fly on an errant cast. Consider waiting until the emergence reaches its seasonal peak (usually early June), and plan to arrive onstream while the adults are still fluttering in the morning air. The emergence will have subsided and the egg laying will be on the wane; but this pattern, wriggling on the surface, will tempt even overstuffed trout.

CHAPTER EIGHT

Baitfish

Rainbow Smelt.

MEDICINE FOR MINNOW-EATERS

Big fish eat little fish. Everyone knows this, but, if the ubiquitous Wooly Bugger is your favorite facsimile of the latter, you won't be prepared when the big piscivores get picky. Sure, the Wooly Bugger's a great fly—who could deny that? Whenever opportunistic fish are vulnerable to the hypnotic suggestion of movement, the Bugger trips the trigger. But no fly survives such popularity without suffering the dulling effects of overexposure. Good medicine can lose its effectiveness; overexposure breeds immunity, and sends us in search of more potent remedies. So it is with flies, and every season the next generation of mutant superbuggers is touted as irresistible. And they can be—briefly. Once the novelty of ostentatious display wears off, they are no better than the basic tie and often not as good. The original endures, but the rubber-legged, flash-bodied, cone-headed variety is probably a thing of the moment, awaiting the next aberration.

Beyond this cycle of endless pattern proliferation, many common baitfish beg the question of imitation. Trout that feed on abundant prey, whether bugs or minnows, are prone to fixation. When this occurs, specific characteristics trigger specific responses. If the treatment of caddisflies and stoneflies is often perfunctory, then the rendering of baitfish can be positively primitive. Curiously, the recent popular explosion that has occurred in saltwater fly fishing (which had no long-standing tradition of accurate imitation) has spawned a host of increasingly realistic baitfish patterns. These for fish whose exposure to the fly is negligible when compared to the harried trout. The upshot of this is that baitfish patterns designed for trout currently lag behind their upstart saltwater kin when it comes to accurate imitation.

The flies that begin the baitfish progressions were formulated with these thoughts in mind. The first fly shares some of the raw elements found in the basic Wooly Bugger, without any added gimmicks. The fly that begins the second series combines synthetic ingredients in the manner of more recent saltwater solutions. From these origins, the flies evolve into more specific and specialized compounds. The little fish these flies imitate fire predatory impulses in the big fish we all love to catch. When the small fry bring the behemoths out of hiding, you'll have the right remedy. The rest is up to you.

BOTTOMFISH
Style 1—Basic Bottomfish

Basic Bottomfish: (left) *Red-and-White Bottomfish*, (right) *Black Bottomfish*.

This Spartan style originated during my minimalist phase—a period in my early twenties when I did all of my trout fishing with only four flies. The Light Cahill and Henryville Special served for dry-fly fishing, and two variations of the Gold-Ribbed Hare's Ear were my only nymph imitations. At times, I found myself in want of a streamer of some sort, and this simple fly was created to occupy that empty niche. The phase didn't last long. I still have fond regard for those flies, but the simple streamer is the only fly that survived to be included in my fly boxes today. It has a broad, flattened shape suggestive of a sculpin, but it can be tied in any color or combination, from earthy, naturalistic shades to outlandishly bright attractor colors. The inverted tie helps to keep the fly out of trouble when bounced along the bottom, and the marabou tail and fins contribute movement even when the fly is drifting with the current.

Tying Sequence

Start with a standard 3X-long nymph/streamer hook (like the Daiichi 1720 or Tiemco 5263). Bind a twisted-wire weight to the top of the hook. It should cover the front two-thirds of the shank. Tie a whole small marabou feather (either a marabou "blood" or Chickabou) behind the weight in the vertical plane. I find it easier to handle these feathers when they are wet. Trim the butt to allow a tapered transition onto the weight.

Wrap a fat body of thick rabbit-fur dubbing forward to a point about one-third back from the eye of the hook. Tie in the marabou fins on either side of the dubbed body. Trim the feather butts, and dub a fat head. In order to prevent the dubbing wraps from slipping as they reach the end of the weight, you may find it helpful to fill the small gap at the front with a little dubbing before dubbing the rest of the head. Whip-finish at the eye and cement.

The finishing touch is to aggressively brush out the sides of the body and of the head with a Velcro dubbing brush, and trim them to a rounded taper toward the tail. A coating of Flexament on the top (which will become the underside of the finished fly) helps to hold the shape.

One additional suggestion that you may find useful: I usually leave all of the marabou feathers slightly long when tied to the hook, and singe them to length. I do this by pinching the feather between my fingers so that only the unwanted excess is exposed and touching a flame to the ends. I suppose a wing burner or some other aid could be used instead of your fingers. After burning, I brush the carbonized residue from the tips. The result is rounder and more attractive than a cut feather.

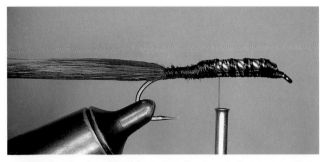

1. *Weight the hook with twisted wire tied on top of the shank, and tie in a marabou feather behind the wire.*

2. *Cover the rear two-thirds of the body with thick dubbing, and tie in marabou on the sides for the pectoral fins.*

3. *Build up the head with thick dubbing, and then apply whip-finish.*

4. *Brush out dubbing to the sides, trim to shape, and coat with Flexament on the underside.*

Red-and-White Bottomfish

Hook: Daiichi 1720, #6-10
Thread: white 6/0
Weight: twisted lead-free wire
Tail/fins: white marabou
Body: white and red (head) dubbing

Pattern notes: From pike spoons to bass poppers, red and white is an enduring color combination that seems to have universal appeal. In the semaphore of fishdom, white represents vulnerability and red, injury. To a predator, this distress signal demands prompt attention.

Black Bottomfish

Hook: Daiichi 1720, #4-10
Thread: black 6/0
Weight: twisted lead-free wire
Tail/fins: black marabou
Body: black dubbing

Pattern notes: In basic black, this is an all-purpose pattern. The larger sizes make exceptional night-fishing flies. By the way, if you'd like a really nice leech imitation, tie the marabou tail in the horizontal plane and omit the fins.

BOTTOMFISH
Style 2—Hardheaded Bottomfish ①

Hardheaded Bottomfish: (left) *Mottled Sculpin,* (right) *Slimy Sculpin.*

Sculpins are a common bottomfish in most trout streams. Regionally, they are known by such nicknames as bullheads, stargazers, and miller's thumbs. Because they lack a swim bladder, these homely little fish typically swim in short hops along the bottom. Sculpins have a reputation (perhaps undeserved) for eating trout eggs, and trout have a reputation (deserved) for eating sculpins. In this rough system of checks and balances, trout streams maintain their equilibrium, and the two fishes are cast in the aquatic equivalent of Tom-and-Jerry roles. The Hardheaded Bottomfish is a fly-tying cartoon of the Jerry-fish—a little cuter than the real fish, but the identity is unmistakable. Its distinguishing features are exaggerated, and it is designed to move in a sculpin-like way along the bottom. Hopping and taunting, it plays its little underwater game while waiting for Tom trout to pounce.

Tying Sequence

Turning the Basic Bottomfish into the Hardheaded Bottomfish is a process that happens after the fly exits the vise. The tying steps are the same, except that you use grizzly marabou for the tail and fins, and alternating bands of dubbing cover the body. At the conclusion of

the tying process, you have a Basic Bottomfish in the colors of a sculpin. It is important that you brush out the fur of the head and shape it carefully so that there are no gaps in its flattened, rounded outline.

After removing the fly from the vise, invert it and coat what is now the top of the head with Flexament. When dry, the top of the head receives another coating—this one of thickly applied five-minute epoxy. Because I don't like the shine of epoxy on this dull-hued imitation, I add a third coating of Testor's Dull Cote to give the head a matte finish. (This is a spray lacquer, so I squirt a little

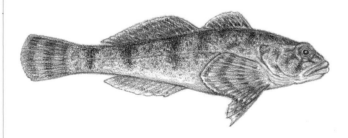

The mottled sculpin (C. bairdi) *is a common trout-stream species. Due to their lack of a swim bladder, sculpins move about in short hops along the bottom.*

into the plastic cap and apply with a brush.) Apply yellow eyes with black centers (acrylic paint) with round toothpicks cut to two different diameters. Apply a dome of five-minute epoxy over each.

1. Construct fly exactly the same as the Basic Bottomfish but use grizzly marabou for the tail and fins, and apply alternating bands of dark and light dubbing to the body.

Mottled Sculpin (Cottus bairdi)

Hook:	Daiichi 1720, #6-10
Thread:	tan 6/0
Weight:	twisted lead-free wire
Tail/fins:	tan grizzly marabou
Body:	tan and dark brown dubbing
Eyes:	yellow and black acrylic paint, epoxy

Pattern notes: This pattern suggests a common coloration of this species, but the appearance of sculpins is so variable that it may be considered as a color-specific rather than a species-specific pattern. I usually paint the belly of the fly with light-colored acrylic paint, but the trout will never see this if the fly is fished where it belongs—on the bottom.

2. After brushing out and trimming the body to shape, coat the underside of the body and the top of the head with Flexament.

Slimy Sculpin (Cottus cognatus)

Hook:	Daiichi 1720, #6-10
Thread:	brown 6/0
Weight:	twisted lead-free wire
Tail/fins:	reddish brown grizzly marabou
Body:	reddish brown and blackish brown dubbing
Eyes:	yellow and black acrylic paint, epoxy

Pattern notes: This is another common trout-stream species and another common color pattern. Distinguishing between *cognatus* and *bairdi* is pretty difficult to do by eye, and I fish these patterns interchangeably, based upon bottom color or the specimens I observe in the water I'm fishing. A slow drift with an occasional hop is usually more productive than active stripping in the conventional streamer style.

3. Then coat the top of the head with five-minute epoxy, followed by a coat of Testor's Dull Cote. Apply paint spots for eyes, and cover with a dome of epoxy.

BOTTOMFISH
Substyle 2a—Heavy Hardheaded Bottomfish

Heavy Hardheaded Bottomfish: (left) *Funereal Sculpin,* (right) *Sanguine Sculpin.*

The Hardheaded Bottomfish style can be tweaked in a number of ways to adjust its versatility and appeal. For use in deeper or faster water, adding external weight can enhance the bottom-hopping capabilities. This not only facilitates a deeper presentation, but also accentuates the headfirst diving action of the fly when it is released from a hop or twitch. During a drift, the weight allows the fly to wobble erratically as it rolls along the bottom. Another worthwhile modification is to complement the imitative qualities of the fly by borrowing a few traits of attractor flies. Flash is out of place on a sculpin imitation, but a hint of red to suggest injury, or a subtle shift of color and contrast to make the fly stand out, can be enticing.

Tying Sequence

The only change to the actual tying process for this variation is the addition of a small amount of red marabou tied in over the fins to suggest blood from the gills flowing over the fins. One pattern also alters the colors so that, instead of serving as camouflage, the contrast between them calls attention to the fly.

Both have half a tin shot glued to the belly of the fly near the head as additional weight. Either Zap-A-Gap or five-minute epoxy can secure the shot. Afterward, you can paint it with acrylic and coat it with either Flexament or epoxy, if you wish.

1. Follow the construction for the Basic Bottomfish, and tie in red marabou along side of the marabou fins.

2. Shape and coat as before, and add eyes.

3. Glue a tin shot half to the forward part of the underside, and paint shot and belly with acrylic paint (if you wish).

Sanguine Sculpin (Cottus *spp.*)

Hook:	Daiichi 1720, #6-10
Thread:	brown 6/0
Weight:	twisted lead-free wire (internal) and tin shot half (external)
Tail/fins:	reddish brown grizzly marabou
Body:	reddish brown and blackish brown dubbing
Bleeding gills:	red marabou
Eyes:	yellow and black acrylic paint, epoxy

Pattern notes: This bloody baitfish imitation is intended to simulate a wounded sculpin that can no longer resist the pull of the current. The added weight assists this presentation, creating a feeble, rock-and-roll action during the drift by interacting with the bottom or by varying tension on the line.

Funereal Sculpin (Cottus *spp.*)

Hook:	Daiichi 1720, #6-10
Thread:	white 6/0
Weight:	twisted lead-free wire (internal) and tin shot half (external)
Tail/fins:	grizzly marabou
Body:	dark gray and white dubbing
Eyes:	yellow and black acrylic paint, epoxy

Pattern notes: The shape and markings of a sculpin are retained in this pattern, but the unnatural colors create a contrast that is highly visible against most backgrounds and under most lighting conditions. Blurring the line between imitation and attraction, this fly can't hide from the fish.

BOTTOMFISH
Style 3—Wiggling Hardheaded Bottomfish Ⓐ

Wiggling Hardheaded Bottomfish: (left) *Margined Madtom,* (right) *Tesselated Darter.*

When we consider the baitfish that share the stream with trout, the fishes we tend to think about and seek to imitate are shiners, dace, and sculpins. But there are others whose images and distinctive habits are rarely represented by the contents of a fly box—miniature catfish known as madtoms, strange house-building stickle-backs, and the myriad, often colorful, little members of the perch family, the darters. The most extreme variation of the bottomfish theme, this style permits a very exacting imitation of such species. Not only does the fly appear realistic, but the construction also captures the movement and unique habits of the prey. The basic dubbed-fur body becomes a sculptural medium that

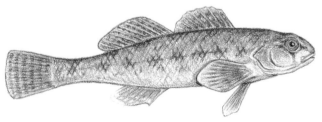

The tesselated darter (E. olmstedi, *pictured) and the johnny darter* (E. nigrum) *were formerly considered the same species. When at rest, darters usually sit on the bottom supported by their forward fins.*

can be shaped in individualized ways to match very different forms. Adding a hinge to these forms allows them to swim in a convincing fashion. Duplicating the fins is more than an imitative embellishment; they contribute subtle movement to the fly, or, in the example of the Tesselated Darter pattern, enable it to assume a characteristic posture when at rest.

Tying Sequence
The tying steps used to construct this style vary somewhat according to the baitfish being imitated, but the basic principles remain the same. Use two hooks: The rear one is a straight-eye hook (such as the Eagle Claw 214EL for larger sizes or the Tiemco 101 for smaller flies), and the front hook is a standard wet-fly hook (such as the Daiichi 1530 or Tiemco 3761). Begin the fly by wrapping the front two-thirds of the hook shank with weighting wire and tying the marabou tail behind the wire.

Wrap the body with thick dubbing. For the madtom imitation, tie two small clumps of marabou to either side near the front (for the pelvic fins), and wrap a small amount of dubbing ahead of these before whip-finishing. Omit these on the darter, and pick out the dubbing on the top and bottom to represent the rear dorsal and anal fins. Coat these with Flexament, and trim them to shape. On either fly, I paint the belly the appropriate color with acrylic and remove the hook bend.

Tie a twisted wire weight to the front hook. You may be tempted to simply wrap the wire around the hook, but that will reduce the effective gap on the finished fly. For the madtom imitation, tie a tuft of marabou slightly around the bend to become the dorsal fin. (This is not needed on the darter pattern because you will create its spiny dorsal by picking out the dubbing of the forebody.) Attach the mono loop material, build up a spacer of dubbing, and slip the rear portion onto the mono (remember that this is an inverted fly). Size and secure the loop as with previous hinged flies. The forward half is now completed in much the same manner as the previous styles, except for details that are specific to the particular fish being imitated.

On the madtom imitation, the pectoral fins are smaller and the head is not as broad as in the sculpin patterns. In addition, the long barbels, or whiskers, are represented by long biots tied forward on either side of the hook eye. Similarly, tie coated threads (two on the nose and four on the chin) forward to become the smaller barbels. Then fold back the biots and the threads, and make the finishing wraps behind the hook eye to position the barbels.

For the darter pattern, tie in two thin slivers of coated grizzly marabou below the pectoral fins to become the pelvic fins, which support the front end of the fly at rest (mimicking the darter's distinctive posture). Do not brush out the head and forebody of the darter in the manner of previous patterns, but retain a rounded, dartlike shape. Pick out the representation of the spiny, front dorsal fin, and coat, and trim it, as with the fins on the rear half of the fly.

Add external weight to either fly by gluing half a tin shot to the underside of the fly. For the darter pattern, position this weight farther back, behind the stiffened pelvic fins. This allows the fly to perform its trick of settling to the bottom perched on its forward fins. While you can use round or egg-shaped shot interchangeably for most external weighting, an egg-shaped half (with the wide end forward) works best for the darter imitation. After affixing the shot, paint the belly of the fly. Brushing a little Flexament on the body prior to duplicating the markings of the darter will prevent the marker from bleeding.

1. Attach a marabou tail to weighted rear hook.

2. Cover most of body with thick dubbing. Tie in a marabou clump on both sides near the front of the hook, and wrap thick dubbing up to the eye of the hook.

3. After attaching a twisted wire weight to the front hook, tie in a marabou clump slightly around the bend. Attach the completed rear segment with a monofilament loop.

4. Complete the forward half of the fly like a slimmed down version of the Heavy Hardheaded Bottomfish, but add biot whiskers and thread barbels at the front.

Margined Madtom (Notorus insignus)

Hooks:	Eagle Claw 214EL, #10 (rear), and Daiichi 1530, #6 (front)
Thread:	brown 6/0
Weight:	lead-free wire (internal) and tin shot half (external)
Tail/fins:	dark brown (tail/dorsal) and light brown (pelvic/pectoral) marabou
Body:	dark reddish brown dubbing, off-white belly (acrylic)
Whiskers:	dark brown biots
Barbels:	coated brown (upper) and off-white (lower) sewing thread
Eyes:	yellow and black acrylic paint, epoxy

Pattern notes: This little catfish is the only common madtom species in the trout streams I frequent. It is a safe bet that the trout have never seen its imitation before, and a novel fly can stimulate trout that have grown apathetic toward standard streamers. Because madtoms seldom expose themselves in the harsh light of day, low-light periods are prime times for this pattern.

Tesselated Darter (Etheostoma olmstedi)

Hooks:	Tiemco 101, #10-12 (rear), and Daiichi 1530, #8-10 (front)
Thread:	tan 6/0
Weight:	lead-free wire (internal) and tin shot half (external)
Tail/ pectoral fins:	tan grizzly marabou
Body/dorsal and anal fins:	tan dubbing, off-white belly (acrylic), brown marks
Pelvic fins:	coated grizzly marabou
Eyes:	yellow and black acrylic paint, epoxy

Pattern notes: Darters favor slower water than sculpins, often tending to be pool dwellers. Like sculpins, their swim bladders are absent (or underdeveloped), contributing to the movement for which they were named. While it lacks the bright colors of many darter species, this pattern matches the most common darter in many Pocono and Cumberland Valley streams. The very similar dark-mottled species, the johnny darter *(Etheostoma nigrum)*, is another common trout-stream darter.

SCHOOLFISH
Style 1—Synthetic Schoolfish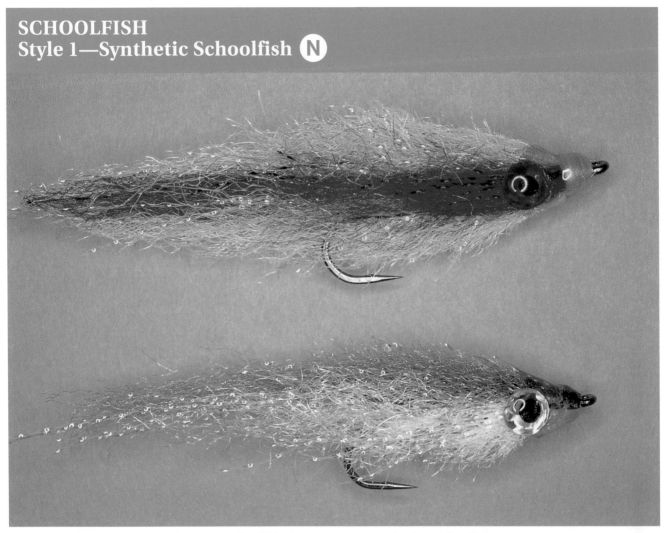

Synthetic Schoolfish: (top) *Mickey Finn Schoolfish,* (bottom) *Olive-and-White Schoolfish.*

The roots of this style reach all the way back to simple saltwater streamers made of bucktail. Saltwater fly tiers wanted a longer, deeper-bodied fly and began to stack clumps of bucktail along the hook shank to achieve this result. Joe Brook's Blonde series and the Keys Hi-Tie are examples of this approach. It was the much more recent saltwater designs of Enrico Puglisi, however, that demonstrated how this old technique, combined with modern synthetics, could produce remarkable results. Puglisi's synthetic-fiber imitations of menhaden, mackerel, herring, sardines, and anchovies are part of a larger trend toward more realistic baitfish flies for the salt. On the freshwater scene, simple, flashy streamers constructed with the same techniques can suggest common trout stream minnows such as shiners, chubs, and dace. Many traditional attractor patterns can also be translated into brilliant synthetic versions through this style of tying.

Tying Sequence

Start with a straight-eye streamer hook (such as the Daiichi 1750 or Tiemco 9395) that has been bent upward slightly ahead of the center. This bend enhances the action and the stability of the fly. Wrap weighting wire so that it extends an equal distance on either side of the keel-shape bend. Tie the belly-color synthetic fibers and a few strands of Krystal Flash at the rear, butting against the weighting wire. Add the back-color fibers and flash strands on top of that. (The Mickey Finn pattern has red fibers and flash sandwiched between a top and bottom bundle of yellow fibers and flash.)

Continue adding successive bundles of fiber and flash along the shank to build the body. The sequence I prefer is to tie the back bundle, then the belly, followed by the sides. Repeat this sequence until you fill the shank. You can tie in each bundle separately, but I prefer to use a version of the fold-over technique. Tie in the back bundle so that the fibers project fore and aft of the tie in point. Tie the belly bundle underneath the hook in the same way. Wrap thread over both bundles to the point where the next group would be tied in if you were applying separate bundles. Fold back the forward part of the top and bottom bundles, and wrap thread over the fold to hold the bundles to the rear. Tie the side bundle to the near side, and fold it back along the far side, wrapping over the fold (the same way that you tied fiber wing cases to several pupal styles in chapter 6). While this process is a little complicated to describe, it is faster than tying in separate bundles. It also means that two bundles are stacked top and bottom for every one on the side. This is an appropriate distribution of materials.

Once you reach the front of the hook, shape the contours of the head with thread, and apply a whip-finish. Trim the fly with scissors until you achieve the desired shape. Coat the head with five-minute epoxy or several coats of Flexament. Color the top of the head with marker to match the back of the fly, and add plastic eyes with epoxy or Zap-A-Gap.

1. Tie the back and belly fiber and flash bundles to the rear of the bent and weighted hook.

2. Add the back fiber and flash bundle followed by the belly bundle and then the sides.

3. Continue adding back, belly, and side bundles until the hook shank is filled.

4. Shape the head with thread, and then trim the fly to shape. Coat the head with thick Flexament or five-minute epoxy (color the top of the head if needed). Glue plastic eyes to the sides of the head.

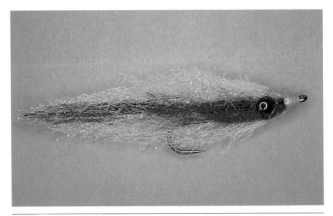

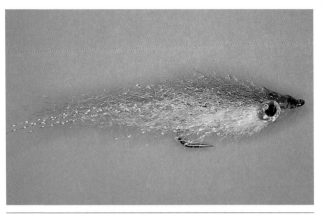

Mickey Finn Schoolfish

Hook:	Daiichi 1750, #4-10 (bent)
Thread:	yellow 6/0
Weight:	lead-free wire
Back:	yellow Hi-Vis and Krystal Flash
Belly:	yellow Hi-Vis and Krystal Flash
Sides:	red Hi-Vis and Krystal Flash
Eyes:	red 3-D Hologram Eyes

Pattern notes: An old, but enduring bucktail pattern popularized by John Alden Knight, the original continues to be an effective fly. This updated interpretation adds synthetic sparkle and appropriately bloodshot eyes to the bright colors of the bucktail named for a spiked drink. This pattern, like its namesake, is usually at its best as an early-spring or late-fall attractor.

Olive-And-White Schoolfish

Hook:	Daiichi 1750, #4-10 (bent)
Thread:	white 6/0
Weight:	lead-free wire
Back:	olive Hi-Vis and Krystal Flash
Belly:	white Hi-Vis and pearl Krystal Flash
Sides:	white Hi-Vis and pearl Krystal Flash
Eyes:	silver or gold 3-D Hologram Eyes

Pattern notes: This more subtle and imitative application of the Synthetic Schoolfish style is suggestive of a number of trout-stream minnows. In particular, it is an effective imitation of the important, fast-water species, the longnose dace *(Rhinicthys cataractae)*, which is found almost everywhere in trout country. In the larger sizes, this fly is a decent smelt imitation. Tied with green Hi-Vis and Krystal Flash instead of olive, it is a good match for the emerald shiner *(Notropis atherinoides)*.

SCHOOLFISH
Style 2—Tailed Synthetic Schoolfish ①

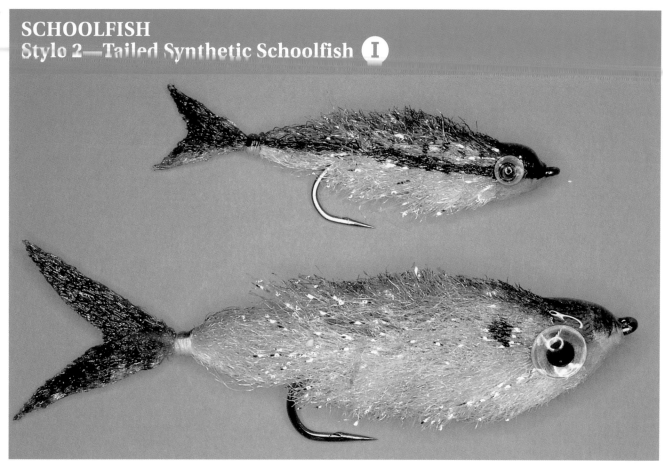

Tailed Synthetic Schoolfish: (top) *Blacknose Dace,* (bottom) *Alewife.*

As a young angler, I once watched an old-school bait fisherman use his split-cane fly rod to roll a salted minnow along the bottom of the Yellow Breeches with great skill. He was deadly, and I have since wondered why streamers aren't more often fished in the same manner. I suppose that one reason, aside from the absence of a fishy smell, is that traditional feather-wing or bucktail streamers lose some of their effectiveness when

they are not actively stripped. But the more aggressive presentation of streamers goes stale rather quickly with prolonged exposure. This decline in potency can be accelerated in waters where the fish are also regularly exposed to similar tactics employed by hardware anglers using spinners. The old-timer's more subtle and vulnerable presentation, however, coupled with a more convincing imitation, is a very productive way to seduce fish

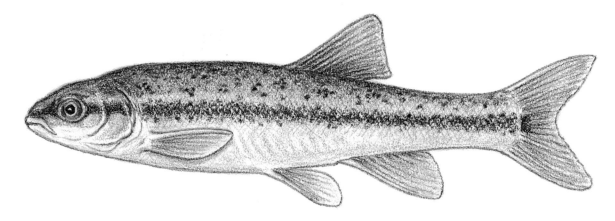

*The blacknose dace (*R. atratulus, *pictured) is a common and classic trout-stream baitfish. Its cousin, the longnose dace (*R. cataractae), *is a widespread species that favors fast water.*

that have learned to shun the more blatant approaches. The Tailed Synthetic Schoolfish works well when stripped in the conventional streamer fashion, but my favorite tactic is to use it as a synthetic substitute for a salted minnow—in tribute to the masterful old angler who showed me how to do it.

Tying Sequence

This style uses the same bent and weighted hooks as the prior style. You also construct the body in the same manner, except that you assemble the shaped tail section with a simple needle-tying procedure (see chapter 4 for additional details).

Lash the back and belly fiber bundles (two colors for the dace pattern and three for the alewife) to a needle, and apply the whip-finish over the thread wraps. After removing the wrapped bundles from the needle, coat the wraps and the fibers on one side of the wraps with Flexament, and flatten them. When the tail is dry, trim it to shape, and color it with marker. Also color the top of the wrap to match the back fibers.

After bending and weighting the hook shank, attach the tail section to the rear with the fibers butting against the weighting wire. Tie the successive back, belly, and side bundles along the hook as before. When you have tied in the last bundles, shape the head with thread, whip-finish, and trim the fly to shape.

To finish the fly, coat and color the head, and attach the eyes. You can mark the more detailed and specific patterns to match the species being imitated with spots, stripes, and other accents with marker. A little Flexament brushed along the sides gives the fly a tighter shape and aids in applying the markings.

1. Wrap fiber bundles on a needle, and whip-finish. Coat one end of the wrapped fiber bundle with Flexament, flatten, and trim to shape.

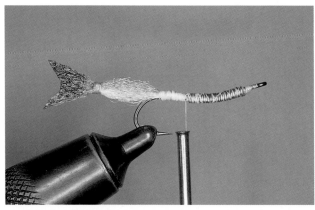

2. Attach the finished tail section to the rear of the bent and weighted hook.

3. Proceed to cover the hook shank with back, belly, and side fiber and flash bundles.

4. Shape the head, and trim the fly to shape. Coat the head and add whatever markings are necessary. Attach plastic eyes.

Blacknose Dace (Rhinicthys atratulus)

Hook: Daiichi 1750, #8-10 (bent)
Thread: white 6/0
Weight: lead-free wire
Tail section: brown over white Hi-Vis, tail tinted gray
Back: brown Hi-Vis and silver Krystal Flash, black specks
Belly: white Hi-Vis and pearl Krystal Flash
Sides: tan Hi-Vis and silver Krystal Flash, black stripe
Eyes: yellow or gold 3-D Hologram Eyes

Pattern notes: This is the classic trout-stream minnow, immortalized in bucktail, marabou, and more recently, by Clouser Minnow versions. All of these flies are effective, but none is as convincing as this pattern when presented with a slow, teasing drift along the bottom. As the drift works its way toward the tail of a pool, the fly is eased into action, as though the little dace had recovered its equilibrium and was struggling to avoid being swept over the brink.

Alewife (Alosa pseudoharengus)

Hook: Daiichi 1750, #2-6 (bent)
Thread: white 6/0
Weight: lead-free wire
Tail section: blue over light gray over white Hi-Vis, tail tinted gray
Back: blue Hi-Vis and Krystal Flash, top darkened
Belly: white Hi-Vis and pearl Krystal Flash
Sides: light gray Hi-Vis and silver Krystal Flash, black spot behind eye
Eyes: silver 3-D Hologram Eyes

Pattern notes: Alewives are important forage fish for big trout and salmon in large lakes and rivers. When alewives spill from the Cannonsville Reservoir into the West Branch of the Delaware, trout feast on the small shad, and an accurate imitation has a distinct advantage over the White Marabous and Wooly Buggers offered by most anglers on this popular stream. On the Great Lakes and on Finger Lakes such as Cayuga and Seneca, this pattern is exceptional for tempting trout and salmon, especially when alewives crowd the lakeshores and tributaries as they prepare to spawn in the spring.

SCHOOLFISH
Substyle 2a—Inverted Tailed Synthetic Schoolfish Ⅰ

Inverted Tailed Synthetic Schoolfish: (left) *Spottail Shiner,* (right) *Yellow Perch.*

As you probably know by now, I am a stream angler, by preference and disposition, but I also like variety in my fly fishing. Big waters present interesting challenges and can offer big fish as a reward for solving their problems. They can also be a way of escaping pressure by virtue of their size alone. In big-water situations, whether deep rivers or large lakes, there are times when a heavy fly is beneficial. Heavy flies can quickly penetrate to depths that are rarely encountered on small streams and ponds. A heavy fly can also help to represent the habits of forage fish that tend to school near the bottom, such as yellow perch. When schoolfish suspend over deep water, a heavy fly can be useful for reaching their location and for keeping the fly in that area. The Inverted Tailed Synthetic Schoolfish is a heavy baitfish imitation that is designed for big-water applications. It is wrapped with weighting wire, but most of its weight and its action comes from the metal barbell eyes that keep it diving headfirst toward the bottom whenever it is not under tension from the line.

Tying Sequence

This upside-down version of the Tailed Synthetic Schoolfish uses a standard, down-eye, nymph/streamer hook such as the Daiichi 1720 or Tiemco 5263. The down-eye

becomes an up-eye when you invert the fly, which is advantageous for the jiglike action of this fly. There is no need to bend this hook because the heavy barbell eyes provide the orientation.

After gluing plastic eyes to the ends of the machined metal barbells (Real Eyes) with epoxy or Zap-A-Gap, secure them with cross wraps of thread and Zap-A-Gap to the top of the shank (which will be the underside of the inverted fly). Wrap weighting wire behind the eyes through the midsection of the hook shank. Prepare the shaped tail section the same as before—just remember that you are constructing an inverted fly when you tie it to the hook.

Tie fiber bundles along the shank (as before) until you reach the barbell-eye position. Tie in full-length bundle of fibers by its middle to become the pectoral fins. Leave these fibers long so they can be held out of the way as you trim the body to shape. Wrap a length of red Estaz (or similar sparkle chenille) behind the eyes over the fin-fiber tie-down wraps.

When adding the fiber bundles that fill out the head in front of the eyes, a gap develops where the barbell eyes hold the belly fibers away from the body. I solve this problem by tying the belly fibers down behind and in front of the eyes (Clouser-style) and then folding the forward portion of the fibers back to cover the wraps. Apply Zap-A-Gap in the notch between the eyes, and press the folded fibers into the glue, filling the gap. Tie in the back fibers near the front (note that you do not need side fibers to complete the head in this style). Shape the head with thread, and whip-finish it. Trim the body, followed by the pectoral fins. Coat the head, and apply markings as with the previous style.

1. Tie the barbell eyes to the hook, and wrap weighting wire behind them. Construct the tail section as before, and tie it in (upside down) behind the weighting wire.

2. Add back, belly, and side fiber and flash bundles to a point a little behind the barbell eyes. Tie in a long fiber strand for the pectoral fins, and wrap red Estaz behind the eyes.

3. Finish the head with back and belly bundles, and shape with thread. Trim the fly to shape, and then trim the pectoral fins. Coat the head, and add markings.

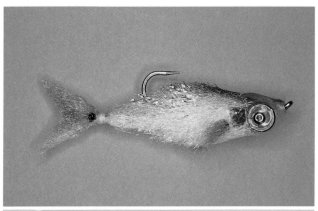

Spottail Shiner (Notropis hudsonius)

Hook:	Daiichi 1720, #6-10
Thread:	white 6/0
Weight:	lead-free wire and Real Eyes barbells
Tail section:	gray over white Hi-Vis, tail tinted gray except for lower edge, dark spot at base
Back:	gray Hi-Vis and pearl Krystal Flash, top darkened
Belly:	white Hi-Vis and pearl Krystal Flash
Sides/fins:	gray (fins) and light gray Hi-Vis and silver Krystal Flash
Gills:	red Estaz
Eyes:	yellow or gold 3-D Hologram Eyes (glued to barbells)

Pattern notes: These large-eyed shiners are a very common baitfish in lakes and rivers. Their range extends throughout much of the East, Midwest, and into Canada. This pattern was originally designed as a tool to reach trout feeding on schools of these shiners in deep lakes, but it is also effective in the deep pools and runs of large rivers like the Delaware. Schools of spottail shiners are often found over gravelly shoals in late spring, where trout, perch, and smallmouth bass take advantage of their abundance.

Yellow Perch (Perca flavescens)

Hook: Daiichi 1720, #2-6
Thread: white 6/0
Weight: lead-free wire and Real Eyes barbells
Tail section: olive over yellow Hi-Vis, tail tinted olive, black bars
Back: olive Hi-Vis and Krystal Flash, black bars
Belly: yellow (rear) and white (front) Hi-Vis
Sides/fins: orange (fins) and yellow Hi-Vis and Krystal Flash
Gills: red Estaz
Eyes: yellow or gold 3-D Hologram Eyes (glued to barbells)

Pattern notes: During a visit to the Royal Coachman fly shop in Skaneateles, New York, I found Mike DeTomaso, proprietor and master angler, tying a Clouser-style bucktail imitation of a yellow perch—a primary forage fish in Skaneateles Lake. When he finished, he gave the fly to me, and I keep it in a box of fly-fishing mementos. This is my version, and, while I tied it with the big lake's rainbows and landlocked salmon in mind, it has also enticed many pugnacious, hard-pulling smallmouth bass.

SCHOOLFISH
Style 3 — Wiggle-Tailed Synthetic Schoolfish A

Wiggle-Tailed Synthetic Schoolfish: (left) *Brown Trout Parr,* (right) *Rainbow Smelt.*

It takes an exceptional purpose to justify the extra time required to construct this exceptionally detailed imitation. The two patterns described here were conceived for very specific and personally significant missions.

I have long entertained a quixotic quest for landlocked salmon. It is much like the obsession that some have for the regal, sea-run variety, but the landlock is more blue-collar, more of a people's fish. The Rainbow Smelt pattern is like a synthetic Sancho Panza, serving as my squire in that adventure. There are only a couple of places in Pennsylvania where these fish can be found. Harvey's Lake, in Luzerne County, is one of these, and it is only a short drive from my former Pocono home. Better opportunities exist in a few of New York's Finger Lakes, such as Cayuga, where I caught my first landlock on a fly. Smelt are first-line forage for the salmon in both of these lakes.

The other mission is to test the upper size limit of the wild brown trout that occupy my favorite stream. The choice of a small trout as the model for the fly that would assist in that research was motivated by two intriguing events. One was the capture, on that same stream, of a wild rainbow (an unusual event in itself) that bore the unmistakable imprint of a huge trout's jaws on either side of its body. The other occurred on the Lit-

tle Lehigh, when an enormous brown engulfed a little specimen of the same species that I was dragging toward a hasty release. The monster carried off its hapless kin and all of my fly line before the link between me and this cannibalistic assault was severed. I figured that if big trout were going to bite little ones, it would only be fitting if one of those innocent victims bit back.

Tying Sequence
For this hinged, two-part version of the Tailed Synthetic Schoolfish, use an Aberdeen hook (such as the Eagle Claw 214EL) for constructing the rear portion and a bent

Little trout parr, like this baby brookie, can be prey for their larger kin. Imitating them is one way to turn the tables on the neighborhood bullies.

1. *Tie a back fiber bundle to the top of the hook, wrapping from the middle of the hook shank to the eye. Tie a belly fiber bundle underneath the hook, wrapping through the forward third to the eye. Trim some of the fibers from the rear portion of the top bundle to thin it.*

2. *Shape the adipose and anal fins by coating the rear fibers with Flexament and trimming them to shape. Divide the forward sections of the bundles, and fold them to the rear around the fins, tying them down at the back of the hook. Coat and flatten the tail section, and trim it to shape.*

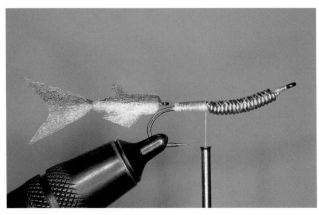

3. *Attach the completed tail section to a bent and weighted hook with a mono loop.*

4. *Add a back, belly, and side fiber and flash bundle, followed by the dorsal and pelvic fin strands. Continue adding bundles up to the head position, and add the pectoral fin strands. Wrap red Estaz for the gills, and add the final bundles at the head.*

5. *Shape the head with thread, and trim the fly to shape. Coat and trim the fins, and coat the head.*

6. *Add paint or markings and the plastic eyes.*

and weighted straight-eye streamer hook (such as the Daiichi 1750 or Tiemco 9395) for the front section.

After covering the rear hook shank with thread, wrap a bundle of back fibers down from about the middle of the shank to the hook eye so that fibers project fore and aft of the wrap. Tie on the belly fibers under the hook slightly ahead of the beginning of the previous wraps. (The exact distance depends on the desired shape of the anal fin—farther back for the narrower fin of the trout and farther forward for the wider fin of the smelt.) Shape the adipose fin by trimming away some of the rear-facing back fibers, coating the remaining fibers with Flexament and trimming the fin to shape. Shape the anal fin the same way, but do not remove fibers before coating. Flatten the fin before trimming it to shape.

Once you have shaped the fins, divide and fold the forward section of the back fibers to the rear around the adipose fin. Tie these fibers down at the rear of the hook. Divide, fold, and tie the belly fibers the same way. Make a whip-finish at the rear of the fly. Coat the tail fibers and finishing wraps with Flexament, and shape the tail as with the other tailed styles. Remove the hook bend.

Tie monofilament to the rear of the bent and weighted front hook to form the connecting loop. Build up thread over the tie-down wraps to serve as a spacer between the sides of the mono loop. Slip the completed tail section onto the mono and secure and size the loop as in all previous hinged styles.

Tie the first back, belly, and side bundles around the hook. Tie the bundle that forms the dorsal fin in front of these. (I usually coat and trim one end of this bundle prior to tying it in.) Tie in the long bundle that forms the pelvic fins by its middle in front of the dorsal fin. Stack back, belly, and side bundles forward to the rear of the head, and attach another long bundle there for the pectoral fins. Wrap red Estaz for the gills, followed by the back, belly, and side bundles that form the head. Wrap thread to finish the head, and make a whip-finish at the eye of the hook. Trim the body to shape, then coat and trim the remaining fins, and coat the head.

After brushing a little Flexament along the sides, apply markings, and in the case of the smelt imitation, paint the cheeks and stripes with silver model paint (Testor's). Attach plastic eyes with epoxy or Zap-A-Gap to finish the fly.

Brown Trout Parr (Salmo trutta)

Hooks:	Eagle Claw 214EL, #10 (rear), and Daiichi 1750, #4-6 (front)
Thread:	white 6/0
Tail section:	brown over white Hi-Vis, anal fin tinted orange, adipose accented with red
Weight:	lead-free wire
Back/ dorsal fin:	brown Hi-Vis, top darkened, black spots
Belly:	white Hi-Vis
Sides:	tan Hi-Vis and yellow Krystal Flash, black and red spots, purple parr marks
Pectoral/ pelvic fins:	orange Hi-Vis
Gills:	red Estaz
Eyes:	yellow or gold 3-D Hologram Eyes

Pattern notes: Using an imitation of a trout to catch a trout is nothing new. Some old wet flies even imitated trout parts—the Trout Fin, Brook Fin, and Bergman Fontinalis were imitations of a brook trout's fin. (George La Branche made some amusing comments about these flies in *The Dry Fly and Fast Water*.) There's a classic streamer pattern called the Brook Trout that featured red-and-blue painted spots on its feather wings. Later, Pennsylvania's own Sam Slaymaker produced the flies in his Little Trout series, which are still tied and fished by anglers hoping to incite a cannibal trout. The Brown Trout Parr is my entry in this odd category. It is a handsome pattern, suitable for framing, but it looks best clamped in the kype of a ferocious brown.

Rainbow Smelt (Osmerus mordax)

Hooks: Eagle Claw 214EL, #8-10 (rear), and Daiichi 1750, #2-4 (front)

Thread: white 6/0

Tail section: olive over white Hi-Vis, tail tinted grayish olive, anal fin tinted gray, side tinted pink with silver stripe (model paint)

Weight: lead-free wire

Back/
dorsal fin: olive Hi-Vis and Krystal Flash, top darkened

Belly: white Hi-Vis and pearl Krystal Flash

Sides: pink Hi-Vis and pearl Krystal Flash, silver stripe and cheeks (model paint)

Pectoral/
pelvic fins: gray Hi-Vis, tinted light olive

Gills: red Estaz

Eyes: yellow or gold 3-D Hologram Eyes

Pattern notes: Classic New England streamers recall the glory days of Eastern fly fishing—days of rustic camps on wilderness waters and casting or trolling beautiful feather-wing flies from wooden canoes in pursuit of huge brook trout and acrobatic landlocked salmon. Names of tiers like Herb Welch and Carrie Stevens and names of waters like Sebago, Kennebago, Moosehead, Richardson, Rangeley, Parmachenee, Cupsuptic, and Mooselookmeguntic are forever tied to the romance of the region. On many of the fabled waters, the thing that fueled the trout and salmon, inspired the famous and forgotten tiers, and ultimately drove the development of the streamer fly was the rainbow smelt. Those days are gone, but wherever big trout and salmon chase rainbow smelt, there is still a chance to recapture a moment of that glory. In those places, and even in this very modern fly, a personal piece of that heritage survives in a different day and for a different generation of fly fishers.

GENERALIZED EASTERN EMERGENCE TABLE

There are so many problems inherent in assembling aquatic insect emergence charts that I considered avoiding the issue entirely. I contemplated ways of adjusting the tables so that they would be useful to anglers in different parts of the country, at different latitudes, or on different types of waters. While such adaptations are possible, much of that work would inevitably be based on secondhand knowledge. In the end, I decided to simply record the experiences I have had with the hatches I fish.

These tables are based on scattered and sundry notes that I have assembled over many years—some are more than thirty years old and others are of fairly recent vintage. Those notes reflect the hatches of my home waters in the Cumberland Valley and the Poconos primarily, but they are also drawn from places that I fish regularly in other parts of Pennsylvania and New York. Even within this range, there is considerable variation in the timing of these hatches. Because the waters that I know best range roughly from the Catskills to southern Pennsylvania, I have attempted to split the difference between these extremes. This means that the chart is most accurate for the Pocono region. Of course, not all of these hatches are found in the Poconos, but most are, and that region serves as a convenient and familiar baseline for comparison to other regions.

For example, about a month separates the typical peak emergence of the early-season Hendrikson hatch (*E. subvaria*) in southern Pennsylvania (mid-April) and the northern Catskills (mid-May). The timing of the peak on Pocono streams is usually midway between the two (around the end of April or beginning of May). Waters north of the Catskills will see hatches peak later (late May or even early June), and waters south of Pennsylvania will peak earlier (early April). A similar pattern exists as one moves north and south in the Midwest. This would seem to offer an easy way of adjusting the charts for most parts of the East and Midwest, but there's a catch.

The difference in peak hatch timing between these regions diminishes as midseason approaches. Consider that the July peak of the yellow Hex hatch (*H. rigida*) on the Finger Lakes in central New York is virtually identical to the peak of the hatch on the Yellow Breeches in south-central Pennsylvania. Similarly, the late-July peak of the dark olive morning dun hatch (*D. lata*) in the Poconos is approximately the same as it is in Maine or Michigan. This doesn't mean that regional adjustment of this chart is impossible, it just means that early-season hatches (April and May) will vary more than later-season hatches (July and August).

Prevailing weather conditions and variations in water type can be just as significant as the variations from region to region. Unseasonably warm or cool weather can shift a hatch as much as a week or more. Water temperature differences within a region or even within the same watershed can have a remarkably dramatic effect. For example, the olive morning dun (*D. cornuta*) typically reaches its peak on the lower Brodheads around the end of May. But if you follow that same hatch into the headwaters, you'll find it peaks around mid-July. That's a month-and-a-half difference in about twenty miles!

Tailwaters with unusual flow and temperature regimes can also influence hatching schedules in surprising ways. On the West Branch of the Delaware, cold water releases often increase dramatically in early June during hot, dry seasons. Three insect species that are affected by these releases are the aforementioned olive morning dun, the pale evening dun *(E. dorothea)*, and the yellow quill *(E. vitreus)*. The cold water interrupts these hatches, and they return later on revised schedules. While the yellow quill is normally an evening hatch that peaks in June, I have fished fine hatches of this mayfly on mid-September afternoons on the West Branch. The pale evening dun, which usually hatches around dusk in June, returns as a midday hatch, and the olive morning dun becomes an evening hatch! Such crazy schedules are just another of the many challenges that keep West Branch anglers on their toes.

So, with these abundant cautions about the reliability of hatch charts, I present you with mine. I hope they will bring some additional organization and understanding to the fly patterns that represent these hatches. I trust that you will use these tables in the same way as the rest of the book—as food for thought, exploration, and experimentation. I fully recognize that these charts, like the fly patterns, may not serve anyone quite so well as they serve me. That is as it should be. Take what you need, adapt what you can, and create the rest. Above all, enjoy the quest and the ever-changing adventure of fly fishing.

GENERALIZED EASTERN EMERGENCE TABLE

- - - --- potential activity
--====-- typical peak activity

MAYFLIES

Name	Mar	Apr	May	Jun	Jul	Aug	Sep	Oct
B. tricaudatus	- - -	-===- -		- - ----- - - -		- - ----- - - -		
Baetis spp. (other)		- - ---------- - - -	---------- - - -	- - - - -	- - - - -	------ - -	- - - - -	
P. adoptiva		--====-- -						
E. pleuralis		- --===- - -						
E. subvaria		- --===- -						
E. septentrionalis			-===- - -					
E. invaria			--====- - - -					
M. vicarium			- -===-- - -					
L. recurvata			- -===- - - -					
E. dorothea			- -=====-- - - - -					
E. guttulata			- -==- -					
E. simulans				-=- (- -==- -) (cold lakes)				
I. bicolor				- -=====-- - - - - - - ----====--- - - -				
S. quebecensis				- ---------- - - - - - - -				
E. vitreus				- -====-- - - - - - - - -				
D. cornuta				- -===-- - -				
S. deficiens				- -===--- - - -				
D. cornutella				- -===- - -				
Paraleptophlebia spp.				- --=====------ - - - - - - - - - ---------- - - -				
S. interpunctatum				- -======--- - - -				
M. ithaca				- --=====-- - - -				
A. attenuata				- - - ----- - -				
L. hebe				- - -=====-- - - - -				
E. varia				- --=====---- - -				
A. distinctus				- -=====--- - - -				
H. rigida				- -======--- - - -				
T. stygiatus					- ---========----- - - - -			
D. lata					- -==---			
H. atrocaudata						- -=====--- - -		
E. leukon						- - - --=====--- - - -		

GENERALIZED EASTERN EMERGENCE TABLE

- - - --- potential activity
--=====-- typical peak activity

CADDISFLIES

Name	Mar	Apr	May	Jun	Jul	Aug	Sep	Oct
A. incerta		-=====---						
Hydropsyche/Ceratopsyche spp.			---==================----------- - - - -					
C. aterrima		- --=====----- - - -						
B. appalachia		- -=====-- -						
B. numerosus		- -=====-- -						
B. lateralis		- -=====-- - -						
Cheumatopsyche spp.		- ---===============----- - - - -						
Micrasema spp.			- - -------- - - - - - - - - - - - --------- - - -				
Rhyacophila spp.			- -===============----- - - - - -				
P. labida, frontalis			- --=====-- -					
H. argus			- -------- - - - - - - -				
O. avara				- - --========--- - - - -			
Nectopsyche spp.				- - - ---===========------ - - -			
D. distinctus				- - - - - - - - - - --------------- - - - - - -			
M. sepulchralis					- ---==========--- - - -		
P. scabripennis							- - ---=====-- - -	

STONEFLIES

Name	Mar	Apr	May	Jun	Jul	Aug	Sep	Oct
Allocapnia spp.	--=====-- - - -							
Taeniopteryx spp.	- ---======- - - - -							
T. nivalis	- - ---=====-- -							
S. fasciata	- --=====- - - -							
Isoperla spp.			- ---========--------- - -				
I. bilineata			- ---=======--- - -				
Alloperla spp.			- - -------------- - - - -				
Pteronarcys spp.			- - -=====--- - -				
P. dorsata			- --===-- - -				
P. media			- -=====- - - - - -				
A. lycorias			- ---------------------- -				
A. capitata				- ---=====--- - - -			
P. immarginata				- --=====--- - - - - - - - - - --			
P. placida					- - - -=========-- - -		

INDEX OF STYLES
AND SUBSTYLES

INDEX OF FLY PATTERNS

INDEX OF SCIENTIFIC NAMES